The Slain and Resurrected God

The Slain and Resurrected God

Conrad, Ford, and the Christian Myth

Robert J. Andreach

New York · New York University Press
London · University of London Press Ltd
1970

Acknowledgments

Excerpts from Ford Madox Ford's *The Young Lovell,* copyright © 1913 by Chatto and Windus Ltd. and the Literary Estate of Ford Madox Ford. Reprinted here with permission.

Excerpts from Ford Madox Ford's *The Good Soldier* and *Parade's End,* copyright © 1951 and 1961 by Alfred A. Knopf, Inc. Reprinted here with permission.

Excerpts from Joseph Conrad's *Complete Works* and *The Nature of a Crime* by Joseph Conrad and Ford Madox Ford, copyright © by the Trustees of the copyrights of the late Joseph Conrad, and J. M. Dent & Sons Ltd. Reprinted here with permission.

Excerpts from Robert J. Andreach's "The Two Narrators of Conrad's 'Amy Foster,' " in *Studies in Short Fiction,* vol. II (spring 1965), copyright © 1965 by Newberry College and the editors of *Studies in Short Fiction.* Reprinted here with permission.

Excerpts from Robert J. Andreach's "Ford's *The Good Soldier:* The Quest for Permanence and Stability" in *Tennessee Studies in Literature,* vol. x (1965), copyright © 1965 by the University of Tennessee and the editors of *Tennessee Studies in Literature.*

I wish to thank Oscar Cargill for his invaluable advice, encouragement, and assistance.

My former colleagues, John Hagan, Jr., Robert Kroetsch, Bernard S. Levy, Paul F. Mattheisen, Manuel Schonhorn, and William Bysshe Stein, for sharing their ideas with me.

Miss Claire Moriarty of New York University Press for her helpful suggestions in the preparation of the manuscript.

Contents

For Constance, Kevin, and Jason

Introduction

On November 8, 1923, Ford Madox Ford wrote to Joseph Conrad asking him if he would agree to the publication in book form of the third, and the least significant, of their three efforts at literary collaboration, a short story which had originally appeared in the April and May 1909, numbers of the *English Review* and was later reprinted in the *transatlantic review*. "But I think," Ford explained, "that to reprint the *Story of a Crime* as a collaboration with a note to the effect that it is old & was published under a pseudonym [Baron Ignatz von Aschendrof] would have a certain literary and sentimental interest and I should very much like to do it." [1] Conrad consented and the book was published by Duckworth and Company in 1924, with each man furnishing a prefatory note. "After signing these few prefatory words," Conrad wrote, "I will pass the pen to him in the hope that he may be moved to contradict me on every point of fact, impression and appreciation. I said 'the hope.' Yes. Eager hope. For it would be delightful to catch the echo of the desperate, earnest, eloquent and funny quarrels which enlivened those old days. The pity of it that there comes a time when all the fun of one's life must be looked for in the past!" [2] Ford found nothing to contradict: "And I really do not believe that either my Collaborator or myself ever made an objection, which was not jointly sustained. That is not quarrels. When I last looked through the bound proofs of *Romance* I was struck with the fact that whereas my Collaborator eliminated almost every word of action and 80 per cent. of the conversations by myself, I supplied almost all the descriptive passages of the really collaborated parts—and such softer sentiment as was called for. And my Collaborator let them get through." "All this took place long ago," he concluded; "most of it in another century, during another reign; whilst an earlier, but not less haughty and proud, generation were passing away." [3] Although their paths had long since diverged, in June, 1924, both men could look back with genuine feeling on this period of their lives. Indeed, one of Conrad's biographers calls his meeting with Ford in 1898 "the most important event" in his literary career,[4] and one of Ford's critics considers the first of their joint efforts, *The Inheritors,* "a fresh start altogether" for the subject of his study.[5]

According to Ford's memorial volume on Conrad, Edward Garnett, reader for T. Fisher Unwin, the publisher of both men's earliest books, arranged the meeting which led to Conrad's renting Ford's house, Pent Farm, near Aldington, Kent, and a collaboration which produced *The Inheritors* (1901), *Romance* (1903), and *The Nature of a Crime* (1924).[6] In 1898 Conrad, aged forty, married, with an infant son, was permanently settled in England and thoroughly engaged in the new career which had begun for him with the publication in 1895 of *Almayer's Folly*. Born Jozef Teodor Konrad Nalecz Korzeniowski in December, 1857, in the Polish Ukraine, he left Poland in the spring of 1862 with his parents when his father, Apollo, an extremist in the cause of Polish Independence, was sentenced to exile in a distant Russian province. After his mother, Evelina, died in 1865, he spent most of the next four years with his father until his death in 1869, at which time he was put under the guardianship of his grandmother and his maternal uncle. His father, a translator of Shakespeare and Victor Hugo, had been deeply concerned about his son's education, but it was not until Thaddeus Bobrowski assumed responsibility for his nephew that Conrad received what little formal education he ever had. It amounted to very little because in October, 1874, at the age of sixteen, he left Cracow for Marseilles and the second phase of his life, a four-year period of maritime apprenticeship in southern France and the adventures which are supposedly fictionalized in *The Arrow of Gold* (1919). A berth on the British freighter, the *Mavis*, brought him to England in 1878 and a fifteen-year period as a professional seaman and master mariner. This phase came to an end when Conrad disembarked in London from the *Adowa* on January 17, 1894, for within the year the manuscript he had commenced writing in 1889 was accepted by Unwin. This novel was followed by *An Outcast of the Islands* (1896) and *The Nigger of the "Narcissus"* (1897) so that by the time he met Ford he had published three novels; completed a volume of short stories, *Tales of Unrest* (1898); and was working on a fourth novel, *The Rescuer*. Furthermore, during the period of collaboration, he finished "Heart of Darkness" (1899) and *Lord Jim* (1900) and started *Nostromo* (1904).

In 1898 Ford, aged twenty-four, married, with one

daughter, had not yet discovered his talent as a novelist. Born Ford Hermann Hueffer in December, 1873, in Merton, Surrey, he grew up in the midst of a rich literary and artistic environment of Victorian England. His father, Dr. Franz Hueffer, a transplanted German, was chief music critic of the London *Times,* author of *The Troubadors: A History of Provencal Life and Literature in the Middle Ages,* and friend of Carlyle. His mother, Catherine, was the daughter of Ford Madox Brown, the Pre-Raphaelite painter, and half sister of the wife of William Michael Rossetti, the brother of Dante Gabriel and Christina Rossetti. His education, though irregular, was superior to that received by Conrad: he attended Praetoria House in Folkestone, University College School in London, and the Sorbonne in Paris. Given the atmosphere in which he was reared, it is not surprising that at eighteen he had published his first book, a children's fairy tale, *The Brown Owl* (1891). This book was followed by two more fairy tales, *The Feather* (1892) and *The Queen Who Flew* (1894) so that by the time he met Conrad he had published, in addition to the three fairy tales, a collection of poems, *The Questions at the Well* (1893), and a biography of his maternal grandfather, *Ford Madox Brown* (1896). But with this background it is not surprising either that he had not discovered his talent, for although he continued to publish during the years of the collaboration—a historical and descriptive record of Kent and Sussex port towns, *The Cinque Ports* (1900); another collection of poems, *Poems for Pictures* (1900); and art criticism and biography, *Rossetti* (1902)—by 1898 he had published only one novel, *The Shifting of the Fire* (1892). It was not until 1905 that he published his second novel, *The Benefactor,* and it was not until 1915 that he published his first major novel, *The Good Soldier.* A passage in a volume of reminiscences may explain his exceptionally long period of apprenticeship in the art form that would one day establish his genius: "You see there were in those days a number of those terrible and forbidding things—the Victorian great figures. To me life was simply not worth living because of the existence of Carlyle, of Mr. Ruskin, of Mr. Holman Hunt, of Mr. Browning, or of the gentleman who built the Crystal Palace. These people were perpetually held up to me as standing upon unattainable heights, and at the same time I was perpetually being told that if I could not attain to these heights I might just as well not cumber the earth. What then was left for me? Nothing. Simply nothing."[7]

The reasons usually advanced for the collaboration are Conrad's financial straits and his desire to become more fluent in English, Ford's difficulty in placing his manuscripts and his admiration for the older man. Whatever the reasons, each immediately sensed the other's dedication to the art of writing, and despite their differences in temperament, together they finished two novels, which though inferior productions repay careful reading, for they reveal an incipient archetypal pattern which will increasingly shape their fiction.

The Inheritors is a political satire directed at the modern age as symbolized by the Fourth Dimensionists, a group ruthlessly committed to the overthrow of the old order, the values and virtues of which are " 'diseases' " (V.10)[8] to the Dimensionists. Love is the primary disease because the hero, Etchingham Granger, who tells the "extravagant story" in the first person, is corrupted through his emotional involvement with the heroine, a member of the Dimensionists who poses as his sister. A commercially unsuccessful author who takes a commission to do a series of studies of celebrities for a paper edited by another member of the group, Granger is gradually drawn into her circle until he must make a decision. His decision is the climax of the novel. The Dimensionists are the power behind a project to convert Greenland into a productive state. Headed by a foreign financier, the Duc de Mersch, and backed by Chancellor of the Exchequer Gurnard, the *Système Groënlandais,* which purports to be bringing light to a dark spot on the earth while reclaiming barren land, is in fact an unscrupulous plan to undermine public confidence in the administration of Gurnard's antagonist, Foreign Minister Churchill, who has endorsed the project. Granger's political and moral sympathies are with Churchill, but because he wants to prove his love to his sister, at the crucial moment he decides not to stop the publication of an article which, by exposing the horrors perpetrated by the *Système,* topples the government. When he confronts her, however, she informs him she was counting on his love to execute her plan: " 'I chose you because you would do it. That is all . . . I knew you; knew your secret places, your weaknesses. That is my power. I stand for the Inevitable, for the future that goes on its way; you for the past that lies by the roadside' " (V.209). Overcome by despair, he accepts his fate.

Ford's comment that the book appeared to him "to be an allegorico-realist romance" [9] provides an insight into the design of the novel. *The Inheritors* opens and closes with an interview scene between the hero and heroine. In Chapter I Granger relates his experience with the woman to whom he had been attracted in the cathedral at Canterbury:

> We had climbed the western hill. Below our feet, beneath a sky that the wind had swept clean of clouds, was the valley; a broad bowl, shallow, filled with the

purple of smoke-wreaths. And above the mass of red roofs there soared the golden stonework of the cathedral tower. It was a vision, the last word of a great art. I looked at her. I was moved, and I knew that the glory of it must have moved her.

She was smiling. "Look!" she repeated. I looked.

There was the purple and the red, and the golden tower, the vision, the last word. She said something—uttered some sound.

What had happened? I don't know. It all looked contemptible. One seemed to see something beyond, something vaster—vaster than cathedrals, vaster than the conception of the gods to whom cathedrals were raised. The tower reeled out of the perpendicular. One saw beyond it, not roofs, or smoke, or hills, but an unrealized, an unrealizable infinity of space.

It was merely momentary. The tower filled its place again and I looked at her.

"What the devil," I said, hysterically—"what the devil do you play these tricks upon me for?" (V.7–8)

She proceeds to tell him about the Fourth Dimensionists, prophesying he will eventually enlist with her.

Between this scene and the final one is the body of the novel, a movement which suggests a descent into the underworld. Within a year after his encounter with the heroine, during which time he does the series, Granger is introduced to de Mersch and Gurnard. The former, a man with a florid face and red beard, "glows all over"; the latter, a man "with an icy assurance of manner," gives "the impression of never having seen the light of day. . . ." (V.80–2) Jealous of their interest in his sister and confident he is still "clean-handed in the matter" (V.57), he welcomes the opportunity to join her in Paris; rather than being "a better sort of paradise" (V.93) as he hoped, the

French city is a lower level of the descent. Granger learns of the exploitation of Greenland; he recognizes de Mersch for a "trafficker in human blood" (V.119); he struggles "against the numbness of frost" (V.127) as he listens to his sister's plan to destroy de Mersch, the *Système,* and Churchill. His attempt to resist her appears to succeed, since he returns to London following her announcement that she will marry Gurnard, and once out of the "underworld" (V.166), once back in the "upper world" (V.172), he has "a sense of recovered power from the sight of them [the land steward and the manor house], of the sunlight on the stretches of turf, of the mellow, golden stonework of the long range of buildings, from the sound of a chime of bells that came wonderfully sweetly over the soft swelling of the close turf" (V.156). The truth, however, is that he craves his sister so intensely he cannot resist her influence. For a short while after the crucial moment, he believes he has risen above the impulses of his conscience, but the realization of the consequences of his betrayal brings him crashing to the earth—to the closing interview. In this scene, after reminding him of her prophecy, she consigns him to the realm of the dead. Having betrayed his past and therefore his future, he is silenced by a judgment he now knows was inevitable: "I had not looked at her; but stood with my eyes averted, very conscious of her standing before me; of her great beauty, of her great glory" (V.211).

The novel's design traces the contours of the archetypal pattern which will become the dominant structural principle of Conrad's and Ford's major works. The hero encounters a female who offers him a glimpse into another dimension of reality. He then descends into the underworld, where he is expected to subdue the dark forces of evil, a necessary trial before he can rejoin her. Having accomplished the goal expected of him, he returns to her with "a sense of recovered power . . ." for "either a reward or just due" (V.206). In its broad outlines, this is the pattern of the quest of the traditional hero of myth, the stages of which are schematized by Joseph Campbell: "The standard path of the mythological adventure of the hero is a magnification of the formula represented in the rites of passage: *separation—initiation—return:* which might be named the nuclear unit of the monomyth. *A hero ventures forth from the world of common day into a region of supernatural wonder: fabulous forces are there encountered and a decisive victory is won: the hero comes back from this mysterious adventure with the power to bestow boons on his fellow man."* [10] From this sketch it is apparent Granger bears little resemblance to the traditional hero in that he fails his ordeal, he does not experience a rebirth, and his action does not reintegrate society. Yet even should the critic argue that *The Inheritors* is an intentional inversion or parody of the myth of the hero, the presence of the pattern bears witness to Conrad's and Ford's mutual concern with the viability of the myth in the modern age. This concern is further attested to by their second collaboration, for *Romance* clarifies three areas to be developed before the myth can be re-created, before it can be given ritual form in the twentieth century. In this novel the "I" narrator, John Kemp, relates his adventures in the West Indies from the time he left home until the time he is reunited with Seraphina Riego, the woman who is the "essence" (VII.532) of his life. Each one of the novel's five sections revolves around an episode in Kemp's quest for romance: departure for the West Indies with Carlos Riego and Tomas Castro; encounter with Seraphina, her father, and O'Brien, ringleader of a pirate organization with headquarters in Rio Medio; sojourn at the "enchanted castle" (VII.171) of Don Balthasar Riego,

where he is betrothed to the old man's daughter; entomb-
ment in a cavern with Seraphina and Castro while fleeing
from the pirates; and trial in England on the charge of
being " 'John Kemp, *alias* Nichols, *alias* Nikola el Escoces,
alias el Demonio, *alias* el Diabletto' " (VII.516).

The first area is the relationship between the past and
the future. When Granger takes his commission, he believes he is "leaving an old course of life . . . actually
and finally breaking with it . . ." (V.48). As he walks home
to the club on the morning the article is published, he
feels his thoughts moving "serenely as in a new light, as
men move in sunshine above the graves of the forgotten
dead" (V.192). Yet when he realizes the consequences of
his betrayal, he realizes "it is permitted to no man to break
with his past, with the past of his kind, and to throw away
the treasure of his future" (V.200), for the irony of the
novel is not only that by trying to break with his past he
betrays his future, but that by failing to confront his past
he cannot be free for a new future with his sister. The very
love which proves his loyalty is his undoing, since it is a
" 'disease' " to her, an emotion which belongs to the dead
past. Standing before her, he becomes "a ghost in a bottomless cleft between the past and the to come" (V.209).
Unlike Granger, Kemp has a "foretaste" of how his past
"would rise up to crush" him (VII.514) as he awaits his
trial. Of course, the trial is a case of mistaken identity
since he is not Nikola, but it functions as a vehicle for the
establishment of his origin; so by convincing the court
he is John Kemp and not el Diabletto, he is acquitted for
a new future with Seraphina. This novel also widens the
scope of the myth because Part Three returns to mankind's origin. Seraphina is "a strange new being, a marvel
as great as Eve herself to Adam's wondering awakening"
(VII.158); O'Brien is "an evil spectre" (VII.185) whose de-

sire for Seraphina precipitates the expulsion from Eden. Excited by the inflammatory speeches of Manuel-del-Popolo, O'Brien's lieutenant, the bandits charge the palace, demanding Kemp's life. In the ensuing battle, Kemp flings the pirates' leader out of the Casa Riego and slams the gate behind him, but with both Carlos and Don Balthasar dead and O'Brien sworn to vengeance, Kemp, Seraphina, and Castro must seek safety elsewhere. Their flight takes them deep into a subterranean darkness, the second stage in Campbell's division of the mythic quest and the second area to be developed.

Paul L. Wiley and Charles G. Hoffmann are of the opinion that in *The Inheritors* the impressionistic condensation defeats the political satire. For Hoffmann the hero "is remote from the heart of darkness and can only report his impressions of the horror second and even third hand. Even the general outlines of de Mersch's scheme are reported somewhat vaguely by Granger to the reader, and what is missing—but should not be missing—in such a political satire is the sense of the reality of the horror being revealed." [11] From the mythological perspective, the reality of the horror is not revealed because Granger never confronts the evil in himself. Finding it "unpleasant . . . to have been mixed up in this affair," he wants to recover his "old self" (V.110), but once he returns to the upper world he tries to soar above his conscience and memory until the realization of his betrayal brings him back "to the earth, overwhelmed, crushed by an immensity of ruin and of sorrow" (V.193). There is always hovering over the interview scenes between Granger and de Mersch or Gurnard and Granger and his sister the suggestion of a doubling technique, but it is only a faint suggestion at best, perhaps because Granger never discovers himself. "What could the man know about me?" he wonders to himself as he seems to feel Gurnard's glance boring "through the irises" of his eyes "into the back" of his skull (V.82). When he confesses to his sister, he is not so much guilt-stricken as he is hopeful of a reward. Part Four of *Romance* conforms more closely to the initiation stage than does the corresponding section of *The Inheritors*. On their attempted escape from the pirates, Kemp, Seraphina, and Castro hide in "an abode of darkness" (VII.361), a cavern "big enough to contain, in its black gloom of a burial vault, all the dust and passions and hates of a nation . . ." (VII.366), a grave "with inexorable death standing between" them and "the free spaces of the world" (VII.382). Since the hero must confront Manuel before he and Seraphina are able to leave the cavern "like two people newly arisen from a tomb, shrinking before the strangeness of the half-forgotten face of the world" (VII.417), the doubling technique is more developed in *Romance* than it is in *The Inheritors*. In fear Manuel makes the sign of the cross to protect himself from the apparition of Kemp creeping toward him from the depths of the darkness. Kemp has to defend himself against the charge that he is el Diabletto. While on trial he has the sensation that O'Brien's blood is "still sticky" on his hands (VII.538). And before he is reunited with Seraphina, he must admit to the truth of her reproach: " 'You broke our compact' " (VII.541).

Just as the key to the discovery of a new future is the confrontation with fabulous forces, so the key to the confrontation is the role of the woman, the third area to be developed before the myth can be re-created. On the summit of the hill, the heroine introduces Granger to a dimension of reality, an "infinity of space," beyond the horizon, alien to human experience. When she tells him she has arranged for the exposure of the *Système Groënlandais,* he has an idea that the solution is beyond him, "as if the controlling powers were flitting, invisible, just above my head, just beyond my grasp" (V.124). Hence he never descends into himself, never redeems his past so that he can discover a new future. Following his failure to stop the presses, he feels himself a new man, "risen" (V.192) above his conscience and his memory. He subsequently crashes to the earth, but he never descends into his heart of darkness to discover himself because the heroine does not offer him a glimpse into the "infinity of space" within himself. Only for an instant does he see beyond the crumbling buildings "into unknown depths," but he turns away from a descent. " 'This is too absurd,' " he says to himself. " 'I am not well' " (V.195). Ironically, by turning away he encounters the death he has been trying to evade—in the person of his sister, whose vision of reality remote from earth is his death. Kemp is somewhat like Granger at the opening of *Romance* in that for him the journey in search of romance is comparable to "trying to catch the horizon" (VII.62). The nature of the journey changes, however, when the three fugitives descend into the "darkness of infinite space" (VII.373) within the cavern. Since the cavern is on Seraphina's estate and since she sits "concealed in the very heart of her dominions" (VII.364), the implication is that Kemp is descending, through her agency, into the heart of darkness within himself, into his "dust and passions and hates. . . ." Certainly the implication of his embracing the "dry lips" of her "emaciated face" is that he accepts mankind's "appointed fate" (VII.391) as Granger does not until his final interview. The nature of the journey changes in *Romance* because Seraphina is not exclusively an agent of death as Granger's sister is. She has a dual role: agent of death and agent of life, of man's fall and of his redemption. Her presence at Casa Riego provokes the conflict between Kemp and

O'Brien; her image enables the former to recover his innocence during the trial.

So far I have been analyzing these novels as if they were the products of one author. *The Inheritors* is largely Ford's work with Conrad contributing the last twenty pages,[12] but *Romance* is a collaboration. Conrad assigned the authorship of the five sections in a letter quoted in the Appendix to *The Nature of a Crime:* " 'First Part, yours; Second Part, mainly yours, with a little by me on points of seamanship and suchlike small matters; Third Part, about 60 per cent. mine with important touches by you; Fourth Part, mine, with here and there an important sentence by you; Fifth Part practically all yours, . . . with perhaps half a dozen lines by me. . . .' " Ford concurred with Conrad's ascriptions "if conception alone is concerned. When it comes, however, to the writing, the truth is that Parts One, Two, Three and Five are a singular mosaic of passages written alternately by one or other of the collaborators. The matchless Fourth Part is both in conception and writing entirely the work of Mr. Conrad." [13] From these summaries it would appear that Ford, who wrote almost all of *The Inheritors* and the early draft of *Romance,* entitled *Seraphina,* before he met the older man, is responsible for the conception of the female in these novels. Yet since Conrad contributed the descent stage to *Romance,* I think we must recognize a shared attitude toward the woman's role in the hero's journey. Carol Ohmann, who notes that the heroine of *The Inheritors* "differs from the usual Conradian woman and foreshadows a number of heroines whom Ford was subsequently to create," sees in the relationship between the narrator and the heroine of this novel "certain resemblances to Conrad's habitual treatment of love." [14] In the two novels the female is an idealized being: Granger's sister is "an inscrutable white figure, like some silent Greek statue, a harmony of falling folds of heavy drapery perfectly motionless" (V.153–4); Seraphina is "an apparition of dreams" (VII.158), a fairy-tale princess who never " 'set foot to the open ground' " (VII.244) before leaving Casa Riego. There is a slight progression, though, from idealized female to real woman in the second novel. Whereas Granger sees his sister as an allegory or symbol whose distinguishing physical characteristics are her eyes and smile, Kemp dreams in prison that he suddenly sees Seraphina's "full red lips, her quivering nostrils, the curve of her breasts, her lithe movements from the hips, the way she set her feet down, the white flower waxen in the darkness of her hair, and the robin-wing flutter of her lids over her gray eyes when she smiled" (VII.489). This progression fuses with another progression in the woman's role: the heroine of *The Inheritors* is likened to Diana or Venus; the heroine of *Romance,* to the Madonna. Following the direction of Seraphina's hand after she unties him in Part Two, Kemp's eyes fall upon "the image of a Madonna; rather large—perhaps a third life-size; with a gilt crown, a pink serious face bent a little forward over a pink naked child that perched on her left arm and raised one hand" (VII.98–9). Later, in court, he has a vision of the drowned Seraphina: "I thought I was bound again, and on the sofa in the gorgeous cabin of the *Madre-de-Dios.* Someone seemed to be calling, 'Prisoner at the bar . . . Prisoner at the bar. . . .' It was as if the candles had been lit in front of the Madonna with the pink child, only she had a gilt anchor instead of the spiky gilt glory above her head" (VII.537).

Though these three areas are still inchoate by the time the two novelists had ended their collaboration, the emergence as organizing principle of an archetypal **pattern** from separation to transformed reunion foreshadows a movement within each man's fiction from love as a disease to love as a cure, a movement which when completed will restore the tradition overthrown in *The Inheritors,* the cardinal virtue of which is love. The key to its completion is the heroine's role in guiding the hero through a region of supernatural wonder within himself. Granger's sister attacks the basis of Western culture: the Christian tradition. " 'But you contracted diseases,' " she tells her brother, " 'as we shall contract them,—beliefs, traditions; fears; ideas of pity . . . of love. You grew luxurious in the worship of your ideals, and sorrowful; you solaced yourselves with creeds, with arts—you have forgotten!' " (V.10). Her matter-of-fact statement, " 'Oh, we are to inherit the earth, if that is what you mean' " (V.6), is a parody of Christ's Sermon on the Mount. Her vision of a future beyond the horizon, in which the tower of Canterbury Cathedral reels, demolishes the symbol of England's spiritual center. Her victory signals the disintegration of the Christian era, disinheriting Churchill and Granger. When the role taken by Seraphina in *Romance* is developed so that the heroine can give a particular configuration to the hero's interior journey, the myth will be re-created. Once the myth in its Christian configuration is re-created, the hero will regain his lost heritage because he will have discovered his potential for love and self-sacrifice. He will have discovered the center of his tradition—Christ, the slain and resurrected God—within himself.

The importance of the heroine's role in the hero's quest is demonstrated in James Joyce's *Ulysses,* a novel in which the myth is re-created, the tradition reaffirmed, the original state lost in the past recovered. "History . . . is a nightmare from which I am trying to awake," Stephen Dedalus tells Mr. Deasy early in the day on June 16, 1904.[15]

A little later, in the newspaper office, the man whose path
will cross Stephen's, Leopold Bloom, muses over the piety
that brought the Jews "out of the land of Egypt and into
the house of bondage *alleluia*." Before their day is over,
however, the two of them exit from "the house of bondage"
into the garden. There the husband "elucidates the mystery
of an invisible person, his wife Marion (Molly) Bloom,
denoted by a visible splendid sign, a lamp." Free at last,
the former leaves on a new beginning while the latter,
hearing the "double reverberation of retreating feet on the
heavenborn earth," sees the "disparition of three final stars,
the diffusion of daybreak, the apparition of a new solar
disk," heralding the end of his journey and the beginning
of his new life. Back inside, he falls asleep next to Molly,
"the childman weary, the manchild in the womb."

This novel, probably the most widely read of twentieth-century novels, defines man's actuality and potentiality
or, in terms of the myth, the states preceding and following
the initiation stage. Between these two states—the old life
trapped within the nightmare of history and the new life
in which the wound is healed and time reordered—a man
has choices: he can try to escape his consciousness, hiding
until his destiny inexorably overtakes him; he can resist
the pressure to begin his journey until his circle of movement is so diminished that he must act; he can submit to
the invisible pressure, thereby beginning his journey to a
new destiny. To submit is to accept the woman, for she
guides him to self-discovery, to his rebirth. Not the center
of the imaginative world but the agent who awakens him
to find the center, she is a mediatrix. William York Tindall's incisive comments on the trinity in *Ulysses* hold,
with a change in names, for the works in this study: "Likely
at first to single Stephen out, we discover Bloom next, and
finally, after many readings, Mrs. Bloom. Understanding

her is the sign of understanding and its achievement." [16]

Putting aside the various interpretations of her role in *Ulysses,* we can say critics agree that we must make an attempt to understand Molly Bloom in order to understand the novel, that we cannot dismiss her, that she is as important as Stephen and Leopold. Unfortunately, there is not this agreement about the heroine's role among critics of the two subjects of this book, particularly of Conrad, whose works have received much more critical attention than those of Ford. According to Thomas Moser, whose reading of his fiction appeared in 1957, "There is something about the theme of love that elicits only bad writing from Conrad, something that frustrates his most strenuous efforts to create." [17] For him the worst novels contain a menacing feminine sexuality lurking beneath the surface, which belies the author's conscious intention to affirm the importance of love between man and woman. Since he finds love to be the uncongenial subject for Conrad, he wonders why the novelist, "rather than subordinating women and love in the full-length novels, did not cut them out altogether and produce only perfect works like *The Nigger of the 'Narcissus'* and 'The Secret Sharer.' " [18] That the thesis advanced by Moser is controversial is evidenced by subsequent criticism,[19] but whether or not we agree with his conclusions, he singles out imagery every critic of Conrad's fiction must take into account. Recently, Dr. Bernard C. Meyer published a psychoanalytic biography of Conrad. I am not qualified to endorse or refute his findings, since he studies the details of the fiction as symptoms of the author's personality disorders, but he singles out a characteristic of the Conradian heroine I think inseparable from the menacing feminine sexuality: she inspires more awe than sexual desire in the male.[20]

There is another controversial judgment in Conrad

criticism which should be noted. According to critics such as Douglas Hewitt, Moser, and Albert J. Guerard, Conrad's artistry deteriorates in the novels written after *Under Western Eyes* (1911). Hewitt's position on *Victory* (1915) is an example of this judgment: "But if Heyst's flaw is never made real, if Conrad seems to remain unable to convince us of any evil in his hero, there is no lack of villainy in his villains." [21] Although I agree that Conrad's artistry deteriorates in his late novels, I think many critics' low regard for *Victory* is partially the result of three related misreadings: Heyst's flaw is never made real; evil is external to him; and the envoys arrive at the island by chance.[22] And none of these readings (or misreadings) satisfactorily accounts for the role of Lena. The rhetoric of *Victory* may be turgid, but the pattern within the novel deserves the closest scrutiny, for the heroine as agent whose reality circumscribes the hero until he discovers himself is at the heart of Conrad's work as well as Ford's.

I want to indicate here the reading I hope to substantiate in the chapter on Conrad. The woman does menace the hero because she challenges his ideal conception of himself; in her eyes he sees reflected his actuality and potentiality. For the man who must have his illusion to survive, this confrontation is intolerable. The internal conflict in *Victory* is externalized in the struggle between Lena and the envoys, life and death, to claim Heyst. Lena will not leave Heyst alone until he confronts his betrayal of Morrison because she embodies a concealed reality which she reveals when she unveils herself. When he looks at her closely, he seems "to read some awful intelligence in her eyes"; the potential for love and self-sacrifice from which he has been running throughout the novel.

What I am arguing for is a reexamination of Conrad's and Ford's imaginative worlds focused on the woman as mediatrix. We can see why when we extract representative scenes from their works and place them side by side. The first is a composite of Conrad's Lord Jim in Patusan dropping the clock he wishes he could mend; fixing the circular fence round the grave; being angry with Jewel for waking him to warn him his life is threatened; standing on the beach waving farewell to Marlow; looking at, but not seeing Jewel when she begs him to fly with her; letting the pen fall when he realizes the futility of trying to explain; handing the girl over to his servant, Tamb' Itam, so that he can finally behold " 'the face of that opportunity which, like an Eastern bride, had come veiled to his side.' " In the second, Dowell, the narrator of Ford's *The Good Soldier,* tries to decipher the past while his mind goes "round and round in a weary, baffled space of pain." He is aware of being very much where he "started thirteen years ago."

These scenes dramatize the old life, the state preceding the initiation stage, in which the male sits, like Granger, crippled by guilt yet refusing to confess, or hopelessly bewildered, in a confined, darkening interior with time closing in on him. His life moves in an endless circle, an endless return to itself, an endless reenactment of the past in the present. Since he will not make the journey, he cannot escape the circularity except by falling into despair, where he remains immobile until death claims him.

There are scenes that dramatize the new life, the state following the initiation stage. The archetypal pattern begins to assume definitive form with the hero, like Kemp, moving toward the discovery of Christ in himself. " ' "This is glorious," ' " cries Marlow as he prepares to leave Patusan after his interview with Jewel, his eyes " 'roaming through space, like a man released from bonds who stretches his cramped limbs, runs, leaps, responds to the inspiring

elation of freedom.' " Turning about to come out of the
heart of darkness, he leaves Lord Jim for " 'the world
where events move, men change, light flickers, life flows in
a clear stream, no matter whether over mud or over
stones.' " Confessing to Natalia, which frees him " 'from
the blindness of anger and hate' " and from despair, Razumov of *Under Western Eyes* is " 'washed clean' " in the
rain. Instead of wandering about the streets of Geneva or
secluding himself on an island, he goes directly to the conspirators' headquarters to make a public confession. Reading "some awful intelligence" in Lena's eyes, Heyst, who
now cannot bear separation from her, joins her in the
purifying fire. Tietjens in *Parade's End* is reborn as the
new Adam on top of the sunlit mound "honeycombed
with springs." Once he elects to leave no man's land because he wants to talk with Valentine, he descends into
hell, where Sylvia awaits him, ascends mount purgatory,
and then, after being reborn, descends to bring Valentine
upstairs to the reunion celebration.

The journey is undertaken precisely because the hero
accepts the heroine's guiding power. " 'I could never
succeed in driving away your image,' " Razumov writes to
Natalia in his journal, and a few paragraphs later, " 'the
truth shining in you drew the truth out of me.' " Valentine's image constantly "wriggling in," Tietjens follows it
to the bottom of hell and from there to the top of mount
purgatory. In other words, the hero accepts the supernatural aid offered him by the woman. Since man is
bounded by time, he cannot get outside it to reorder it.
Some reality higher than time—eternity—has to enter into
time. In the Christian tradition this reality is the Incarnation, the entrance of the eternal into time or the
gathering up of time into eternity. Since man is bounded
by consciousness of himself, he cannot get outside himself

imagination. . . ." [29] His comments on Beatrice are more interesting, though. He wishes that "we could say definitely and once for all that Beatrice was purely an allegory—that she represented an idea or an ideal such as that of the Christian church or, say, the philosophy of Aristotle. The whole attitude of Dante, his confessions of infidelity to his Beatrice, and still more his Beatrice's almost acid reproaches for those infidelities on the occasion of their meeting in Heaven—all these things would at once become plain and recognizable." But he cannot say definitely: "Nevertheless, we cannot regard Beatrice as being all through allegorical." [30] His conclusion is as much an interpretation of Dante's conception of the heroine as it is a reaction against the Victorian idealization of the pure female, a reaction that determines his conception of the female.

By comparing each novelist's conception of the heroine's role against Dante's, the critic can see how the Christian tradition destroyed in *The Inheritors* is infused with life in *Parade's End*. After an abortive attempt to create a medieval Beatrice in the heroine of *The Rescuer,* Conrad progressively suggests in his fiction a nineteenth-century Beatrice, a woman who when she unveils herself allows the male a glimpse into his own concealed reality. [31] Ford's Valentine is the twentieth-century Beatrice, the woman who not only leads Tietjens through his descent into the hell within himself to his discovery of Christ within himself but who must descend into her own hell to discover herself. As might be expected from this summary, Ford is more heavily influenced by Dante than is Conrad. In fact, if we ignore the images and allusions in *Parade's End,* we can conclude that "Ford did not have a vision of his world," [32] that "religious materials, if more common in his fiction than his collaborator's, are still infrequent, and incidental," [33] that he "is writing a psychological novel which may be read as a political, but not so easily as a religious, parable." [34] Yet in the opening chapter of the immense novel, Tietjens and Macmaster disagree about Dante's and Rossetti's treatment of Paolo and Francesca, and from then on allusions to Beatrice, the frozen circle, the angel guarding the gate, the ascent of mount purgatory map out the design of the novel informed by Ford's vision, which will not divorce the political from the religious dimension. Of the works analyzed, this novel is the fullest treatment of redemption in the Christian sense. Employing the Dantean structure, it creates in a modern setting the journey from the dark woods to the sunlit garden, from sin to grace.

Conrad's debt to Dante is less substantial than Ford's, but it is operative and in a way that indicates the shift in emphasis in each novelist's work from the idealized female once she becomes a real woman to the hero who discovers himself by accepting her guidance. It is this shift, foreshadowed in the novels of collaboration by the shift from Granger's sister to Seraphina, from Granger to Kemp, which brings the myth to life and restores the tradition. Granger's failure to discover himself spells his ruin, for even more so than his sister, he brings the tradition to a dead end. When he tries to soar above his conscience and memory, he fulfills her prophecy. He is consigned to "a bottomless cleft between the past and the to come" by a disembodied voice which says to him, " 'As for you—you are only a detail, like all the others; you were set in a place because you would act as you did. It was in your character. We inherit the earth and you, your day is over. . . .' " (V.206–7) Dante elects to descend the rocky slope of the inferno on his journey to reunion with Beatrice. The climax of the descent is the confrontation with Satan, into whose face he must look on the frozen circle of Cocytus

before he can begin the ascent to the garden of Eden.
Conrad contributed Part Four, the descent, to *Romance*.
After Kemp and Seraphina leave the cavern, they descend
the rocky slope to an "icy cold" stream (VII.418), hoping
to follow it to freedom. As Kemp rounds a bend, he comes
upon the twisted body of Manuel, who, still alive, looks up
at him. Their penetration "into Manuel's inferno" (VII.
424) saves them. Had they not stopped so that Seraphina
could minister to him in his death throes but turned back
or continued on into the ravine, they would not have been
spotted by the vaqueros from above the cave. In Part Five
Kemp gains the courage to tell his story from the presence
of a little girl who reminds him of Seraphina. While telling his story, he impales his hand on the spikes of the dock
rail, but the blood does not deter him because the girl's
eyes are "fixed, fascinated," on his hands (VII.530). His
bleeding hands convince the court of his innocence: at the
conclusion of his narration, his father, who has not spoken
but who has been suffering through the "extremity of his
only son" (VII.509), acknowledges him, " 'I am the prisoner's father' " (VII.538). Redeemed after his trial, Kemp
stands with Seraphina in awe "before the greatness of a
change from the verge of despair to the opening of a
supreme joy" in "a union that was to be without end.
. . ." (VII.540–1)

   To say that certain modern authors share a common
literary antecedent as the model for the experience in their
works, is to say that they take their inspiration from the
archetypal pattern given form and meaning and consciousness in the poem and from the imagination of the author
who composed the poem. I would not argue for Dante's
fourfold method, but I would insist Conrad and Ford
share with the medieval poet a mind that conceives of
reality as twofold: that literal or surface reality contains

another dimension which we can call symbolic or allegoric and that when we penetrate the surface we unveil this other dimension. Since every artist finds the method of creating which best expresses his talent and his vision, I intend to show how the two novelists' methods shape and refine the materials of their fiction so as to uncover the center of their imaginative worlds, which radiates outward through the mediatrix, forcing the hero to begin his quest.

We now have to commence our quest. I take the position that the modern hero's experience can be fully appreciated only when it is juxtaposed with the one alluded to in the fiction. Just as Beatrice is Dante's experience of grace on earth, so are the heroines in these works the heroes' experience of a metaphysical reality. This experience in the human concrete reconciles past and future in the present, for it is in the human concrete that "the impossible union / Of spheres of existence is actual"—to use the language of *Four Quartets*.[35] It is perfectly consistent that the author of *Ash-Wednesday* and *Four Quartets* should remark in an essay on Baudelaire that the nineteenth-century poet "arrived at the perception that a woman must be to some extent a symbol; he did not arrive at the point of harmonizing his experience with his ideal needs. The complement, and the correction to the *Journaux Intimes,* so far as they deal with the relations of man and woman, is the *Vita Nuova,* and the *Divine Comedy."* [36] In Conrad's imaginative world the woman is a symbol to the extent that she is the guiding power on the hero's descent into the pagan world that reigns in his heart of darkness, the first step on a journey that will bear fruit in Ford's imaginative world.

1.

Joseph Conrad

Although "Amy Foster" (1901), a tale from Joseph Conrad's early period—reprinted in the 1903 *Typhoon and Other Stories* volume—has never enjoyed the respect or the popularity of "The Secret Sharer" and "Heart of Darkness," some critics think it noteworthy for what it reveals of the author's emotional state following his flight from Poland.[1] I do not wish to comment on this matter because it has been done thoroughly and because the tale contains much more than transmuted autobiography. I consider it as important to a study of his works as these other two stories, for it is a good example of a seemingly hopeless world we can assume is Conrad's if we do not read carefully. A first-person narration, told by a Doctor Kennedy to a nameless companion, it is the story of the harrowing adventures of Yanko Goorall, an emigrant from Central Europe bound for America, from the time he had been washed ashore on the Kentish coast until the time he was deserted and left to die by his wife, Amy Foster. We see the picture of the betrayed hero through the eyes of a bewildered narrator, whose narration unfolds within another narration. An intricate framework story, the tale offers two perspectives, the second of which, by the nameless "I" narrator, modifies the first, by the doctor, who can understand the betrayal only within the framework of his hopeless view.

Since "Amy Foster" is a first-person narrative, it raises the question of the epistemological problem in limited narration: what does the narrator (not the author) know, how does he know, is his consciousness the sole authority? We cannot make a judgment about the responsibility for the betrayal until we decide whether the narrator is a reliable witness. The way to do this is through his mental processes and emotional attitudes as they are manifested in his narrative. Doctor Kennedy does not force existential experience to conform to his notion of what it should be as does the narrator of Henry James's *The Sacred Fount;* nor does he distort the events to fit his need for order as does Dowell in *The Good Soldier.* Yet since his narrative is as self-revealing as theirs, we must examine what he reveals about himself before we can examine the function of the nameless "I" narrator.

Our clue occurs at the beginning of his narration, in the language he uses to generalize about tragedy. Telling his companion about Amy's father, who had been disinherited by his father, Kennedy moves into his tale of Amy and Yanko: " 'There are other tragedies, less scandalous and of a subtler poignancy, arising from irreconcilable differences and from that fear of the Incomprehensible that hangs over all our heads—over all our heads . . .' " (XX.107–8).[2] He is so burdened by his awareness that the human drama is acted out under the shadow of the Incomprehensible that his narrative is saturated with a sense of the mystery at the center of life. Since Amy is a dull, passive woman, which should make her incapable of any strong emotions, her aptitude for pity, compassion, and love is " 'an inscrutable mystery' " (XX.109). Trying to get at the " 'definiteness' " in her face is comparable to peering " 'attentively at a vague shape' " while " 'walking in a mist' " (XX.108). The steamer that rammed the ship carrying the emigrants went out " 'unknown, unseen, and fatal, to perish mysteriously at sea. Of her nothing ever came to light . . .' " (XX.122). The lone survivor, Yanko, was " 'a lost stranger, helpless, incomprehensible, and of a mysterious origin, in some obscure corner of the earth' " (XX.113). When Amy's employer confronted him, he " 'felt the dread of an inexplicable strangeness' " (XX.120). " 'Perhaps it was only an inexplicable caprice' " (XX.127) which prompted the employer's neighbor, Swaffer, to give him a place to live. Miss Swaffer had " 'an inscrutable face' " (XX.131) with " 'a mysteriously ironic curl' " to her lips (XX.128). Amy's face was " 'the only comprehensible face amongst all these faces that were as closed, as mysterious, and as mute as the faces of the dead who are possessed of a knowledge beyond the comprehension of the living' " (XX.129).

The mysteries surrounding Amy's betrayal of Yanko are how she could love him, who he was (everything connected with his appearance in England), why their marriage failed, and why he died. For each of these questions Kennedy suggests two answers. One offers a hypothetical explanation that discursive reason can grasp, and one eliminates the need for explanation by removing the mystery beyond the realm of discursive reason—by ascribing supernatural qualities, divine or mythic, to the events. Since for him human relationships are as incomprehensible as the center, we should read his narrative as a groping attempt to understand the significance of the betrayal according to either one of the two schemata.

Despite her dullness Amy must have had imagination: " 'She fell in love under circumstances that leave no room for doubt in the matter; for you need imagination to form a notion of beauty at all, and still more to discover your ideal in an unfamiliar shape' " (XX.109). The other possibility is she came under the influence of " 'a powerful spell; it was love as the Ancients understood it: an irresistible and fateful impulse—a possession!' " (XX.110).

Concerning Yanko's appearance in England, there is information about his life in Europe, the fraudulent methods used to recruit emigrants, the miserable conditions of travel, and the probable cause of the shipwreck. For the other, he was so different " 'his humanity suggested to me the nature of a woodland creature' " (XX.111). " 'It is possible that a man . . . might have floated ashore on that hencoop' " (XX.123); he was " 'cast out by the sea' " (XX.113). He " 'struggled instinctively' " to survive after he reached shore; it was " 'another miracle he didn't get drowned' " in the dyke (XX.112). The villagers found him different because of his foreign dress, language, and customs; he was " 'like a man transplanted into another planet' " (XX.132). A man " 'who knew nothing of the earth' " (XX.111–2), his words sounded as if they were the words of " 'an unearthly language' " (XX.117).

Their marriage failed because his love for his son created a wedge between himself and his wife and because " 'his difference, his strangeness' " repelled " 'that dull nature they had begun by irresistibly attracting' " (XX.137–8). Or, if " 'it was in her to become haunted and possessed by a face, by a presence, fatally, as though she had been a pagan worshipper of form under a joyous sky,' " then it was in her

" 'to be awakened at last from that mysterious forgetful-
ness of self, from that enchantment, from that transport,
by a fear resembling the unaccountable terror of a brute
. . .' " (XX.110). On the night of his death, she felt an
" 'unreasonable terror' " and an " 'unaccountable fear' "
come " 'creeping over her' " (XX.139).

" 'Physiologically . . . it was possible' " (XX.138)
Yanko contracted lung trouble. " 'His heart must have indeed failed him . . .' " (XX.141). On the other hand,
" 'from that moment' " after his arrival when he started
toward New Barns Farm, he was " 'plainly in the toils of
his obscure and touching destiny' " (XX.119), a destiny
that ended in disaster.

In each instance the reason the doctor turns to a supernatural cause, one that eliminates the necessity of a comprehensible natural cause, is his failure to find a natural
one. Amy must have loved Yanko because she married him
in spite of the fact that for " 'a hundred futile and inap-
preciable reasons' " everyone else considered him " 'odi-
ous.' " After Swaffer gave him an acre of ground, " 'no
power on earth could prevent them from getting married.' " Only Amy and Kennedy " 'could see his very real
beauty' " (XX.134–6). Why, then, did she grow to fear
him? She was tender to every living creature, especially
helpless ones, and he clearly needed compassion. What
went wrong? Kennedy suggests Yanko's affection for his
son, his strangeness, his difference, but whenever he offers
a natural cause, his repetition of a phrase reveals his doubt.
" 'A man . . . might have floated ashore on that hencoop.
He might' " (XX.123). " 'It was possible. It was possible' "
that he contracted lung trouble (XX.138). " 'I wondered.
. . . I wondered' " whether it was his strangeness that
alienated his wife (XX.137–8). This is why he turns to a
supernatural explanation. Amy was " 'haunted and pos-

sessed' " in order to love Yanko and " 'awakened at last' " from the possession to fear him (XX.110).

Kennedy's predicament, however, is that he cannot accept a supernatural cause either, since he turns to it only as a substitute for a missing natural cause. Unable to uncover any explanation for the betrayal, he finishes his tale with a cluster of questions. " 'Is his image as utterly gone from her mind as his lithe and striding figure, his caroling voice are gone from our fields?' " How can a woman who loved him passionately enough to marry him in the face of tremendous obstacles forget him? Why has her husband " 'vanished from her dull brain as a shadow passes away upon a white screen?' " " 'Does she ever think of the past?' " He has no answers, but looking at the son, he seems " 'to see again the other one—the father, cast out mysteriously by the sea to perish in the supreme disaster of loneliness and despair' " (XX.141–2). He cannot mean the son bears a physical resemblance, for that would contradict his statement that the " 'crooked cross . . . is all that remains now to perpetuate the memory of his name' " (XX.133–4). He must mean Yanko's experience is the universal one. All men are cast out by the sea onto foreign shores, treated with contempt, locked in cages, reviled and spat upon, finally to perish because the " 'fear of the Incomprehensible . . . hangs over all our heads—over all our heads . . .' " (XX.108). Here is the significance of Yanko's experience: it is incomprehensible and purposeless.

Kennedy can find no natural cause for this disaster, nor can he believe in a supernatural one, and the knowledge that life is a mystery transcending reason corrodes his soul. He can see no purpose to life; he can discern no divine plan. Yet the overpowering fact of existence is that men perish in loneliness and despair, for images of helplessness punctuate his narrative. Yanko is described as " 'an animal under a net' " (XX.112), " 'a bear in a cage' " (XX.120), and a man trapped in " 'the net of fate' " (XX.137). The son, like the father, like all men, is " 'a bird in a snare' " (XX.142).

He wants to believe but he cannot. For him the universe is a wasteland; " 'the earth is under a curse . . .' " (XX.111). On the night he found Yanko lying face down in a puddle, he called out for Amy, " 'and my voice seemed to lose itself in the emptiness of this tiny house as if I had cried in a desert.' " The dying man cried out " 'in the penetrating and indignant voice of a man calling to a responsible Maker.' " His last word was " ' "Merciful," ' " but since Kennedy did not speak, we can infer that for him there is no responsible Maker. He heard only " 'a gust of wind and a swish of rain' " (XX.140–1). Overwhelmed, he sees mankind perishing in tragedy.

If we do not take into account the epistemological problem in first-person narration, we can read the story the way Frederick R. Karl does: "Its pretentiousness is manifest in the narrator, Kennedy, whose 'wisdom' is often more suffocating than Marlow's. The too frequent classical allusions add ponderous weight to the thin trappings, while the excess of rhetoric inundates an essentially simple story of the heart." [3] But the classical allusions—to Greek tragedy, for example—are Kennedy's attempt to remove the necessity for seeking a natural explanation for the events; and the excess of rhetoric—repetition, questions, negatives—demonstrates he cannot comprehend what he witnessed. Just as the narrator's language in *The Sacred Fount* reveals a man who sees existential experience in terms of a priori categories and Dowell's distortion of dates in *The Good Soldier* reveals a man determined to find a pattern in events he witnessed, so do this narrator's allusions and rhetoric reveal his predicament. In defending the artistic reason for Yanko's death, Richard Herndon asserts that it "reflects . . . a literary propensity for ending tragic action with the protagonist's death." [4] But the death is one more unintelligible event. It is a mystery: " 'Physiologically . . . it was possible. . . . Eventually I certified heart-failure as the immediate cause of death' " (XX.138–41).

Doctor Kennedy mythicizes the events because if interpreted naturally they would be unbearable. His constant allusions to the number three, the cross, and Yanko's being a creature of the woods or trees suggest that for him the castaway may have been a Christ-like figure " 'different from . . . mankind' " (XX.111) who descended into the underworld: he was washed ashore mysteriously, was taller than the others, sang and danced among the dead, got with child a woman who can no longer remember him, and died mysteriously. But since Yanko's suffering had no healing effect on the community, since his experience is incomprehensible and purposeless, Kennedy has no faith in the possibility of redemption on earth. He wants to believe in a higher intention for life, though. Hence his narrative keeps returning to the central symbol of Christianity, the cross, for the agony of the Passion makes possible redemption and resurrection. This may be a land of the dead, but he would like to hope there is redemption beyond the horizon.

If there were no other point of view, the reader would have to accept as unexplainable the events culminating in the hero's betrayal by his wife. There is another narrator, however, to whom Kennedy recounts the events, who functions somewhat like a chorus in Greek tragedy. The nameless "I" narrator begins by remarking that Amy " 'seems dull,' " which supports Kennedy's question about her aptitude for love, but as he provides the framework for the latter's narrative, he demythicizes his interpretation. Noting that the roof of Amy's cottage is "shingle" and her figure "squat," he puts her in the wasteland with the rest of the villagers: "The high ground . . . crowds the quaint High Street against the wall which defends it from the sea. Beyond the sea-wall there curves . . . the barren beach of shingle. . . . A dilapidated windmill near by, lifting its shattered arms from a mound no loftier than a rubbish-heap, and a Martello tower squatting at the water's edge. . . ." His description of the terrain gives the reader another perspective from which to understand the tragedy: although man projects himself "on the background of the Infinite with a heroic uncouthness," the melancholy "of an over-burdened earth" weights his "feet," bows his "shoulders," bears down his "glances" (XX.105–10). For all of his aspirations, man is a creature of the earth, destined to live and die on earth.

The nameless narrator interrupts Kennedy's narrative three more times, each time to clarify the tragedy. Looking at the sea, from which Yanko came, he sees "a belt of glassy water at the foot of the sky. The light blur of smoke, from an invisible steamer, faded on the great clearness of the horizon like the mist of a breath on a mirror . . ." (XX.111). It is not given to man to see beyond life. Whatever lies beneath the water or behind the horizon is a mystery. His final comment, "The Doctor came to the window and looked out at the frigid splendour of the sea, immense in the haze, as if enclosing all the earth with all the hearts lost among the passions of love and fear" (XX.138), repeats the "frigid splendour of a hazy sea" (XX.113) of his penultimate remarks. Further, he can say with certainty that the sea is "immense" and "frigid" and he can say with certainty that the world contains "all the hearts lost," but he is not certain whether the sea "encloses all the earth." Like Kennedy, he cannot discern a higher purpose to existence.

If I disagree with Karl because I do not think he does justice to Kennedy, I disagree far more with those critics who discuss the events of "Amy Foster" as one discusses the events in a piece of fiction not utilizing the point of view of limited narration, for the story is about the doctor's response to the events—his imagination.[5] The nameless narrator complements him because, viewing the picture from another angle, he arrives at the moral judgment of the story. He does not mythicize the events, nor does he hedge as the doctor does. He is far less emotionally involved in what he says; he is far more objective about what he sees. He neither contradicts Kennedy nor deflates his illusion, since, as I showed above, the doctor does not believe in his created myth. When one narrator despairs because he cannot discern either natural or supernatural causes for the events he witnessed and another narrator, who did not witness the events, flatly reports that the sea, the origin of Yanko and scene of the shipwreck, is "frigid" and "glassy" and that the land contains "all the hearts lost," we must conclude that man, who does not and cannot comprehend the explanation for existence, can " 'perish in the supreme disaster of loneliness and despair' " (XX.142).[6]

Mankind does not have to perish this way, though. In ruling out a discernible supernatural intention for life, the nameless narrator uses an image, found throughout Conrad's fiction, to place the responsibility for Yanko's betrayal where it belongs, in man himself. When he looks down he sees "glassy water"; when he looks up he sees a "mirror." No matter where he looks for an explanation for Yanko's betrayal, he sees his own reflection. Thus Yanko could have been saved by the men and women in his adopted community had they been willing to recognize themselves in the abandoned derelict. Redemption is not to be found beyond the horizon, but rather in mankind on earth. By making the reader reexamine the picture from his more hopeful perspective, the nameless narrator makes him perceive that all of the villagers are responsible for the tragedy by failing to sympathetically identify with the castaway " 'of a mysterious origin' " who appeared to them as a " 'mass of mud and filth from head to foot' " (XX.120).

"Amy Foster" is not merely an early tale or a minor tale but a very important story in the Conrad canon. "You must remember that I don't start with an abstract notion," the novelist wrote to R. B. Cunninghame Graham. "I start with definite images and as their rendering is true some little effect is produced." [7] Showing the disastrous consequences not only to Yanko but also to Kennedy, who cannot free himself from the burden of the past, the story suggests the values and virtues that must be preserved in a darkening world and the prerequisites for moral knowledge. Since it is not given to man to solve the mystery of existence, he must learn his limitations by looking into the mirror of mankind, which will unite him in compassion, pity, and love for all men, who are perishing in the supreme disaster. The great irony of the story is that Yanko's heart failure was not the cause of his death; it was the failure of the hearts of those in whose midst he appeared, including Doctor Kennedy, who, certifying heart failure, cannot see the real cause.

"Amy Foster" presents one response to the moral test Conrad's characters undergo in that the villagers failed the test without being aware they were being tested. "The Secret Sharer" (1910), a first-person tale from Conrad's middle period—this one reprinted in the 1912 *'Twixt Land*

and Sea volume—presents a second response. With an ease unparalleled in Conrad's major works, the captain recounts how he shared the fate of a stranger, who, like Yanko, came out of the sea one night shortly after he had been appointed captain, and in sharing discovered himself so that by the end of his experience he was able to take command of himself and his ship.

Since Kennedy does not descend into himself, he does not know himself. And the more one lacks self-knowledge the more one ascribes divine or mythic qualities to a stranger. That is, the less is one able to recognize the common bond of humanity uniting all mortals. At the other extreme, the captain was willing to allow Leggatt, with whom he sympathetically identified, to come to the surface immediately because before they met he had admitted he was a stranger to himself and his ship, symbolized by his staring into the "glassy" sea (XIX.97), and he felt some guilt for not adhering to the ship's routine, which accounted for the rope ladder being left over the side. He was surprised by Leggatt's appearance and at one point even questioned whether he had a bodily existence, but at no time did he look upon him as divine; he never considered him a castaway " 'transplanted into another planet,' " speaking " 'an unearthly language.' " On the contrary, he calls Leggatt his "double" (XIX.112), his "other self" (XIX.105), his "secret self" (XIX.114). Extending sanctuary to his "secret self," the mate of the *Sephora* who had killed a man during a storm, he discovered that he was capable of seizing the steward by the throat, that he could take his ship to the brink of destruction, that his test was "a matter of conscience" (XIX.139).

These two stories present two versions of another Conrad theme. Kennedy's narrative is controlled by a sense of the inexorability of fate. For the doctor it is destined that a man who should have gone down in a shipwreck to a watery grave should be denied a glass of water by his wife and should be found " 'lying face down and his body in a puddle' " (XX.140) the night he died. Not knowing his heart, Kennedy does not know he could have altered Yanko's and his own moral destiny. To him the stranger was " 'plainly in the toils of his obscure and touching destiny' " the moment he headed toward New Barns Farm because to him all men are fated " 'to perish in the supreme disaster of loneliness and despair.' " In his journey to self-knowledge, the captain accepted the outcast as his "other self," thereby freeing himself from the prison of the solitary self. Because Leggatt came to him for assistance and because he extended compassion, both men overcame loneliness and despair. Ready to take their "punishment," because they knew they were responsible for their actions, they became "free" (within the human condition, which no man can ever escape) to strike out "for a new destiny" (XIX.143).

A psychological phenomenon in Conrad's imaginative world is the divided self. Kennedy does not know his heart because the "penetrating power of his mind" (XX.106) has corroded his faith in himself and in others. Since "his intelligence is of a scientific order" (XX.106), he expects a scientific explanation for natural events. Unable to find one he turns to a supernatural explanation, but here too he finds nothing because he cannot believe in a supernatural reality. In his skepticism he knows all men are perishing in loneliness and despair, but this skepticism prevented him from responding to the perishing man. His head passes a scientific judgment on what should have been an affair of the heart. Early in "The Secret Sharer," the captain contrasts his "intuition" (XIX.99) with the chief mate's "painstaking turn of mind" which inquired into "the why and the wherefore" of everything (XIX.94). After allowing Leggatt to rise, he thought suddenly of his "absurd mate with his terrific whiskers and the 'Bless my soul —you don't say so' type of intellect" (XIX.101). Kennedy and the captain knew they were confronting a mystery, yet the latter, unlike the former, responded with his heart to the castaway: "A mysterious communication was established already between us two—in the face of that silent, darkened tropical sea" (XIX.99). Together they overcame their loneliness in an indifferent universe and became free.

I can only begin to indicate now the direction the dual nature of illusion will take in Conrad's works. Except for the captain's wondering whether he would "turn out faithful to that ideal conception of one's own personality every man sets up for himself secretly" (XIX.94) and his rejoicing "in the great security of the sea" (XIX.96), illusion is negligible at this pole in Conrad's moral spectrum. In his best works he dramatizes a hero's agonizing struggle to redeem his past, which demands the shedding of illusions about himself.

"Amy Foster" is a more subtle story. Kennedy's illusion is destructive. His trust in his ability to unravel the mystery of existence prevented him from responding with his heart to Yanko. Yanko's illusion was redeeming for himself and potentially redeeming for those whose assistance he sought. His faith in mankind brought him to Amy. Believing in God, he saw her as " 'an angel of light' " (XX.124). Her heart was his " 'gold' " (XX.133). The true Christian in a community professing to be Christian, he was " 'seduced' " by what he took to be " 'the divine quality of her pity' " (XX.135). Although he mistook Amy, his illusion gave them both the opportunity to be moral, for through her " 'act of impulsive pity he was brought back again within the pale of human relations with his new sur-

roundings' " (XX.125), Kennedy explains to the nameless
"I" narrator. (It is ironic that Kennedy can make this
statement about Yanko without seeing its relevance for
himself.) Yanko's faith in man made his heart " 'buoyant' "
(XX.111), his love genuine, and his conduct moral. That
Amy failed him was not his fault. Since we are dependent
on the doctor's narrative for what happened, we can say no
more about her. Perhaps she was too dull to have any illusions about herself or her husband.

Yet a woman did betray Yanko, and since Conrad
added the character Amy to a story which was originally
Ford's idea [8] and since there is no woman in "The Secret
Sharer," we can be misled into concurring with the critics
who hold that she prevents the hero from discovering himself if we discount an image in this second tale—and the
image is the main carrier of meaning in Conrad's work—
an image as pervasive as the mirror: twin hills separated
by a fissure. When the captain realized Leggatt could not
remain on board ship, he decided nearby Koh-ring was his
" 'best chance' " for a new life: " 'It has got two hills and a
low point. It must be inhabited. And on the coast opposite
there is what looks like the mouth of a biggish river—with
some town, no doubt, not far up' " (XIX.134). Here as elsewhere in Conrad's fiction the journey to self-discovery is
an interior journey into death and life on a feminine landscape (the fullest description of which is given in Chapter
XXI of *Lord Jim* and Chapter I of *Nostromo*). Before he
could turn about to freedom, the captain had to take his
ship to the "black mass of Koh-ring," the "very gateway
of Erebus," to pass his initiation. As he did he remembered that he "was a total stranger to the ship. I did not
know her. Would she do it? How was she to be handled?"
With Erebus behind him, however, "alone with her," he
was confident "no one in the world should stand now be-

tween us, throwing a shadow on the way of silent knowledge and mute affection, the perfect communion of a seaman with his first command" (XIX.141–3). His letter to Edward Garnett notwithstanding,[9] Conrad does not "cut out" the female from "The Secret Sharer," as Moser reads the tale.[10] He grounds her in a symbolic landscape. The third story in the 1912 *'Twixt Land and Sea* volume, "Freya of the Seven Isles" (1912), contains the following passage: "The beauty of the loved woman exists in the beauties of Nature. The swelling outlines of the hills, the curves of a coast, the free sinuosities of a river are less suave than the harmonious lines of her body, and when she moves, gliding lightly, the grace of her progress suggests the power of occult forces which rule the fascinating aspects of the visible world" (XIX.210). I prefer Leo Gurko's reading of the sea tales over Moser's. Gurko concludes that "the ship serves as a loose symbol of the feminine principle in a variety of incarnations: mother, mistress, home, haven, protectress, the object on which officers and crew can practice their skills and expend their emotions." [11]

In 1899, two years earlier than "Amy Foster" and eleven years earlier than "The Secret Sharer," Conrad published "Heart of Darkness," the tale that delineates the archetypal pattern he continued to refine throughout his career. The hero, Marlow, relates his experience journeying up the Congo River in quest of another white man, Kurtz, a fellow employee of a trading Company in the Belgian Congo. " 'I felt,' " he tells his audience, " 'as though, instead of going to the centre of a continent, I were about to set off for the centre of the earth' " (XVI.60). Having journeyed into the interior as far as a man is able to and still turn about, he can sympathize with Kurtz in his desire to remain at the Inner Station: " 'But the wilderness had found him out early, and had taken on him a terrible vengeance for the fantastic invasion. I think it had whispered to him things about himself which he did not know, things of which he had no conception till he took counsel with this great solitude—and the whisper had proved irresistibly fascinating. It echoed loudly within him because he was hollow at the core . . .' " (XVI.131). Critics usually interpret this passage to mean Kurtz and Kurtz alone was hollow, but I think for the story to engage the reader in the quest the passage must mean all men have hollow cores behind their hearts. Marlow himself is described as having a "worn, hollow" face (XVI.114). As I read the story, it is by knowing one's heart that a man becomes truly human. There are limits to his knowledge, though: " 'I assure you that never, never before, did this land, this river, this jungle, the very arch of this blazing sky, appear to me so hopeless and so dark, so impenetrable to human thought, so pitiless to human weakness' " (XVI.127). Self-knowledge is necessary to teach him he is free to be good or evil—" 'the pulsating stream of light, or the deceitful flow from the heart of an impenetrable darkness' " (XVI.113-4)—so that he can impose restraints on himself.[12] As one journeys into his heart, he journeys into a realm of increasing darkness, solitude, and freedom, for behind his heart lies an impenetrable mystery described as a " 'hollow core.' " One should know his heart well enough to respond to other hearts, but he should not dare to possess the mystery of his being because he is then tempted to possess the hollow cores of other men. The frequency of the word " 'soul' " in the section in which Marlow relates his experience with Kurtz at the Inner Station suggests it is the inscrutable mystery behind the heart.

Kurtz had gone into the interior believing himself an apostle of light. His illusion was destructive. Not knowing himself, he was unprepared for the ordeal. A white man among black natives, he was received as if he were a god. " ' "What can you expect?" he [the Russian sailor] burst out; "he came to them with thunder and lightning, you know—and they had never seen anything like it—and very terrible" ' " (XVI.128). Kurtz's conduct with the natives was exactly the opposite of Yanko's with Amy. The natives' illusion, that he was a god when he arrived at the Inner Station, gave him the opportunity to be moral, but he failed the test because he went beyond the limits of his heart. " 'Invading' " his hollow core, he " 'wandered alone, far in the depths of the forest' " (XVI.127).

The confluence of his illusion and theirs seduced him into participating in " 'unspeakable rites' " (XVI.118). Marlow distinguishes between " 'pure, uncomplicated savagery . . . a positive relief' " and the " 'subtle horrors' " of these rites (XVI.132). They must have been so diabolical they went beyond the bounds of mere savagery. They must have been the very essence of evil, which in Conrad's world means the violation of another person's being. Acting on his discovery that all humans have hollow cores, Kurtz filled the younger, more vigorous natives with himself so they could take his place in the tribal ritual of the slaying of the man-god.[13] The condition of the Russian sailor yields this reading. Like the natives, the Russian saw Kurtz as a god. Kurtz's " 'last disciple,' " he offered himself to his " 'idol' " (XVI.132), who proceeded to oblige his victim by breaking down his identity—the Russian had " 'no features to speak of' " (XVI.122)—and remolding him—he was a creature of patchwork—in his own image. The sailor's eyes were " 'perfectly round' " (XVI.125) like the " 'round carved balls' " (XVI.121) of the heads Kurtz collected, heads which were not " 'ornamental but symbolic' " (XVI.130). The heads themselves resembled his idol's head, which was like " 'a ball—an ivory ball' " (XVI.115). The Russian confessed to Marlow his master " ' "enlarged" ' " his " ' "mind" ' " (XVI.125), which implies Kurtz was planning to add his head to the collection. The following passage supports this reading: " 'The man filled his life, occupied his thoughts, swayed his emotions' " (XVI.128). Or to locate the activity in terms of the metaphysical structure of heart and soul: " 'He had the power to charm or frighten rudimentary souls into an aggravated witch-dance in his honour; he could also fill the small souls of the pilgrims with bitter misgivings: he had one devoted friend at least, and he had conquered one soul in the world that was neither rudimentary nor tainted with self-seeking' " (XVI.119). Kurtz was able to possess him because the sailor, lost in his illusion, did not know himself.

Marlow did not transgress his limits. He " 'peeped over the edge' " (XVI.151), but he turned about and came back. Throughout his narration he maintains he does not fully understand his experience. If he did he would be completely Kurtz, who paid the price in madness and death for " 'stepping over the edge' " (XVI.151). He had an advantage in that he had had glimmerings into himself before leaving for the Congo. Admitting the charm of the blank mystery and his being part of a conspiracy made it easier for him to accept his " 'kinship' " with the natives in their " 'wild and passionate uproar' " (XVI.96), which in turn disposed him to accept Kurtz as his other, or potential, self. The heart of darkness exercised its lure on him, too, but he was able to restrain himself because he recognized its fascination and abomination. He fought his desire to join in unspeakable rites; he " 'struggled' " with his soul (XVI.144). As much as I respect Bruce Harkness' editorial work on Conrad, I disagree with his judgment that there is a crucial difference in interpretation between the passage, " 'to go through the ordeal of looking into myself,' " and the correct version of this passage, " 'to go through the ordeal of looking into it [Kurtz's soul] myself' " (XVI.145).[14] Kurtz's soul is potentially his soul, and by looking into it, Marlow was looking into his potentiality for evil.

Since he saw himself in Kurtz's soul, when he returned to Europe he was alerted to his potentiality for evil. At the door of the flat of the girl Kurtz called his Intended, the dead man's image " 'stared' " at him from " 'the glassy panel' " (XVI.156). Once inside, the temptation to be Kurtz, to destroy her belief in her fiancé and to be her man-god, became more vividly alive every moment of their conversation because she presented herself to him as the Russian had to his master: " 'She seemed ready to listen without mental reservation, without suspicion, without a thought for herself' " (XVI.155). He could have captured her soul, but by feeling " 'infinite pity' " (XVI.161) for a girl lost in her illusion, he broke the spell of the deepening darkness. " 'It would have been too dark—too dark altogether . . .' " (XVI.162) had he told her the truth about her fiancé. It would have been moral death for him. The " 'right thing' " he said to Kurtz the night he struggled with his soul was, " ' "You will be lost . . . utterly lost" ' " (XVI.143).

For Conrad no man can escape his human destiny, but men are free to be moral or immoral. Both Marlow and the captain in "The Secret Sharer" travel as far as is morally permissible, to the brink of the inscrutable mystery, refrain from invading it, and then come about to fulfill their new destinies. For the journey to self-knowledge is a journey to acceptance of the physical and moral limits of life. While Kurtz was wandering alone in the exhilaration of

his freedom, kicking " 'himself loose of the earth' "
(XVI.144), he was hastening his end. He was becoming
" 'an animated image of death' " (XVI.134). The man who
became more than a man with the savages fulfilled his destiny more rapidly than he had ever dreamed he would, by
joining all other mortals in " 'the mould of primeval
earth' " (XVI.147).

Since no man can ever know himself totally, can ever
totally decipher the mystery of existence, he can never
know another totally. Confronting the mystery of being
constitutes a religious experience: the feelings experienced
by the limited before the unlimited, before one's soul or
that of another person. If a man dares possess the core, the
center, he dies morally and physically: he is no longer a
man. Kurtz became the mystery he set out to conquer: the
wilderness " 'had taken him, loved him, embraced him,
got into his veins, consumed his flesh, and sealed his soul
to its own by the inconceivable ceremonies of some devil-
ish initiation' " (XVI.115). Just as the heart is the organ
of physical life, so it is also the organ of moral response.
It is only by knowing his heart within the metaphysical
structure of heart and soul that one can embrace his submerged, or other, self in humility and respond to another
human being with compassion, pity, and love. By participating in unspeakable rites so that he could continue his
domination as man-god, Kurtz lost his humanity.

In the remainder of this chapter, I want to concentrate on the religious experience that makes moral action
possible in Conrad's fiction. The return stage of the tri-
partite archetypal pattern may not reintegrate society in
Conrad's imaginative world, but it does reintegrate the
hero because by discovering himself in the initiation stage,
he becomes a whole man capable of moral action. In order
to study this experience in the major novels, I must first

trace the accretion of images, symbols, and motifs as they grow from story to story. Conrad never wrote a *Parade's End,* the one work that standing apart from the rest of an author's canon creates a world in itself. His collected works form a mosaic, and it is not until we have the pieces in place that the journey to the center will be fully revealed. For example, the two images we have been looking at will progressively fuse. The mirror image will be grounded in the feminine landscape so that when the heroine uncovers her eyes the hero will see himself in all his actuality and potentiality.[15] Journeying through his heart to her, he will discover his soul, his center, reflected in her eyes. Like Marlow, I cannot capture the center, but by following the guides up the river to its source, I hope to show how each one of the major works will bring into ever sharper focus the " 'implacable force brooding over an inscrutable intention' " (XVI.93) so we can glimpse its suggestiveness before it recedes.

For Conrad illusions are necessary and either destructive or salutary. Kennedy's illusion that rationality can decipher the mystery is destructive as is Kurtz's illusion that he was a supernatural being. These illusions reflect their pride. With the pilgrims in "Heart of Darkness," they lack faith. Instead of filling other hollow cores, Kurtz should have been filling his own soul with faith. Yanko's illusion that Amy had a heart of " 'gold,' " the Russian's illusion that Kurtz was " 'one of the immortals' " (XVI.138), and the Intended's illusion that her fiancé's " ' "goodness shone in every act" ' " (XVI.160) reflect their humility and faith. The second two were saved temporarily because they met Marlow, who had journeyed to self-knowledge, which is ultimately a journey to humility and awe before the mystery of existence: a religious experience. He accepted the Russian's " 'improbable, inexplicable' " existence

(XVI.126) because he had accepted the " 'human secret,' " the " 'unfathomable enigma' " (XVI.104–5) of the cannibals who did not attack white men. Even though he sensed the nature of Kurtz's unspeakable rites and therefore had few illusions about him when he confronted the Intended, he bowed his head " 'before the faith that was in her, before that great and saving illusion that shone with an unearthly glow in the darkness . . .' " (XVI.159).

Marlow's quest being a journey " 'in the night of first ages' " (XVI.96), the dual nature of illusions operates on historical and political levels also. Since every man is a savage, civilization brings the illusion of progress. Necessary to keep man from running amuck in the jungle, it can be beneficial if it prevents him from collecting heads. It can be destructive if he deludes himself into believing that because he is civilized he is not a potential savage. With political, that is, human, activity, the blank space necessarily becomes " 'a place of darkness' " (XVI.52). Although the activity is little more than rapacious and pitiless folly, the " 'idea at the back of it' " (XVI.51) redeems because it brought Kurtz to the wilderness, the man who penetrated the mystery, whose " 'extremity' " Marlow " 'lived through' " in order to have his religious experience. His " 'affirmation,' " his " 'moral victory' " (XVI.151), gave Marlow his choice of nightmares. Had the former not gone to the Inner Station, the latter would not have followed him to self-discovery and would not have had the opportunity to act on his knowledge. Marlow had to journey into the interior to approach the light, for it is found at the heart of darkness.

Which brings us back to the female. A bearer of light, she guides the male into the interior. "Heart of Darkness" is a journey up a snake-like river to the mystery of life and death, death and rebirth. Although one man recounts his experience with another, the woman is at the heart of it. The journey began with Marlow's aunt securing him an appointment with the Company. He embarked from the dead city, where two women guarded the door of darkness, to travel to the Central Station, where he saw the portrait of the blindfolded woman carrying a lighted torch, and then on to the Inner Station, made unforgettable by Kurtz and by the apparition of his high priestess, the gorgeous Negress, at whom " 'the immense wilderness, the colossal body of the fecund and mysterious life seemed to look . . . pensive, as though it had been looking at the image of its own tenebrous and passionate soul.' " The mystery is figured in her person: " 'She stood looking at us without a stir, and like the wilderness itself, with an air of brooding over an inscrutable purpose' " (XVI.136).[16] Away from her, Kurtz, who had sworn to possess the interior, died whereas Marlow, who turned about, came out of the darkness to confront her counterpart, the girl for whom Kurtz had entered the jungle.

This scene with the Intended is necessary to complete the hero's journey from separation from the Western European moral code to initiation into the region of fabulous forces, the pagan world that reigns in his heart of darkness, to return to the Western European moral code. Conrad explained the function of this scene in a letter to William Blackwood: "I call your own kind self to witness and I beg to instance 'Karain'—*Lord Jim* (where the method is fully developed)—the last pages of 'Heart of Darkness' where the interview of the man and the girl locks in—as it were—the whole 30,000 words of narrative description into one suggestive view of a whole phase of life, and makes of that story something quite on another plane than an anecdote of a man who went mad in the Centre of Africa." [17] In the darkness of her death-like room, Kurtz's fiancée " 'seemed to catch all the remaining light' " (XVI.160) in her hair, gathering up in her person the beacons along the journey from the dead city to the center. Marlow had a choice: to violate the bearer of light or to humble himself before her. Having journeyed through his heart to his soul, he knew he did not belong in that place of mystery " 'not fit for a human being to behold' " (XVI.157). Knowing his heart, he responded with infinite pity for her, freeing himself from the temptation to repeat Kurtz's unspeakable rites. Saving her, he did not repeat " 'the horror' " (XVI.156) and thereby created a new life for himself. He walked away from the sarcophagus as he had turned away from the heart of darkness.

The themes, images, symbols, and motifs isolated above are present from the beginning of Conrad's career as an artist, in his first novel, *Almayer's Folly* (1895). Since Almayer, a Dutch trader in Borneo, is lost in his illusion of amassing a fortune that will return him in splendor to the "earthly paradise of his dreams" (XI.10), Amsterdam, with his half-caste daughter, he does not know himself or her. When he accuses Nina of deceiving him with the Malay prince, Dain Maroola, she tells her father he failed to respond to her when she needed him. Losing his faith in her, he turns from the self-deception of illusions to the self-forgetfulness of opium.

Nina listens to her heart: "With the coming of Dain she found the road to freedom by obeying the voice of the new-born impulses, and with surprised joy she thought she could read in his eyes the answer to all the questionings of her heart" (XI.152). His appearance to her as a "gorgeous and bold being" (XI.55) draws her out of her loneliness until she recognizes "with a thrill of delicious fear the mysterious consciousness of her identity with that being"

The illusion that another person is a 'wholly other' being, which can be destructive or salutary, moves us to the paradox in Conrad's imaginative world, illustrated in what would have been his third novel had he finished it according to schedule. Begun in 1896 as *The Rescuer* but not published until 1920 as *The Rescue,* this novel details the undoing of King Tom Lingard, whose plan to restore Prince Hassim as ruler of Wajo is threatened when a yacht becomes stranded off the coast where the factions involved in the restoration are assembled. Although it is imperative that Lingard act decisively with the factions, he is paralyzed. When he looks into the violet eyes of Edith Travers, the wife of the yacht's owner, he feels "his mind overpowered and troubled as if by the contemplation of vast distances" (XII.144). To him she is "a waking dream" (XII.431). His predicament reaches its climax the night she joins him in the native stockade, where he is using his influence to protect the lives of her husband and d'Alcacer, another member of the party from the yacht. Unable to resume his conversation with Belarab, the chieftain whose support is essential to the success of the venture, he breaks off the interview to sit at her feet. He is "in the state of a man who, having cast his eyes through the open gates of Paradise, is rendered insensible by that moment's vision to all the forms and matters of the earth; and in the extremity of his emotion ceases even to look upon himself but as the subject of a sublime experience which exalts or unfits, sanctifies or damns . . ." (XII.415). Failing to receive any answer to the signal sent with Mrs. Travers, Jörgenson, his associate, detonates the ammunition stored on the *Emma,* ending the venture forever. Thus Lingard is "undone by a glimpse of Paradise" (XII.449).

Undone as King Tom or Rajah Laut (King of the Sea), a god whose word is law to the natives, Lingard comes to know himself as a man. He replies, " 'For, listen, Jaffir, if she had given the ring to me it would have been to one that was dumb, deaf, and robbed of all courage' " (XII. 450), to the information from Hassim's servant that the white woman was supposed to give him the signal sent by Jörgenson. And by knowing himself as a man, he discovers a reality within himself because by looking into her eyes, he discovers emotions and sensations of which he was unaware. When she arrives on the beach for their last meeting before they part, he says to her, " 'I am looking at you for the first time. . . . I never could see you before. There were too many things, too many thoughts, too many people. No, I never saw you before. But now the world is dead' " (XII.463). Yet even though the world is dead, for him Edith Travers " 'stands above death itself' ": " 'What has hate or love to do with you and me? Hate. Love. What can touch you? For me you stand above death itself; for I see now that as long as I live you will never die' " (XII. 465).

The paradox can be summed up this way: the less one knows himself the more he ascribes 'wholly other' qualities to the stranger, the more he makes of him a saviour " 'different from . . . mankind.' " As he comes to know himself, however, he realizes the stranger is not different because while journeying into his heart of darkness, he discovers he too has a 'wholly other' core, a concealed reality in himself, which he can never totally know. The heroine is the catalyst for this self-discovery: if he does not reject her, she will guide him to the region of supernatural wonder within himself. This initiation is his religious experience. The male who persists in his illusion that he does not have anything in common with the rest of mankind does not redeem himself because he does not have the experience that makes the moral response possible. Refusing to humble himself before the mystery in her person, he misses the opportunity to humble himself before his own mystery, which would be an acknowledgement of his kinship with all of mankind and the beginning of a moral response. By invading her being or by ignoring her reality, he finds what he is fleeing, death, since he does not realize himself as a human being in moral action.

When Jim in *Lord Jim* (1900) confided in Marlow, the narrator of the events, that he had " 'nothing in common' " (XXI.103) with the shipmates with whom he had deserted the *Patna,* he denied his potentiality for betrayal. Although he was the only one of them to stand trial before the court of inquiry, he could not accept the fact that he had impulsively jumped from a ship he thought was sinking. He therefore could not tolerate the presence of his other self, Gentleman Brown, the fugitive who appeared in Patusan, the jungle village to which he fled in quest of a new life far from constant reminders of his past. He lived in loneliness, destined to jump until he redeemed himself or until he died. His solution was to master his destiny by dying: the sole way to preclude the possibility of leaping again was to commit suicide. In one sense his life duplicated the lives of the criminals, Kurtz and Willems, for he too became a captive of the interior he set out to conquer. The confluence of his illusion and that of the Patusan natives allowed him to become 'wholly other.' He did climb out of the mud bank into which he leaped shortly after his arrival, " 'cracking the earth asunder' " (XXI. 254), but at a terrible price: he forfeited his membership in a human community.

In his desire for one more chance to begin anew, Jim eagerly accepted an offer to go into the virgin forest of Patusan as the new manager for Stein, a wealthy merchant in Samarang and Marlow's old friend. Quickly winning the

confidence of the Bugis chief, Doramin, and his son, Dain
Waris, by driving the Arab half-breed, Sherif Ali, from the
country, he seemed to be escaping his past. He was not.
His destiny inexorably overtook him with the appearance
of Gentleman Brown and his party of cutthroats, who came
to Patusan to ravage the village while replenishing supplies
for their stolen schooner. Surrounded by the natives, who
had been warned in time, Brown pleaded with Jim for
one more chance by hinting at " 'their common blood, an
assumption of common experience; a sickening suggestion
of common guilt, of secret knowledge that was like a bond
of their minds and of their hearts' " (XXI.387). Jim consented to allow Brown free passage to the schooner by
pledging his life to the council of Bugis elders should the
outlaw betray his trust. When he did, by killing Dain
Waris, Jim achieved his goal. He did not falter in his determination to fulfill himself and became a sacrificial
victim. He surrendered to Doramin, who killed him.

Originally conceived as a companion piece to "Youth"
(1898) and "Heart of Darkness," [18] *Lord Jim* yields a richer
meaning when read as an expansion of the initiation stage
to novel length. If the novel is read as the third work in a
sequence, Jim's resolution to conquer the mystery of his
interior has far greater consequences than his own undoing. It was fatal to Jewel also, for the African jungle
becomes the landscape of Patusan, which with its blatantly
feminine contours imagistically defines the process of redemption as a journey to the limits of life and a rebirth
through the agency of the heroine:

"Patusan is a remote district of a native-ruled State,
and the chief settlement bears the same name. At a
point on the river about forty miles from the sea,

where the first houses come into view, there can be seen rising above the level of the forests the summits of two steep hills very close together, and separated by what looks like a deep fissure, the cleavage of some mighty stroke. As a matter of fact, the valley between is nothing but a narrow ravine; the appearance from the settlement is of one irregularly conical hill split in two, and with the two halves leaning slightly apart. On the third day after the full, the moon, as seen from the open space in front of Jim's house (he had a very fine house in the native style when I visited him), rose exactly behind these hills, its diffused light at first throwing the two masses into intensely black relief, and then the nearly perfect disc, glowing ruddily, appeared, gliding upwards between the sides of the chasm, till it floated away above the summits, as if escaping from a yawning grave in gentle triumph" (XXI.220–1).[19]

Intent on knowing himself so completely that he would never again act impulsively, Jim could not perceive its import. " ' "Wonderful effect," said Jim by my side. "Worth seeing. Is it not?" ' " (XXI.221) Blind, he violated Jewel's love, losing his one chance for redemption and destroying her hope.

The final use of this split-hills image occurs after Marlow learned of Jim's decision not to return to life. Now the emphasis is on death. The moon threw its rays across " 'the solitary grave perpetually garlanded with flowers' " (XXI.322). The grave of Jewel's mother, deserted by her husband and hounded to death by Cornelius, Stein's manager in Patusan, becomes the grave of Jewel, deserted by the man who professed to love her, and the grave of Jim, " 'overwhelmed by the inexplicable . . . his own personality' " (XXI.341) he was determined to fathom. Too proud to humble himself, he fell to his death with " 'a proud and unflinching glance' " (XXI.416) on his face, much as the moon in this image " 'disengaged itself from the tangle of twigs' " (XXI.322) to hang suspended, " 'gloating serenely upon the spectacle' " below (XXI.326).

Jim had an opportunity to be redeemed.[20] Jewel offered him the choice between his ideal conception of himself and a new life with her. He refused to run away with her following Dain Waris's death because running away would have been an admission that he had not conquered the unknown in himself so that by demanding redemption on his terms he betrayed his heart and her trust in him. She cannot be blamed. On the night of the attempt on his life by Sherif Ali's men, she had begged him to leave her. He refused, promising never to desert her. She echoes Aïssa when she screams at him, " ' "You are false!" ' " (XXI.414) His choosing death as a way of erasing his desertion of the *Patna* rather than life with her, since accepting life would have meant submitting to the human condition, was another betrayal, another desertion of the *Patna*.[21]

It is clear from these stories of the early period that for Conrad any man who, like Jim, gazes "hungrily into the unattainable" (XXI.19) while denying his human nature discovers precisely what he is denying. To say this another way, any man who looks beyond the woman for his hope misses her reality and does not realize his hope. Almayer, Willems, Kurtz, and Jim fall into despair. Marlow does not fall into despair; nor does he destroy Jewel's faith. Yet he could have, in a scene comparable in intention to his interview with Kurtz's fiancée, by telling her that her hero would one day desert her; instead he tried " 'to soothe her frail soul,' " insisting he would never leave her. Even though he was not engaged to her as Jim was, his awareness of his " 'responsibility' " (XXI.316) to her while confronting " 'the big sombre orbits of her eyes' " (XXI.307) provides a measure for judging the other's betrayal and the consequences of their actions. Like Jim, Marlow is fascinated by the lure of the interior, but unlike the younger man, who is unable to return to life, he turns about to " 'the vastness of the opened horizon. . . .' " (XXI.331) Of the three men who travel up an S-shaped river into the heart of darkness—Kurtz, Jim, and Marlow—two straggle and die whereas the third is reborn.

It is also clear, though, that Jim remains very much of a mystery to Marlow because he became the sacrificial victim Kurtz refused to become: " 'Is he satisfied—quite, now, I wonder? We ought to know. He is one of us—and have I not stood up once, like an evoked ghost, to answer for his eternal constancy? Was I so very wrong after all? Now he is no more, there are days when the reality of his existence comes to me with an immense, with an overwhelming force; and yet upon my honour there are moments, too, when he passes from my eyes like a disembodied spirit astray amongst the passions of this earth, ready to surrender himself faithfully to the claim of his own world of shades' " (XXI.416). Since no one can totally know himself or anyone else, it is just possible he was not " 'one of us,' " a refrain Marlow utters to convince himself he was " 'one of us.' " [22] Any man who pursues his dream to the degree Jim did, any man who " 'goes away from a living woman to celebrate his pitiless wedding with a shadowy ideal of conduct' " (XXI.416) may not be " 'one of us.' " Perhaps he was a fabulously innocent idealist; perhaps he was a " 'superior kind' " of man (XXI.176) or a " 'creature not only of another kind but of another essence' " (XXI. 229). Marlow knows he has not unraveled the mystery: " 'Who knows? He is gone, inscrutable at heart, and the poor girl is leading a sort of soundless, inert life in Stein's house' " (XXI.416-7).

The final paragraph of the novel, a picture in Marlow's mind of the betrayed Jewel, marks a transition in Conrad's collected works. In Jim's reenactment of the past, Conrad gathers up the circular movement that prevails in his early period. In Marlow's return to life, he prefigures the linear movement that will prevail in his middle period. But although different in their responses to Jewel, neither hero completes the mythic quest through the agency of the heroine. Jim becomes the slain god by fleeing from her; Marlow creates a new life for himself by turning away from her as he turned away from Kurtz's fiancée. Here positioned one on either side of the betrayed heroine, the two males will begin to fuse into a single male, a Razumov, a Heyst. This new hero of the middle period will be less extreme than either of the two heroes of the early period. Less remote than Jim, more emotionally engaged to the woman than Marlow, he will move around Jim's circle resisting her pressure until he submits, at which time he will break out of the circle into a movement that develops from Marlow's movement. The Conradian hero will accept the heroine's guiding power on his quest. Once he confronts death within himself, he will confront life. By humbling himself instead of possessing the mystery, he will move toward the discovery of the man-god within himself.

Lord Jim also marks a second transition. Though not as realistically drawn, as substantial a woman as those in the political novels, Jewel is less idealized a female than Edith Travers. I think Conrad tried to suggest in Edith (originally named Beatrix) the otherworldliness of Dante's Beatrice.[23] When Lingard first comes aboard the stranded yacht, she is dressed in blue. Her complexion is "so dazzling in the shade that it seemed to throw out a halo round her head" (XII.139). Her head, which suggests "something medieval, ascetic, drooped dreamily on her breast" (XII. 315). Her eyes receive the most elaborate description. " 'Have you seen the white woman's eyes?' " Immada asks her brother. " 'O Hassim! Have you seen her eyes shining under her eyebrows like rays of light darting under the arched boughs in a forest? They pierced me. I shuddered at the sound of her voice! I saw her walk behind him—and it seems to me that she does not live on earth—that all this is witchcraft' " (XII.241–2). For Lingard the stern lantern of the yacht shines "feebly like a star about to set, unattainable, infinitely remote—belonging to another universe" (XII.203). This attempt to suggest the female's ethereal qualities is the gist of Conrad's problem creating credible women. Edith is shallow and artificial. But he profited from the mistake. Beginning with Jewel, he gives the female a greater reality, more substance as a living woman in this world. As the Conradian female takes on a greater reality as a living woman, she progressively takes on a greater suggestiveness so that by the end of the collected fiction she becomes a nineteenth-century Beatrice with whom the Conradian male can redeem his past. By having the hero discover himself when she unveils herself, Conrad lays the foundation for the experience which will bear fruit in Ford's *Parade's End*.

A cornerstone of this foundation is the imagery with which Conrad describes the heroine. It is imagery traditionally associated with the Virgin Mary. Nina is a pearl to Dain and Aïssa is bedecked with flowers to celebrate the return of Willems's love. Conrad's most telling criticism of the man who looks beyond the horizon for his hope is directed at Jim, who gazes at the stars unaware that next to him he has his Jewel, " 'a wild-flower' " (XXI.309), " 'a

precious gem . . . altogether priceless' " (XXI.277–80).
In the Christian tradition this imagery can be found in
Dante's *Commedia,* a model for Conrad's imaginative
world. In "Amy Foster" one of the young ladies from the
Rectory tried to communicate with Yanko in Italian,
which she had learned by reading Dante (XX.126). In
"Heart of Darkness" it seemed to Marlow that he " 'stepped
into the gloomy circle of some Inferno' " (XVI.66) when
he arrived at the Company's outermost station in Africa.[24]
I detect an allusion in the " 'veiled Eastern bride' " in
Lord Jim to Beatrice in the earthly paradise. In Canto
XXX of the *Purgatorio,* Dante describes the entrance of
Beatrice as the veiled bride from Lebanon whose eyes reflect Christ in His two natures when she unveils herself:
"I once saw at the beginning of the day the eastern parts
all rosy and the rest of the sky clear and beautiful and the
sun's face come forth shaded so that through the temper-
ing vapours the eye could bear it long; so, within a cloud
of flowers which rose from the angels' hands and fell again
within and without, a lady appeared to me, girt with olive
over a white veil, clothed under a green mantle with the
colour of living flame" (22–33). The first time Marlow uses
the image is in his account of Jim's entrance into the virgin
forest of Patusan, where he " 'faced the immovable forests
rooted deep in the soil, soaring towards the sunshine, ever-
lasting in the shadowy might of their tradition, like life
itself. And his opportunity sat veiled by his side like an
Eastern bride waiting to be uncovered by the hand of the
master' " (XXI.243–4). Jim failed to perceive that Jewel
was his Eastern bride. By turning away from her to pursue
his opportunity in " 'a shadowy ideal of conduct,' " he
turned away from life so that it was only in death that he
found paradise. The final time Marlow uses the image is
in the closing paragraphs of his narrative: " 'For it may

very well be that in the short moment of his last proud and unflinching glance, he had beheld the face of that opportunity which, like an Eastern bride, had come veiled to his side' " (XXI.416).

I do not mean to imply that Jewel is Beatrice. At this point in the study of the way in which the Christian myth is being re-created, it is enough to state that by concretizing the mirror image in the heroine, Conrad creates the possibility of redemption for the hero who will look into her eyes. Because she is a woman with whom he can discover himself, she becomes a vessel of hope. Given the imagery with which she is described, she progressively becomes a figure of Mary while retaining her reality as a woman as Conrad moves from his Malayan to his Western European phase.

Almayer's Folly equates the mystery of the sea and the mystery of a woman's heart. "Heart of Darkness" equates economic exploitation that attempts to possess a land's natural mystery and moral exploitation that attempts to possess a person's metaphysical mystery. These equations merge in the first work of Conrad's middle period, *Nostromo* (1904). The opening chapter establishes the theme of the novel. Because the "clumsy deep-sea galleons of the conquerors . . . had been barred out of Sulaco by the prevailing calms of its vast gulf," the town "had found an inviolable sanctuary from the temptations of a trading world in the solemn hush of the deep Golfo Placido as if within an enormous semi-circular and unroofed temple open to the ocean, with its walls of lofty mountains hung with the mourning draperies of cloud." Commercialism, imperialism, colonialism—the activities of the modern state —invade the sanctuary of the temple: "your modern ship built on clipper lines forges ahead by the mere flapping of her sails." Since these activities rob the land of its wealth and the temple of its mystery, they are immoral and the men engaged in them are trapped in a deadly wasteland. Azuera, the masculine landscape guarded by the legendary gringos who perished while searching for forbidden treasure, "lies far out to sea like a rough head of stone stretched from a green-clad coast at the end of a slender neck of sand covered with thickets of thorny scrub. Utterly waterless, for the rainfall runs off at once on all sides into the sea, it has not soil enough—it is said—to grow a single blade of grass, as if it were blighted by a curse." To avoid being trapped, the adventurer should refrain from invading the heart of darkness, the opaque cloud veil which fills the gulf: "The eye of God Himself—they add with grim profanity—could not find out what work a man's hand is doing in there; and you would be free to call the devil to your aid with impunity if even his malice were not defeated by such a blind darkness." Men who venture beyond morally permissible limits will find themselves, with the gringos, becalmed "under the fatal spell of their success," for "their souls cannot tear themselves away from their bodies mounting guard over the discovered treasure." They will not "renounce," the requirement to be "released."

If the adventurer will renounce, the curse can be healed on the Great Isabel, the feminine landscape opposite the entrance to the harbor of Sulaco and outside of the cloud veil. The island has "a spring of fresh water issuing from the overgrown side of a ravine. Resembling an emerald green wedge of land a mile long, and laid flat upon the sea, it bears two forest trees standing close together, with a wide spread of shade at the foot of their smooth trunks. A ravine extending the whole length of the island is full of bushes; and presenting a deep tangled cleft on the high side spreads itself out on the other into a shallow depression abutting on a small strip of sandy shore" (IX.

3–7). In this imagery, then, we have the basis for studying the four main male characters. The three who trespass where man does not belong find slavery and death; the one who accepts the heroine's guiding power finds freedom and life.

"Silver is the pivot of the moral and material events, affecting the lives of everybody in the tale." [25] Confiscated during the period of political turmoil following the death of the dictator, Guzman Bento, and then forced upon Charles Gould, senior, a wealthy merchant in Costaguana, the San Tomé silver mine is reopened by Gould's son partly because it was "the cause of an absurd moral disaster," his father's death, and partly because his idealism hopes to transform the disaster into "a serious and moral success" (IX.66) by keeping the operation of the mine aloof from political machinations. Backed by the American capitalist, Holroyd, the mine brings political stability and prosperity to the South American country until a revolution led by General Montero deposes Señor don Vincente Ribiera, whose government is financed by the San Tomé Administration. To prevent the silver from falling into Monterist hands, two men volunteer to take the ingots across the gulf: Nostromo, a Genoese sailor and captain of the Oceanic Steam Navigation Company's lightermen who sees himself as the only dependable man for the desperate affair, and Martin Decoud, an idle boulevardier and skeptic who becomes involved through his infatuation for Antonia, the daughter of Don José Avellanos. The fourth main male character is Monygham, an English doctor who for years wandered "with almost unknown Indian tribes in the great forests of the far interior where the great rivers have their sources" (IX.311) until given the post of medical officer of the mine.

Charles Gould's illusion that "material interests" will bring permanent peace and stability to Costaguana is

blindness. Believing his silver mine to be the country's
" 'ray of hope' " (IX.84) renders him blind to man's true
hope, the woman standing next to him, for his violation of
the soul of the land is analogous to his violation of the love
given him by his wife, a woman who, "with each day's
journey, seemed to come nearer to the soul of the land.
. . ." (IX.88) Emilia's "prophetic vision" of her future
with Charles is one of "immense desolation" (IX.522):
the mine has been turned into "a wall of silver-bricks,
erected by the silent work of evil spirits, between her and
her husband" (IX.222). Knowing he has compromised his
conscience yet refusing to relinquish the mine, he finds
himself caught in "a grip as deadly as ever it had laid upon
his father" (IX.400). Although sick of the bribing and intriguing necessary to maintain his image of the mine as an
incorruptible moral force, he nonetheless consents to use
the Gould Concession as a party to negotiations with the
Monterists.

In his Preface to *Nostromo,* Conrad singles out Antonia Avellanos, the "being capable of inspiring a sincere
passion in the heart of a trifler" (IX.xiii), and passes judgment on Decoud, a skeptic who recognizes only the truth
of his sensations. He is unable to respond to the one truth
given him in life, Antonia's love. For all of his declarations
of love, his skepticism prevents him from believing in her,
in spite of her faith in him. On the fifth day on the island,
he sees her "gigantic and lovely like an allegorical statue,
looking on with scornful eyes at his weakness." By the
seventh day he does not "dare to think of Antonia. She
had not survived. But if she survived he could not face
her." The "lover of Antonia" becomes convinced she
"could not possibly have ever loved a being so impalpable
as himself" (IX.498–501). By sailing across the darkness of
the gulf, where "no intelligence could penetrate" (IX.
275), he discovers the "retribution meted out to intellec-

tual audacity" (IX.501). Once the skeptic is removed from the object of his sensations, he commits suicide, in the gulf next to the Great Isabel, whose virginal mystery he scorns by burying his silver in her, just as he repudiates Antonia's guiding power by burying himself at the bottom of the water.

" 'You have no heart—and you have no conscience' " (IX.23), Teresa Viola tells Nostromo in Part One of the novel, since he values only his reputation. Gaining heart and conscience in Part Three by admitting that he abandoned her, by refusing to fetch a priest when she was dying, and Decoud, by allowing Dr. Monygham to think he went down with the silver in the gulf, he reaches the stage of his awakening where he should turn about to act on his self-knowledge. He does not. In "a gust of immense pride," he decides there is "no one in the world but Gian' Battista Fidanza, Capataz de Cargadores, the incorruptible and faithful Nostromo, to pay such a price" for their souls. Making up his mind that "nothing should be allowed now to rob him of his bargain" with the San Tomé Administration because he believes his courageous action unrewarded, he discovers the "reward of audacious action" (IX.501–2) for sailing across the darkness of the gulf. He embarks on a life of secrecy, with the final act of his self-betrayal played out on the Great Isabel, where he and Decoud hid the silver.

Nostromo has two opportunities to be redeemed. The first is offered by Linda Viola, Teresa's choice to marry him. But because her love for him "would be violent, exacting, suspicious, uncompromising—like her soul," she "inspires him with a deep-seated mistrust." He knows he would not be able to possess her. The tender of the lighthouse beacon on the Great Isabel, she would expect him to be morally responsible; she would expect him to give up the silver. He cannot. He is so much a slave to it he does not tell Giorgio Viola he prefers the other daughter, Giselle, for fear the old man will bar him from the island. He desires Linda's younger sister, who, "by her fair but warm beauty, by the surface placidity of her nature holding a promise of submissiveness, by the charm of her girlish mysteriousness, excited his passion and allayed his fears as to the future" (IX. 524–5). Believing he can possess her as he has possessed his silver, he yearns to "clasp, embrace, absorb, subjugate" her as his own (IX.529). But Giselle, described as a pearl, a rose, and a star, can also be an agent of redemption if he renounces his possession. When she confesses to him, " 'I love you! I love you!' " her words "cast a spell stronger than the accursed spell of the treasure" (IX.540–1). However, when she asks the location of the silver, he refuses to tell her, losing his chance for freedom:

> The spectre of the unlawful treasure arose, standing by her side like a figure of silver, pitiless and secret, with a finger on its pale lips. His soul died within him at the vision of himself creeping in presently along the ravine, with the smell of earth, of damp foilage in his nostrils creeping in, determined in a purpose that numbed his breast, and creeping out again loaded with silver, with his ears alert to every sound. It must be done on this very night—that work of a craven slave! (IX.542)

He seals his doom. Coming to claim his possession, he is shot by Viola in the shade of the tree "under which Martin Decoud spent his last days" (IX.553).

Dr. Kennedy has faith in his intellect; Jim, in his ability to redeem himself without anyone's assistance;

Gould, in the San Tomé mine; Decoud, in no one; Nostromo, in himself, not in Dr. Monygham, Viola, or the two girls. Unable to pass their ordeals, they fall into despair.

Doctor Monygham is the second major Conradian character to return from the interior journey. Having succumbed to maiming torture during Guzmán Bento's infamous regime, he knows " 'the last thing a man ought to be sure of' " is himself (IX.310). Having " 'met the impossible face to face' " in his grave-like prison cell (IX.318), he knows himself, knowledge which "binds him indissolubly to the land of Costaguana" (IX.375) so that he cares more for the people than for the silver. He would not have denied Teresa's dying wish. He is able to respond to Viola's grief. He is able to pity Mrs. Gould in her loneliness. In his devotion to the woman who "refreshed" his "withered soul" (IX.369), he is willing to sacrifice himself for her happiness, which gives him the opportunity to act. The man "with a broken wing" (IX.411) runs so rapidly in his haste to work his plan that "the tails" of his coat "fly behind him" (IX.461). Knowing he will be accepted as a betrayer, he sacrifices his reputation by offering to lead the Monterist, Sotillo, to the place where he will claim the silver is buried as a delaying tactic until Nostromo can bring help to the beleaguered town. His purpose is to save the mine, not for Charles Gould's but for his wife's sake because the mine presents itself to him in the form "of a little woman in a soft dress with a long train, with a head attractively overweighted by a great mass of fair hair and the delicate preciousness of her inner worth, partaking of a gem and a flower, revealed in every attitude of her person" (IX.431).[26]

The doctor can be contrasted with each of the other three men. He responds to "the delicate preciousness" of

Emilia's "inner worth. . . ." "Living on the inexhaustible treasure of his devotion drawn upon in the secret of his heart . . ." (IX.504), he does not commit suicide when separated from the woman he loves. He acts to save another person. Hence he is the one who experiences rebirth. Freed of his haunting nightmare of Father Beron, Bento's chaplain who conducted the interrogation of political prisoners, he is no longer "the slave of a ghost" (IX.374). Passing his ordeal, he qualifies as a spokesman for the author: " 'There is no peace and no rest in the development of material interests. They have their law, and their justice. But it is founded on expediency, and is inhuman; it is without rectitude, without the continuity and the force that can be found only in a moral principle' " (IX.511).

In Morton Zabel's opinion, *Nostromo* is Conrad's "most complex historical and political drama, a comprehensive matrix of his moral and ethical sensibility, resonant of a profoundly riddled debate of moralities and creeds of conduct. . . ." [27] As *Nostromo* unfolds, we realize we are viewing the ethos and drama of a world we come to recognize as frighteningly real. The novel exposes the roots of those problems currently thwarting the efforts of underdeveloped nations to improve their lot. In a larger sense, it attacks a malaise of the modern world: the logic of economic growth devoid of a moral principle. The philosophy of materialism, symbolized by the silver, corrupts and destroys. The mine brings material improvement while insidiously denying freedom. It rids the country of the military, but it brings a new and more terrible subjugation. In Mrs. Gould's vision, the San Tomé mine becomes "more soulless than any tyrant, more pitiless and autocratic than the worst Government; ready to crush innumerable lives in the expansion of its greatness" (IX.521).

Don Juste and the other members of the Provincial Assembly are willing to compromise for the preservation of their lives and property. Don José mistakenly expatiates upon the value of the mine. His manuscript, "Fifty Years of Misrule," comes to an ignoble end, and, to paraphrase Irving Howe, for all of his liberalism and idealism, he is irrelevant. For all of his noble sentiments and heroic past, Giorgio Viola, a former lieutenant in Garibaldi's army of liberators, is impotent.[28] Of the leaders of the revolution, the Montero brothers are macabre and their deputies in Sulaco, the Señores Fuentes and Gamacho, comical. Pedro Montero's army is ludicrous. The mob expends its energy smashing windows. An ex-waiter captures Sulaco, and an ex-bandit chieftain becomes Minister of War in a new government with a new constitution. New political forces, new secret societies, will produce new revolutions. Of those who know the truth, Mrs. Gould, who sees through Holroyd's " 'purer forms of Christianity' " (IX.80), is ignored by her husband and the cynical doctor, who understands thoroughly the fallacy in the logic of material interests, is mistrusted by the people.

The difficulty with reading any one Conrad story by itself is that we miss the progression and the artistry within the collected fiction. By reworking images, techniques, and motifs into a constantly expanding pattern on a restricted surface constantly being magnified, Conrad so fissures the surface that it progressively threatens to crack wide open, revealing the inscrutable intention behind it.[29] Any one image or technique or motif in any one story discloses a kernel of truth, but when it reverberates backward through the works of the early period and forward through the works of the middle period, it accrues a reality and a suggestiveness it would not have otherwise. The sexual experience becomes a religious experience, since the imagery in the fiction is both sexual and religious; Emilia, a heroine who is associated with the Madonna throughout the novel; Dr. Monygham, a hero who takes Marlow's descent one step closer to Razumov's and Heyst's; and *Nostromo,* a "Heart of Darkness" with an interior journey culminating in rebirth set against many circular movements and arrested descents overpowered by death.

Since the circularity within the political novels is shaped by Conrad's skeptical temper, *Nostromo, The Secret Agent,* and *Under Western Eyes* form a triptych on the ills of our age, articulated in the Preface to *Under Western Eyes:* "The ferocity and imbecility of an autocratic rule rejecting all legality and in fact basing itself upon complete moral anarchism provokes the no less imbecile and atrocious answer of a purely Utopian revolutionism encompassing destruction by the first means to hand, in the strange conviction that a fundamental change of hearts must follow the downfall of any given human institutions. These people are unable to see that all they can effect is merely a change of names" (XXII.x). Yet beneath the skepticism there is a faith shaping the quest that triumphs over circularity and death, giving man hope. The Preface (1920), written years after the political novels, serves at one end of the canon as a commentary on the works preceding it as "Heart of Darkness" serves at the other end as an archetypal experience for the works following it. " 'All Europe contributed to the making of Kurtz' " (XVI.117), who took his European culture to its inevitable extreme, the willful destruction of life. In the midst of the pitiless and rapacious folly that is the Western world's political and economic activity, Marlow overcomes the temptation to impose his will on the natives, experiencing the fundamental change of heart necessary for rebirth. Journeying through the surface to the core to discover the source of man's religious and moral life, he confronts his double, freeing himself to act morally.

The hope is not to be found in any new socio-political systems or in Michaelis's illusion in *The Secret Agent* that " 'everything is changed by economic conditions—art, philosophy, love, virtue—truth itself!' " (XIII.50). " 'Everything merely rational fails' " (IX.315) in Costaguana because the one permanent truth that gives man hope is found in the metaphysical structure of heart and soul. Conrad's treatment of Dr. Monygham, who descends into himself and then with Mrs. Gould's assistance comes out to participate in a human community, points the way for a world locked in the moral insularity of Charles Gould, Martin Decoud, and Nostromo, the man of the people.

For me *The Secret Agent* (1907) is Conrad's most provocative use of the double, his mode of representing a character's potential reality. The character in his imaginative world who does not know himself does not recognize a kinship with his other self. Inexorably, however, he will confront himself in the person of the double. How he responds to his other self, dramatically presented as his double, determines his fate. One way therefore of studying Conrad's fiction is to analyze a character's response to his double. The captain of "The Secret Sharer" offers asylum to Leggatt and in so doing assumes command of himself and his ship, striking out in freedom for a new destiny. Jim does not admit his kinship with Gentleman Brown, who has a " 'ruthless faith in himself' " (XXI.374) and " 'a vehement scorn for mankind' " (XXI.352) so that Brown's assault on the natives—" 'an act of cold-blooded ferocity' " (XXI.403)—provides a measure for judging Jim's betrayal, just as Jim's idealism provides a measure for judging Brown's betrayal.

The Secret Agent marks a third transition in Conrad's collected works. In his early stories Conrad confines the doubling technique to males and the female's function to drawing the male out of his isolation, reconciling him with his other self. Although the confrontation scenes in "Heart of Darkness" suggest that the Negress and the Intended as well as Kurtz are Marlow's doubles, it is not until *The Secret Agent* and *Under Western Eyes* that his years of reworking the technique over a progressively magnified surface while localizing the reflection image in a progressively magnified feminine landscape create a new dimension. The landscape fuses with the surface so that the hero's descent through the surface to the interior becomes a descent through the feminine landscape to self-discovery in a religious experience. In these two novels the heroine retains her function as agent of redemption at the same time that she is the double for the hero's other self. In her eyes he sees reflected his other self, a life he betrayed. This is a necessary advance from earlier stories, preparing for the final stage in *Victory*. In this novel the heroine retains her function as agent at the same time that she is his double, the bearer of the 'wholly other' life he betrayed. In her eyes he sees reflected his soul, the center, the source of his religious and moral life. Since the Conradian heroine progressively becomes a figure of Mary, there develops in the fiction the suggestion that the concealed reality may be Christ, the slain and resurrected god of the Western tradition, the source of redemption in the hero himself.

Conrad establishes the doubling technique as the unifying principle of *The Secret Agent* in a few ways. His Preface details the stages leading to the composition of the novel. A friend's remark, " 'Oh, that fellow was half an idiot. His sister committed suicide afterwards,' " remained an illuminating impression dormant within him until he read the Home Secretary's complaint about secrecy, which crystallized the impression in his imagination. Then "slowly the dawning conviction of Mrs. Verloc's maternal passion grew up to a flame . . ." until "at last the story of Winnie Verloc stood out complete. . . ." (XIII.x-xii) In Chapters VIII and XI Conrad tells us that Winnie and her brother Stevie resemble each other. Throughout the text he never lets us forget the two are inextricably united. Like Stevie, Winnie is capable of compassion and rage. When the mother asks her daughter whether Verloc is " 'getting tired of seeing Stevie about,' " Winnie replies, " 'He'll have to get tired of me first' " (XIII.40). The boy is "connected with what there was of the salt of passion in her tasteless life—the passion of indignation, of courage, of pity, and even of self-sacrifice" (XIII.174). Mrs. Verloc tries to make her husband see Stevie's worth by informing him that she " 'couldn't do without' " her brother (XIII. 179). With this basis in mind, we should study *The Secret Agent* by analyzing Verloc's response to Winnie's double. His response to his brother-in-law is an extension of his response to his wife.

Each one of the three interview scenes between Verloc and Winnie is prefaced by a scene involving Verloc and his brother-in-law, an extreme version of the scene that follows.[30] In Chapter III Verloc, preparing to close the shop for the night, comes upon Stevie " 'capering all over the place.' " He does not know what to say to him because he never gave "a moment's thought till then to that aspect [providing for him] of Stevie's existence" (XIII.55–6). He "extended as much recognition to Stevie as a man not particularly fond of animals may give to his wife's beloved cat" (XIII.39). When Winnie defends her brother's usefulness in the family, she becomes younger, "as young as" she "used to look, and much more animated than the Winnie of the Belgravian mansion days had ever allowed herself to appear to gentleman lodgers," but Verloc, disturbed about his bombing assignment, is blind to her transformation: "it was as if her voice was talking on the other side of a very thick wall" (XIII.58–9). The interview—punctuated by the refrain, "Mr. Verloc made no comment"—terminates on a note of forewarning. Verloc's consenting to put out the light not only foreshadows the death of Stevie, who explodes "like a heavy flash of lightning in the fog" (XIII.87), but also his own. Winnie's eyes, which at the beginning of their conversation "gleam under the dark lids," become "more and more contemplative and veiled during the long pause" (XIII.58–60). When he rips the veil from her eyes in the third interview, he is silenced forever.

In the second scene, in Chapter VIII, the figure of Stevie, arriving home with his sister, is "imperceptible" to Verloc. He is unaware his brother-in-law looks at him with reverence and awe, since he is unaware of the boy's existence. Later that night Winnie, in her loneliness, starts to talk about Stevie, but Verloc continues to undress with "unnoticing inward concentration," with an "expressionless" stare. He forbears unburdening himself because in his indolence he regards her as his "chief possession," just as he regards her brother as a piece of furniture brought along by her into their marriage. The mystery in her person is a "familiar sacredness" for him, just as her brother is a familiar object in the house whose behavior, when he notices it, is baffling to him. This scene takes the reader closer to Stevie's death. Verloc "snaps" an answer at his wife's question about the light, " 'Put it out' " (XIII.174–81).

During the time between the second interview and the third, in Chapter XI, Verloc becomes acquainted with

Stevie's devotion for him, mistakenly believing Stevie loves him for himself. This devotion is the basis of his plan to bomb the Observatory: he counts on the boy's docility and loyalty without questioning his motives. Assuming she too loves him for himself, he counts on Winnie in the same way to take care of the business while he is in prison. In the third scene, though, the situation is reversed. Ripping the veil from the face of his wife, his chief possession whose sacred mystery he made familiar through uncon-cern, he confronts a "mysterious visitor of impenetrable intentions" (XIII.256). Stevie "turns up with a vengeance" (XIII.230) in the person of his sister. Verloc, the betrayer "of his fellow-men" (XIII.245), receives the justice meted out in Conrad's imaginative world to men who violate the mystery. Calling amorously to Winnie while reclining on the sofa, the man who took his wife's heart " 'along with the boy to smash in the dirt' " (XIII.290) is stabbed in the heart with a carving knife.

The piercing of his heart by Winnie is the inevitable consequence of his action, for Verloc completes the tri-partite archetypal pattern without completing the mythic journey. Chapter II opens with Verloc leaving behind him his household and business "on his way westward . . . through a town without shadows in an atmosphere of powdered old gold" to an appointment with his superior at the Embassy, Vladimir, who orders him to blow up " 'the first meridian,' " the Greenwich Observatory. By accepting the assignment, the anarchist commits himself to an action that determines his fate. He retraces "the path of his morn-ing's pilgrimage as if in a dream—an angry dream," to find himself "at the shop door all at once, as borne from west to east on the wings of a great wind," but he does not re-turn a transformed questor reborn into life (XIII.11–37). Verloc does not pass his ordeal. Instead of accepting Winnie's guiding power on a descent into himself to discover his oneness with the son, he destroys his opportunity to become a reintegrated hero.

In his attempt to detonate the Observatory, the tangible, visible symbol of the Prime Meridian, Verloc sacrifices the boy who could have been a son to him. The conversation at the Embassy about the bombing assignment and the description of Stevie both contain archetypal imagery. The Prime Meridian is a circle, a symbol of unity, oneness, and the sun. The description of Stevie, who occupies his time drawing circles, as a youth having a growth of thin fluffy hair "like a golden mist" (XIII.10) on his lower jaw, suggests a god. Implicit in this imagery is the association of sun-son as the source of light. Betraying Stevie and Winnie, Verloc betrays himself. When he calls to Winnie, she comes to him with a vengeance: "As if the homeless soul of Stevie had flown for shelter straight to the breast of his sister, guardian, and protector, the resemblance of her face with that of her brother grew at every step, even to the droop of the lower lip, even to the slight divergence of the eyes" (XIII.262). This reversal of roles produces a comic effect consistent with the novel's tone: Verloc becomes the archetypal slain god against his wishes; he achieves his destiny without realizing it. Winnie's extraordinary resemblance to her late brother fades as soon as she plants the knife in her husband's heart.

The dismemberment of Stevie is the event that sets off the ripples of movement from chapter to chapter, all of which approach the immense circle in the novel. In Chapter V while examining the mangled body, which "might have been an accumulation of raw material for a cannibal feast," Chief Inspector Heat notes "a narrow strip of velvet with a larger triangular piece of dark blue cloth hanging from it" (XIII.86-9). The piece of cloth is a talisman, since it contains Stevie's address. Intended as a safe-guard against his getting lost on his peregrinations with Verloc about the city, it is an invitation to every man to return Stevie to Winnie. Heat pockets the talisman, but he does not pursue the quest for political reasons, prefer-ring to arrest Michaelis, one of Verloc's fellow anarchists. He does relinquish it, however, to the Assistant Commis-sioner, who when he reads the address, 32 Brett Street, de-cides to investigate for himself. Likened to Don Quixote (XIII.115) and Aeneas, whose golden-leafed bough is al-luded to in the "dead leaf" (XIII.148), he leaves "the scene of his daily labors quickly like an unobtrusive shadow. His descent into the street was like the descent into a slimy aquarium from which the water had been run off. A murky, gloomy dampness enveloped him" (XIII. 147). His descent into the underworld in Chapter VII takes him to Brett Street, which "branched off, narrow, from the side of an open triangular space surrounded by dark and mysterious houses" (XIII.150)—to the feminine triangle, through which the hero must pass to approach the mystery of the circle. He does not complete the quest. He too stops short of the goal for political reasons, pre-ferring to make life uncomfortable for the Embassy people behind the bombing incident. But his journey takes the reader to Stevie's resurrection in Chapter VIII, the chapter which temporarily ends the disruption of normal time se-quence begun in Chapter IV with his death. As discussed above, Chapter VIII closes with a scene in which Verloc snaps, " 'Put it out,' " in answer to his wife's question. By interrupting the time-shift, this scene repeats the son's dismemberment and foreshadows the slaying of the father surrogate.

Betrayed by her husband, overlooked by the Chief Inspector and the Assistant Commissioner, Winnie turns to Comrade Ossipon, one of the anarchists. The difference between Ossipon and Verloc is that the former is conscious of his betrayal of her. She made herself available for Verloc to marry; she throws herself at Ossipon, begging him to save her. Given the routine of their lives, it is understandable that Verloc never investigated the origin of his wife's feelings; Ossipon knows he can be Winnie's "saviour" by helping her escape the gallows. Verloc never concerned himself with his fate; when Ossipon peers through the glazed door of Verloc's parlor and sees the dead body, he sees his potential fate. Nevertheless he duplicates his counterpart's betrayal. On the train Winnie lifts her veil granting her would-be saviour a glimpse into the mystery. There is no mystery for him, though, only a simple scientific explanation: she is "the sister of a degenerate, a degenerate herself—of a murdering type." As Verloc put out the light by rejecting the gift proffered by Winnie, so does Ossipon. Blind to the "ray of sunshine" emanating from her unveiled eyes, he falls asleep "in the sunlight" after deserting her (XIII.296–301).

Since Winnie is conscious after murdering her husband, being "compelled to look into the very bottom of this thing" (XIII.267), and Ossipon is conscious, his betrayal brings her to suicide and him to despair and impending madness. Obsessed by the knowledge that he caused her death, he can no longer keep the romantic appointments which formerly satisfied his material and emotional needs. He knows that by betraying her "vigour of vitality, a love of life that could resist the furious anguish which drives to murder and the fear, the blind, mad fear of the gallows," he has betrayed his own "love of life." Alone, he walks into the gutter to meet his "inevitable future," his brain "pulsating to the rhythm of an impenetrable mystery" (XIII.308–11).

Nostromo attacks the logic of material interests devoid of a moral principle. *The Secret Agent* attacks the logic of political anarchism sanctioning its activities on the belief that they are necessary to usher in a future where science and materialism will answer to man's needs. The perversity of the anarchists' insistence on a world reduced to the totally comprehensible and predictable is the subject of some of Conrad's most devastating irony. Verloc foresees all eventualities except the one that returns with a vengeance. Michaelis, who places his faith, which "masters him irresistible and complete like an act of grace" (XIII.45), in economic conditions, is a hermit who cannot tell "whether the sun still shone on the earth or not." His literary labor, which to him is "holy" and "the letting out of his soul into the wide world," is "first awakened by the offer of five hundred pounds from a publisher" (XIII.120). Karl Yundt's imputing "sinister impulses" to every act of "anger, pity, and revolt" is an "evil gift" (XIII.48) in a " 'disgusting old man' " (XIII.59), a " 'posturing shadow' " (XIII.68). For Ossipon " 'without emotion there is no action' " (XIII.50), but when he looks at Stevie or into Winnie's eyes, he has a scientific catchword for what he sees: " 'degeneracy.' " He denies the existence of the soul "on scientific grounds" (XIII.297). The Professor, who has made science into "something secularly holy," loses his assurance in a street peopled by mankind "impervious to sentiment, to logic, to terror, too, perhaps" (XIII.81–2). He is a freak who lives in a room characterized by a "poverty suggesting the starvation of every human need except mere bread" (XIII.302).

The anarchists are not only wrong-headed; they are immoral because they destroy the moral response by eliminating the religious experience. Since they deny the reality of the mystery or attempt to explain it away, they systematically destroy the heroine, in whose person it is most meaningfully experienced. Conrad introduces this theme on the first page of the novel. His shop window containing "photographs of more or less undressed dancing girls," Verloc's business becomes a metaphor for his attitude toward Winnie. The pornography he sells makes a sacred mystery familiar. The irony in the novel is unavoidable, for each of the group depends on the female. Michaelis is befriended by the society woman. Without his "blear-eyed old woman," Yundt would not be able to get around. Ossipon preys on "silly girls with savings-bank books" (XIII.52–3). Verloc relies on Winnie to mind the shop while he is on periodic sojourns. Each man's attitude toward the woman provides insight into the novel. The Professor considers the female an opiate for weak fools like Ossipon. The Assistant Commissioner, who comes closest to being a hero in the novel, pursues the quest to Brett Street because, although not enthusiastic about his marriage, he is afraid his wife will never forgive him if he allows Heat to arrest Michaelis. Even Winnie's ex-boyfriend, the butcher, takes on a significance he would otherwise not have. When he broke off the courtship because he did not want to be saddled with Stevie, he forced Winnie to seek security elsewhere. Stevie's remains, following the explosion, are "the by-products of a butcher's shop" (XIII.88).

Yet despite its betrayals, squalor, and gloom, *The Secret Agent*, like *Nostromo*, offers hope. The mystery of life survives the merely rational attempt to explain it away or to reorder it to fit a scientific schema. Ossipon's revolutionary career is menaced by the rhythm of an impenetrable mystery, which transcends his despair and impending madness and which in the force it accumulates as it builds up in the concluding pages demolishes the Professor's images of ruin and destruction, for the Professor, "a pest in the street full of men," has "no future" whereas the " *'impenetrable mystery is destined to hang for ever. . . .* ' " (XIII.309–11)

The inscrutable intention of "Heart of Darkness" and the impenetrable mystery of *The Secret Agent* are brought into sharper focus in the next major work, *Under Western Eyes* (1911). No matter how far he attempts to run away from himself, the hero, Razumov, knows one day he must confront his betrayal of Victor Haldin, a fellow student at the University of St. Petersburg who seeks refuge with him after assassinating the notorious Minister of State. Even while giving himself up to the "overpowering logic" of the "train of thought" (XXII.33) which will persuade him to betray Haldin, Razumov realizes that to avoid incurring the inevitable consequence, moral solitude, he can rush back to his lodgings and "pour out a full confession in passionate words that would stir the whole being of that man to its innermost depths; that would end in embraces and tears; in an incredible fellowship of souls—such as the world had never seen" (XXII.40). Since he first goes to the home of General T—, who sets a trap for the assassin, he is driven to the one person with whom he can discover his fellowship with the other student, the girl with " 'the most trustful eyes of any human being that ever walked this earth' " (XXII.22)—Haldin's sister, Natalia. When Councillor Mikulin of the General Secretariat asks him, " 'Where to?' " in reply to his resolution to retire from " 'this comedy of persecution' " (XXII.99), the reader should know the answer. If he does not, Conrad has the professor, the narrator of the novel, introduce Mrs. Haldin and her daughter on the succeeding page. They reside in Geneva, a mecca for such exiles from Czarist Russia as the aristocratic Madame de S—, mistress of a revolutionary salon at her Chateau Borel; Peter Ivanovitch, fugitive from Siberia and apostle of feminism; Sophia Antonovna, the dedicated revolutionist; Nikita, terrorist and police spy; and Julius Laspara, pamphleteer and editor of the *Living Word.*

Conrad gradually develops Natalia as her brother's double. Just before the revolutionist mentions his sister's eyes, he affirms his belief that his soul will live on after his death. A few pages after the professor introduces Natalia, she tells him her mother imagines her the " 'slavish echo' " of Victor (XXII.106). Remaining "faithful to his departed spirit" (XXII.140), she shares his faith in the will of the people and his hope in the future. At her first interview with Razumov, she duplicates her brother's display of trust: " 'I've told him,' " she repeats to the professor, " 'that I was in great need of someone, a fellow-countryman, a fellow-believer, to whom I could give my confidence in a certain matter' " (XXII.176). Her "presence in the ante-room," cutting off Razumov's retreat from Mrs. Haldin's room, is "as unforeseen as the apparition of her brother" in St. Petersburg (XXII.341). Razumov's journal records the fullest statement of the connection between Victor and Natalia: " 'And when you stood before me with your hand extended, I remembered the very sound of his voice, and I looked into your eyes—and that was enough. . . . Hate or no hate, I felt at once that, while shunning the sight of you, I could never succeed in driving away your image. I would say, addressing that dead man, "Is this the way you are going to haunt me?" ' " (XXII.358)

Haunted by the phantom of Victor Haldin, whose offer of brotherhood was a " 'test' " of fate (XXII.24), Razumov must work out his redemption until he knows his conscience was engaged in the test, until he discovers the moral bond he betrayed. The novel is a descent into his

actual and potential selves as reflected in the eyes of those
he meets: in the closed eyes of his secret self, Haldin,
whose eyes open after he returns to his lodgings from General T—'s study; the blank eyes of Ziemianitch, the peas-
ant Haldin counts on to get him out of Russia; the gog-
gle eyes of General T—, autocracy incarnate; the red-nosed
student's hollow eyes; the landlady's entreating eyes; the
dim, unreadable eyes of Mikulin, who arranges a secret
meeting at an oculist's office; the hidden eyes of Peter
Ivanovitch, who in his bullying of his secretary, Tekla, is
blind to the female's "sacred, redeeming tears" (XXII.124)
he has written about so eloquently; the glassy eyes of
Ivanovitch's Egeria, Madame de S—, a "galvanized corpse"
(XXII.215); the watchful eyes of the Chateau Borel;
Tekla's scared eyes; the black, glittering eyes of Sophia
Antonovna, the "spirit of destructive revolution" (XXII.
261); Laspara's bloodshot eyes; the professor's Western
eyes. But it is not until his eyes, which he shields throughout the journey, look into Natalia's pure, clear eyes that
he discovers himself.

From Razumov's point of view, Haldin is intransi-
gent. Not knowing himself, he does not recognize the bond
he shares with the revolutionist, his double, his potential
self. Like Haldin, he believes in a better future. Capable
of violence, he thrashes the drunken Ziemianitch and fights
his impulse to strangle Haldin and to stab Ivanovitch. He
can respond instinctively to Tekla's suffering. He assumes
Haldin's position on the bed. The university students
credit the two of them with a "mysterious connexion"
(XXII.82). " 'It is in you,' " Natalia says to him about her
brother, " 'that we can find all that is left of his generous
soul' " (XXII.346).

Priding himself on his ability to order the future by
the "free use of his intelligence" (XXII.83), Razumov

lives in dread of the irrationalities, absurdities, and contingencies beneath the calm surface of daily routine. " 'Life
is a public thing,' " he exclaims (XXII.54), only to discover to his horror that Mikulin recruits him as a police
spy and the revolutionists want to send him on undercover
missions. He considers himself free, only to discover he
cannot be rid of Haldin's phantom and Natalia's image.
He convinces himself his conscience was not engaged in
the trust Haldin extended him, only to discover that his
is a " 'conventional conscience' " racked by guilt (XXII.
288). He holds himself intellectually superior, only to
discover that he has " 'neither the simplicity nor the
courage nor the self-possession to be a scoundrel, or an
exceptionally able man' " (XXII.362). He thinks he has
no time for love, only to discover that he is falling in
love with Natalia. A stranger to himself, he discovers in
his confrontation with Natalia that his betrayal of Haldin
was really self-betrayal. " 'In giving Victor Haldin up, it
was myself, after all, whom I have betrayed most basely.
You must believe what I say now,' " he writes to her after
leaving her house; " 'you can't refuse to believe this. Most
basely. It is through you that I came to feel this so deeply' "
(XXII.361). He comes to feel this so deeply because it was
only when she unveiled herself during the interview that
he renounced his plan to betray her.

Although Natalia is not named Beatrix as Edith Travers was, she is more nearly a Beatrice than the heroine of
The Rescue. She is a development of the shift in emphasis
which began with the picture of the betrayed Jewel in
Marlow's mind in the final paragraph of *Lord Jim*. Dante
is guided through hell, the actual and potential states of
his soul, by Virgil, human reason, and his faith that Beatrice awaits him on the other side of hell. Before he can
be reunited with her, he must look into the face of Dis

on the frozen circle of Cocytus: "How chilled and faint I turned then, do not ask, reader, for I do not write it, since all words would fail. I did not die and I did not remain alive; think now for thyself, if thou hast any wit, what I became, denied both death and life" (*Inf.* XXXIV.22–7). With Satan behind them Dante and Virgil ascend mount purgatory. The reunion takes place in the garden of Eden, Beatrice's entrance signalling Virgil's departure, but before she unveils herself, revealing the mystery of divine Love, she so reprimands Dante that when he looks into the stream he sees his image in all its sinfulness. After he confesses and is immersed in the waters of Lethe, Beatrice unveils herself, in a scene which is a counterpart to the confrontation scene in Canto XXXIV of the *Inferno:* "So fixed and intent were my eyes in satisfying their ten years' thirst that every other sense was quenched in me and on the one side and the other they had a wall of indifference, so did the holy smile draw them to itself with the old net [of love] . . ." (*Purg.* XXXII. 1–6). The *Purgatorio* ends with Dante "remade" (XXXIII. 143), ready to ascend with Beatrice to the heavenly flower.

I have already indicated how the tensions within Razumov make him receptive to the confrontation in the Haldin home. In the eyes of the police state officials and the self-exiled revolutionists, his existence is valuable only in so far as he can perform acts of deception, falsehood, and duplicity. For them he is not a student with a promising career; he is a police spy or a bomb-throwing revolutionist. Sophia, his adversary, gives him advice that would stifle his quest for self-knowledge: " 'You've got to trample down every particle of your own feelings; for stop you cannot, you must not' " (XXII.245). When Nikita enters the grounds of the Chateau Borel, Razumov feels himself choking in the "fumes of falsehood . . . the thought of being condemned to struggle on and on in that tainted atmosphere without the hope of ever renewing his strength by a breath of fresh air" (XXII.269). Concomitant with the awakening of his conscience, which undermines his belief in his superior intellect, is his awakening to the sense of Natalia's presence. "The mysteriousness of his quickened heart-beats" startles him as he approaches the flower bed in the garden where they first met. " 'It is here!' " he thinks "with a sort of awe. 'It is here—on this very spot . . .' " (XXII.204).

As he stands before Mrs. Haldin, to whose lighted window he has been irresistibly drawn, he cannot "shake off the poignant impression" of the mother who in mourning her dead son will not let him forget the betrayal. Alarmed, he retreats, to confront Natalia blocking his escape. Raising his eyes to her, he comes "to himself in the awakened consciousness of that marvellous harmony of feature, of lines, of glances, of voice, which made of the girl before him a being so rare, outside, and, as it were, above the common notion of beauty." Appealing to his " 'generous soul' " while questioning him, she unties her veil, revealing to him "the seductive grace of her youthful figure" (XXII.340–7). With the veil between them dropped, Razumov confesses to the one person " 'in all the world' " (XXII.361) to whom he must confess.

The confession reaches its climax when Razumov says to Natalia, " 'An hour after I saw you first I knew how it would be. The terrors of remorse, revenge, confession, anger, hate, fear, are like nothing to the atrocious temptation which you put in my way the day you appeared before me with your voice, with your face, in the garden of that accursed villa.' " Bewildered, she goes "straight to the point": " 'The story, Kirylo Sidorovitch, the story!' " to which he replies, " 'There is no more to tell!' " The temptation which began " 'on this very spot' " in the garden " 'ends here—on this very spot,' " he concludes, as he presses "a denunciatory finger to his breast . . ." (XXII.354). When the professor, who has assisted Natalia to the sofa, looks down at her, he sees her hands "lying lifelessly, palms upwards, on her lap." She whispers, " 'It is impossible to be more unhappy. . . . It is impossible. . . . I feel my heart becoming like ice' " (XXII.356), implying that she has just seen Satan in the young man who, earlier in the interview, called her " 'a predestined victim . . .' " (XXII.349). Yet instead of filling her soul with venom, Razumov snatches up the dropped veil and returns to his room, there to record in full his confession to her before he ascends the "two flights of stairs from the lower darkness" (XXII.364) to his confession to the revolutionists.

Conrad fuses two confrontation scenes. Since Razumov sees in Natalia's eyes both his potential for betrayal and his potential for love and self-sacrifice, the suggestion is that he sees in her eyes both the potential Satan and the potential Christ within himself. By making Natalia Victor's double, Conrad achieves a harmony of intended victim and agent of redemption. Driven by his need to confess, Razumov moves inexorably toward her. Yet so long as he deludes himself into thinking his intellect alone can control his fate, he is destined to repeat the betrayal. As he journeys into himself, he learns he is not free: he is subject to further interrogation by Mikulin; he cannot leave Geneva without the revolutionists' permission; the phantom of Haldin haunts him; Natalia puts herself in his hands. But he resists this knowledge. To admit to himself he is not free is to admit he is vulnerable to the irrationalities, absurdities, and contingencies he refuses to accept. To admit to himself he is not free is to admit his conscience was engaged in Haldin's trust. Ironically, just when he has good reason to believe in his freedom, he is closest to repeating the betrayal. Sophia informs him she has received a letter intimating Ziemianitch betrayed the student. By lying to her that the information is correct, he removes any lingering doubt about himself in the minds of the revolutionists. Yet it is now that he is least free because the situation parallels that with Haldin. Since Natalia trusts him, she does not suspect him of any falsehood. Like Kurtz's Intended, she is at his mercy if he chooses to " 'steal' " her soul, an intention he gloats over, " 'brooding upon the best way.' " " 'Natalia Victorovna,' " he writes in his journal, " 'I was possessed! I returned to look at you every day, and drink in your presence the poison of my infamous intention' " (XXII.359–60).

Razumov is redeemed, however, for the light emitted from her eyes pierces his obdurate heart. With the gift of insight, he is saved from the temptation to betray his heart again:

> "I remembered the shadow of your eyelashes over your grey trustful eyes. And your pure forehead! It is low like the forehead of statues—calm, unstained. It was as if your pure brow bore a light which fell on me, searched my heart and saved me from ignominy, from ultimate undoing. And it saved you too. Pardon my presumption. But there was that in your glances which seemed to tell me that you . . . your light! your truth! I felt that I must tell you that I had ended by loving you" (XXII.361).

The glimpse she allows him obliterates his pride by revealing to him his self-betrayal, at the same time restoring his faith in himself and mankind with an appeal to his potential for love and self-sacrifice. Humbling himself before the mystery, which transcends the " 'secular logic of human development' " (XXII.95) to which he rigidly adhered, he confesses to her, washing himself clean in the rain that "envelopes him like a luminous veil" (XXII.363). Responding to her, he is " 'freed from the blindness of anger and hate . . .' " (XXII.361). It is but a few steps from his confession to her to his public confession—an act which, Miss Rosenfield suggests, is "like the crucifixion of Christ" because it is "accompanied by thunder and lightning" [31]— to his reunion with the human community. Though not "torn to pieces" by the conspirators (XXII.366), Razumov is the first Conradian hero to accept the potential he discovers when he looks into the heroine's eyes. He becomes " 'a martyr . . . —a sort of hero—a political saint' " (XXII. 61) he predicted Haldin would become. After being deafened by Nikita and maimed, he returns with Tekla to Russia, where he is visited by revolutionists like Sophia who respect his intelligence and his ideas.

The atheist who mocks Haldin's faith begins to believe in " 'an active Providence' " (XXII.350) manifesting Itself in Natalia's person. " 'You were appointed,' " Razumov writes to her, " 'to undo the evil by making me betray myself back into truth and peace' " (XXII.358), implying man's fate lies not in submission to a secular autocrat brought into existence by the "logic of history" (XXII.35) but in acceptance of the saviour within himself. While not converted to the visionary idealism of a Victor Haldin or the vulgar democracy of the beer-drinking Swiss couple, he does learn his fundamental allegiance is to his conscience, not to the state. And since he engages his conscience in the trust extended by Natalia, in whom " 'everything is divine' " (XXII.352), his humility before her is an admission of a mystery which transcends human reason. It would be a " 'sacrilege' " (XXII.360) to violate this mystery initially experienced in the person of the girl who, after cooperating in his redemption, travels to the " 'centre' " of Russia, "sharing her compassionate labours" with those who need her (XXII.378).

It is fitting that the heroine who comes closest to being a modern Beatrice in any single Conrad novel " 'shall never give up looking forward to the day when all discord shall be silenced.' " Although honest enough to recognize that " 'its dawn' " can appear only after " 'many bitter hours,' " after " 'the tempest of blows and of execrations is over,' " she maintains her faith that " 'at last the anguish of hearts shall be extinguished in love.' " It is equally fitting that the professor uses the metaphor from the closing cantos of the *Paradiso* to concretize her faith in the redeeming power of love: "It is hard to think I shall never look any more into the trustful eyes of that girl—wedded to an invincible belief in the advent of loving concord springing like a heavenly flower from the soil of men's earth, soaked in blood, torn by struggles, watered with tears" (XXII.376-7). For Conrad even though paradise on earth may be only a vision, man's hope is realized in the human concrete. The heavenly flower is not to be found in a quest for redemption beyond the horizon; it springs from man's acceptance of his nature, his acceptance of death as a prelude to rebirth, his acceptance of his union with the female. Significantly, Avrom Fleishman quotes Natalia's vision of the future in the conclusion to his fine study of Conrad's politics: "Her faith rests ultimately on a very human, earthy fact—the power of love, of human community— in which Conrad, for all his skepticism, never stopped believing. It is with love that Conrad, like his narrator, parts from his heroine, mindful of the seductive power of her faith, 'an invincible belief in the advent of loving concord. . . .' " [32]

That everyone is a double for everyone else is implicit throughout Conrad's writings, since everyone shares the actual and potential reality of the human condition. In view of the thorough study of "Conrad's extensive reliance upon character doubles" [33] in *Victory* (1915), the last novel I want to examine, I will concentrate on Lena as Heyst's potential reality. " 'The truth shining in you drew the truth out of me,' " Razumov confesses to Natalia (XXII. 361). *Victory* depicts Lena's efforts to draw the truth out of Heyst, "enigmatical and disregarded like an insignificant ghost" (XV.24), by awakening him to the truth in her. She is named Alma (life or soul) or Magdalen, but he prefers to call her Lena, a shortening of Magdalen. If Magdalen is meant to suggest the Biblical story of Christ's redemption of the sinner, then *Victory* begins as an inverted parallel. It is Lena, the potential prostitute whose words thrill Heyst "like a revelation" (XV.76), who cooperates to redeem the man who seems "to have no connection with earthly affairs and passions" (XV.60), the man whose father chided him for believing in flesh and blood, the man whom Morrison took to be an agent of Providence.

The son of an expatriated Swede who died in London, Axel Heyst is a drifter who soon after he had arrived in the Malay Archipelago became enchanted with the islands and the captive of "a magic circle" with a center in Samburan and a radius that touched Manila and Saigon (XV. 7). His first opportunity to break out of his isolation occurred when he impulsively offered to help Morrison pay the fine on his trading brig impounded by the Portuguese authorities on Timor. He failed the test. His embarrassment at Morrison's gratitude prevented him from responding with more than "consummate politeness" to the latter's "emotional collapse" (XV.18). Crippled by his father's advice that he " 'cultivate that form of contempt which is called pity' " (XV.174), he was " 'struck by the comicality' " (XV.198) of his being an answer to Morrison's prayer. In his "native delicacy" he was so sensitive that the grateful man's desire they share trading ventures was not the proper form of human relations he consented simply "to put an end to the harrowing scene in the cabin" (XV.19). From this meeting sprang the Tropical Belt Coal Company with Heyst as manager. Yet his anxiety to keep secret his intervention in Morrison's plight made possible the rumors, started by Schomberg, that he was taking advantage of the desperate man. In his disguised amusement and politeness, he did not respond to the trust extended him. Schomberg calumniates him. To the hotelier in Surabaya who hates him because of his aloofness, Heyst is a common thief who puts on the airs of a Swedish baron.

The affair with Morrison took place before the main action of *Victory*. The novel opens with the Company defunct and Heyst a recluse on Samburan who only occasionally visits Surabaya on business. On one of these trips he wanders into the concert hall of Schomberg's hotel, where he witnesses a member of the ladies' orchestra being abused for not circulating among the customers between performances. When he offers to help her, he encounters his second opportunity. There are a few reasons why he does not fail this test. He has never been able to follow completely his father's teachings; being "temperamentally sympathetic" (XV.70), he naturally gravitates toward someone in trouble. He has "lately become aware" (XV.66) of his loneliness. He feels remorse over Morrison's death, vaguely sensing he was partially responsible by letting him return to England to get financial backing for the Company. Heyst does not yet know himself: the "submerged Morrison" (XV.77) has not been allowed to surface. He does not recognize that the impulse which brings him to Lena is the same one that brought him to Morrison years ago. He shrinks "from the idea of competition with fellows unknown" (XV.85), recoiling from Lena during her account of the dangers she is exposed to. But since neither his instinctive response to a person in distress nor his conscience is dead, he is at the stage where he can begin the journey to self-knowledge.

The catalyst for this journey, and the most important reason Heyst does not fail, is Lena, who by demanding he fulfill his promise to aid her makes him conscious he "engaged himself" (XV.83). Like Morrison, she treats him as a saviour. By trying to live up to this image, he can be drawn out of his moral solitude, the "naked truth" (XV. 80) of which her penetrating voice makes him perceive. A "new experience" for him (XV.71), she begins to awaken him to the life he denies. Her presence seems "to enter his body, to infect his very heart" (XV.84); her "glance of frank tenderness" leaves "a secret touch on the heart" (XV.92). Together they can have " 'a fresh start' " (XV. 88).

Because of his mistrust of life, Heyst will not admit he needs Lena. He will acknowledge her only privately; to acknowledge her publicly would be to admit an incompleteness in himself. In his fastidiousness he dreads returning her glance, at the same time realizing it is "the most real impression of his detached experience—so far" (XV.93). He wants her, yet he wants her secretly. " 'I shall steal you,' " is his compromise (XV.87). She has no choice but to flee with him to the jungle of the grave-like Samburan; the alternative would probably be losing him forever.

The temptation which began for Razumov " 'on this very spot' " in the garden ends " 'on this very spot' " in his breast. The temptation which began for Heyst in the concert hall under the spreading boughs of trees in the enclosure "containing a garden" (XV.35) will end in his heart as well. " 'There must be a lot of the original Adam in me, after all,' " he reflects during one of his meditations on the primitive island, discovering that "this primeval ancestor is not easily suppressed" (XV.173). Three months later he and Lena ascend the forest path to a shaded nook where he explains the influence on him of a father who could write that "of the stratagems of life the most cruel is the consolation of love" (XV.219) and the boredom of his relationship with Morrison. " 'You should try to love me' " (XV.221), she exhorts him back in the house, for although he enjoys her company, he gives her reason to fear he will become bored with her. This widening rift in his moral identity stems from the failure to know himself. For him women are "created with a special aptitude" for deception (XV.81), yet he is the one who deceived Morrison. " 'I was not very far from you,' " Lena reminds him. But he will not summon her so that while she "abandons to him something of herself—something excessively subtle and inexpressible" (XV.187–8) which gives "him a greater sense of his own reality than he had ever known in all his life" (XV.200), he still denies his deception, a garbled version of which she heard at the hotel. Schomberg " 'invented' " the atrocity, he argues (XV.211). If he knew himself he would know both his guilt and his potential for love and self-sacrifice. Of course, so long as he refuses to face his self-image in its actuality, he cannot accept his potential reality. He has not confessed to himself that his pity is disguised contempt, his detachment disguised pride. He senses an "incompleteness," an "imperfection" (XV.212) in his relations with Lena, but because of his factually oriented mind, which is dissociated from his instinctive nature, he does not know the incompleteness is in himself. He playfully refers to Lena's eyes as " 'windows of the soul' " (XV.204), but he avoids looking into them because they are "unreadable as ever" (XV.220), not realizing they are so because he avoids looking into them.

His belief having been destroyed by his father, Heyst lacks faith. It is imperative that Lena awaken it, for while addressing her he is "really talking to himself" (XV.196), whenever she retires to her room the "mood of grim doubt intrudes on him" (XV.186). Out of sight she is "a promise that could not be embraced and held" (XV.222). Without faith he will never be able to love, to sacrifice himself; unable to love he will always be detached from life. " 'You should try to love me,' " she exhorts him; " 'Do try!' " She does not accuse him of murdering Morrison, but she does want him to commit himself to her. Since in Conrad's moral vision one cannot live up to his commitment until he learns the truth of himself, her heart "sinks" at his dismissal of further self-examination: " 'Surely you don't suspect after what I have heard from you, that I am anxious to return to mankind. I! I! murder my poor Morrison! It's possible that I may be really capable of that which they say I have done. The point is that I haven't done it. But it is an unpleasant subject to me. I ought to be ashamed to confess it—but it is! Let us forget it' " (XV.221–3). Her cry, " 'He's here!' " referring to the intrusion of Wang, disrupts his self-sufficiency: the Chinese houseboy announces that a boat has invaded the island's peace.

As soon as Heyst conceals Lena on his island, his two grotesque doubles, Jones and Ricardo, with their attendant, Pedro, appear first in Surabaya and then in Samburan. Incensed by Heyst's theft of Lena, whom he desires, and frightened by the two vagabonds who have converted his concert hall into a gambling den, Schomberg convinces Ricardo that the Swedish baron has amassed a fortune in plunder on Samburan. Ricardo in turn convinces Jones that Heyst will provide him with the amusement he needs to overcome his boredom. Jones's misogyny is an extension of Heyst's reluctance to become a whole man engaged in life. Ricardo's coyly voluptuous expression is an extension of Heyst's surreptitious response to Lena. The relationship of the two vagabonds, "identical souls in different disguises" (XV.130), is an exaggeration of the division in his psyche. Jones, " 'evil intelligence' " (XV.329), is amused by adventures involving the capture of a man's hidden treasure. For him there is a proper way to kill a man. Ricardo, " 'instinctive savagery' " (XV.329), is willing to deceive Jones, by concealing the knowledge of Lena's presence on the island, in order to steal the buried treasure. He claims that his gentleman knows him thoroughly and would never get rid of him, indicating how little they know each other: when the spectral misogynist discovers his secretary's deception, he shoots him. With the doubles' arrival in Samburan, in "a big boat, the greater part of which was hidden from him by the planking of the jetty" (XV.227), Heyst's inexorable fate is catching up to him, and by analyzing the responses of the characters to one another, the reader can chart his movement toward redemption through Lena's self-sacrifice.

Heyst wants Lena, but he does not want to pay the price one must pay in Conrad's world for life. He will not confess to himself his deception of Morrison, nor will he acknowledge Lena. She must stall for "a short period of safety" (XV.308) until he reveals their engagement. She must practice duplicity so that he will not repeat with her his betrayal of Morrison. She wants total commitment from him, which is possible only if he descends into himself to be reborn into the life she bears, a life which, unknown to him, he also bears. Either the public confession or acknowledgement, each one containing the other, would dispel the threat posed by the avengers. Since Jones has an aversion to females, the envoys would disappear from Samburan.

That the confession and acknowledgement contain each other is amply demonstrated in Chapter V of Part Four. Heyst does not understand what Jones meant when he started to volunteer his identity because he " 'did not want to listen to all this nonsense.' " " 'I said that his comings or goings on the earth were none of my business,' " he relates to Lena, deceiving himself his sense of responsibility for her prevented him from laughing at Jones when the latter asked him " 'to look at the state he [Jones] was in.' " He then insists she stay hidden. " 'People will have to see me some day,' " she replies. A few pages later, as he beckons her to the window, he watches her cross the room. "He had never seen such an expression in her face before. It had dreaminess in it, intense attention, and something like sternness." Suddenly seeing Jones and Ricardo moving toward the bungalow, he cuts off her "strange transfiguring mood" by stopping her at the doorway. While they peep out at the two men, who have stopped walking, he protests to her that there is a strain in him which lays him " 'under an insensate obligation to avoid even the appearance of murder,' " at which point the spectre and his secretary return to their bungalow (XV. 318–29).

Heyst wants the three envoys to leave the island, but they will not until he comes to terms with them. So long as he thinks they are " 'divorced from all reality' " (XV. 364), he cannot act. He wants Lena abstracted from life, but she wants to be acknowledged. Not sure whether she is a "dream" (XV.319) or a reality, he cannot commit himself. Until he journeys to death, he cannot be re-born.

His conflict is mirrored in the extreme responses of Ricardo and Jones to Lena and to each other. Cautious about communicating openly with Lena, who exercises her attraction on him "like a concealed magnet," Ricardo approaches her bungalow stealthily. The sight of her "pearly white" arm arousing him, his feral instinct, hith-erto kept in check by Jones, overcomes his self-restraint and he charges through her veil-like bedroom curtain. Interpreting her silence as condoning his attempted assault and not knowing she loves Heyst, the feline secretary concludes she will join forces with him. At the sound of Heyst's voice, he realizes that if he is seen he is "un-masked." With her assistance he manages to climb out the window in time (XV.285–302).

This scene is a condensation of Lena's predicament with Heyst. She cannot give in to Ricardo's sexual assault because that would be death for her lover and herself. On a literal level, Heyst can easily be killed by Ricardo once Jones's henchman has her in his camp or once he learns there is no money, and she would no longer be free. On a symbolic level, it is also death for them. If she abandons herself to the Ricardo part of Heyst, she will lose her chance to awaken the whole man to a total commitment; he might quickly tire of her if her attraction is merely sexual. She decides to stall, letting Ricardo believe he can trust her while hoping to gain Heyst's confidence.

She is successful with Ricardo. The secretary feels "almost tender" toward her (XV.294). His lust transformed "by the proofs of her amazing spirit" (XV.299), he begins to trust her so much so that "his uplifting exultation is

replaced by an awed and quivering patience before her"
and he prostrates himself at her feet. In his "imbecile
worship" of Lena, Ricardo wants to kill Jones, with whom
he feels uncomfortable now that his repressed thoughts
and sensations have been set free (XV.394–5). Instinctive
savagery pushed to an extreme wants to eliminate death.

When the cadaverous Jones discovers his secretary deceiving him with Lena, he realizes he is " 'taken in . . .
fairly caught.' " Forcing Heyst to listen to Ricardo's rap-
turous mutterings before the woman in black enthroned
in the interior of the lighted room, he "distils his ghostly
venom" into the Swede's ear: " 'Mud souls, obscene and
cunning! Mud bodies, too—the mud of the gutter! . . . I
wouldn't trust him near me for five minutes after this!' "
Recognizing "the end of his reign over his excellent secretary's thoughts and feelings," Jones wants to kill Ricardo
(XV.387–92). Evil intelligence pushed to an extreme wants
to eliminate life.

Heyst lies suspended between Ricardo and Jones, and
because he does not admit his kinship with them, his other
selves, he does not acknowledge his kinship with Lena,
his unknown self. Decrying the loss of his revolver, he is
"baffled" by her "penetrating gaze"; he cannot "pierce the
grey veil of her eyes" (XV.330). Just before he leaves to
confront Jones, she "grasps his shoulders . . . staring into his face in the dark," but he orders her to put on her
black dress and veil. As she does his eyes "lose her completely" (XV.371). It is apparent from the rising intensity
of her determination to save him, which parallels his seeking every avenue except the right one, that she must
sacrifice herself if he is to awaken to the life within himself.

Since it is Ricardo who responds to Lena, she plans to
disarm him. On a literal level, she wants to render him

incapable of killing Heyst. On a symbolic level, she wants the Ricardo part of Heyst to surrender to the "new sort of life" (XV.303) she experienced when the sound of Heyst's voice drove the secretary out the window. She wants to transform his sexual address to an engagement of the whole man, for Ricardo's weapon is sexual and deadly when separated from the whole man: "The knife was lying in her lap. She let it slip into the fold of her dress, and laid her forearms with clasped fingers over her knees, which she pressed desperately together. The dreaded thing was out of sight at last. She felt a dampness break out all over her" (XV.400).

Lena can convert Ricardo because of his emotional response to her. She cannot directly effect a change in Jones because she symbolizes the life he rejects. She has to operate through Heyst, sending him to the misogynist, but the Swede must pass the initiation stage, which commences when he interprets the movement of her head during dinner as her intention to guide him through the darkness. Tragically for her, by resisting her efforts to infuse him with life, he is not strong enough to free himself of the ghost's deadly hold, despite the numerous opportunities he has in Chapter XI of Part Four. Jones, dressed in a blue silk gown which resembles Lena's bedroom curtain and Heyst's father's dressing gown, waits "for some sort of overture" from his visitor. Since the latter is silent, the former can only repeat his statement, " 'I am a person to be reckoned with,' " to which Heyst replies, " 'I don't know you.' " After telling him he is " 'a sort of fate—the retribution that waits its time,' " the spectre alludes to Heyst's relationship with Morrison, an insinuation he denies: " 'You have heard a lot of ugly lies.' " Even when Heyst finally divulges Lena's presence—" 'the only effective truth in the welter of silly lies' "—overwhelming Jones with a "sense of utter insecurity," he is disgusted with himself for mentioning her. Denying a " 'love of life,' " he remains "a prisoner captured by the evil power of a masquerading skeleton out of a grave," who marches him to the other cabin to observe Ricardo's worship (XV.377–90). Doubting Lena, he allows Jones, or the Jones part of his psyche, to fire the gun at Ricardo, or the Ricardo part of his psyche, killing her.

Until Lena's voice "cuts deep into his very breast," he is amused, speaking in his polite, Heystian tone. When he discovers she deceived him to save him, he has the insight he has been resisting throughout the novel: "He caught his breath, looked at her closely, and seemed to read some awful intelligence in her eyes" and then tears away the barrier he imposed, her black dress, to get at the "sacred whiteness" of her breast. The man who fought to conceal from himself his deception of Morrison and his need of Lena cannot conceal his despair. He curses the fastidiousness which prevented him from acknowledging her smile in Surabaya and which at this moment chokes the "true cry of love" in his throat (XV.404–6).

Lena's death almost repeats Morrison's death in that it is unintentionally perpetrated by the schizoid Heyst. It is different only because she transforms it into a loving act of self-sacrifice. Since her act lays bare the truth to him, he sacrifices himself to redeem her deception. His last words to her—" 'No one in the world,' " in response to her question, " 'Who else could have done this for you?' " (XV.406)—are a public acknowledgement of his commitment to her. His last words to his friend, the skipper of the *Sissie*—" 'Ah, Davidson, woe to the man whose heart has not learned while young to hope, to love—and to put its trust in life!' " (XV.410)—are a public confession of his deception of Morrison and his betrayal of the life in himself. It is but a few steps from his wish to be alone with the dead, completing the belated fall which began when he impulsively offered sanctuary to Lena, to his atonement in the purgatorial fire. Heyst is the second Conradian hero to accept his potential revealed to him in the heroine's eyes. What began as Magdalen's redemption of Heyst ends as his redemption of her, an act of self-sacrifice which leads Dr. Meyer to write that "in *Victory*, the rescue of the girl Magdalen (later renamed Lena) bears an unmistakable allusion to the fate of her namesake in the New Testament. Like Magdalen, Conrad's heroine, who describes herself as 'not what they call a good girl,' attains an ultimate state of grace through the redeeming action of Heyst (which rhymes with Christ), another ostensible self-portrait of the author." [34]

In his illusion that he is "different from . . . mankind," the Conradian male does not know himself. Morally isolated, he does not know he shares the human condition with its boundaries of birth and death. But since he is unwittingly drawn into life, he always has the opportunity for self-discovery. If he does not make the journey into his heart of darkness or if he fails his ordeal, he will repeat his self-betrayal until time overtakes him, sealing him in death.

The time scheme of *Under Western Eyes* is an example of the novelist's handling of timelessness in time, of eternity circumscribing the tangible, visible world yet contained within it, transforming it when unveiled. By reorganizing the chronology so that Part Four returns to the question posed by Mikulin at the end of Part One, " 'Where to?' " Conrad creates the impression that Razumov is not making the interior journey. Since he is, one can see that so long as he resists the truth reflected in the conspirators' eyes he cannot redeem time. His past is his present.

The grave-like silence of General T—'s study with its mute clock oppresses Razumov, who, by informing on Haldin, betrays the life within himself. Not sharing his fellow student's belief in eternity, he is bounded by his watch, which tells him when to go to class, and the university, where his lectures are held. For him time is a relation of existence to which one pays little more than perfunctory notice. His watch is useful because it can indicate the duration between his looking at it and Haldin's exit. When Haldin leaves, however, his watch breaks, plunging him into a world shorn of conventional signposts. For the first time he "looks wildly about as if for some means of seizing upon time which seemed to have escaped him altogether." And for the first time he is made aware of the passing of time: "He had never, as far as he could remember, heard the striking of that town clock in his rooms before this night" (XXII.65). Razumov is thrust into the timelessness within himself while he moves in a world of time ticking away on him. Until he accepts himself in his actuality and potentiality, he is arrested in his illusion, condemned to reenact with Natalia his betrayal of her brother. Her dropping the veil frees him, enabling him to redeem his past. Given a glimpse into eternity, he is reconciled with time, for he goes to his confession at the hour he sent Haldin to his death. "There was no reason for that choice except that the facts and the words of a certain evening in his past were timing his conduct in the present. The sudden power Natalia Haldin had gained over him he ascribed to the same cause" (XXII.362).

The space in which Heyst can physically move is progressively diminished the more he resists taking the interior journey. The time in which he can make the journey is progressively lessened the more he resists confronting the timelessness of death ahead and the timelessness of life within. The emissaries close in on him. Wang will not let him cross the barricade. Lena disobeys him, waiting in the bungalow under the portrait of his father, whose voice from the past pours venom into his ears. She and the envoys encircle him, cutting off escape from the past. As doubles for his father and Morrison, they are his past; as a victim or a rescuer—and she can be either, depending on his response to her—she is his present or his future. The importance of time in this novel is succintly stated by Karl: "Nowhere else has Conrad so clearly used time in so many ways. Nowhere else does time enter so essentially as character, as influence, and, finally, as the very stuff of the novel's being." [35]

The quest every man must make is a journey to the acceptance of the timelessness of death that ends temporal life and the timelessness of eternal life that redeems time. Conducted in time to the timeless center, it is a descent into a region of fabulous forces to discover both the boundaries of temporal life and the existence of the soul, the life behind the heart that transcends boundaries. Returning from his initiation, he can be reborn by responding to his fellow men—if not to reintegrate society, at least to become himself a reintegrated man. If he dares possess the mystery, he finds death, which cancels his future; if he humbles himself, he finds life, which redeems his past. While Jim is frantically trying to extricate himself from the mud into which he has leaped in Patusan, he longs to be back in the courtyard repairing the clock. He can mend time if he will turn about. Instead, he cracks the earth asunder and dies.

I wrote above that the less one knows himself the more he ascribes 'wholly other' qualities to his other self. Paradoxically, since no one can ever know himself totally, his personality being "a ridiculous and aimless masquerade of something hopelessly unknown," [36] the more he knows himself the more he discovers the existence of life concealed within himself. This life is 'wholly other' because it is "hopelessly unknown" and immortal because, a mystery, it makes possible the new movement set against the circular movement overpowered by death. Immortal, it circumscribes his mortality and informs it. A hero can make this discovery on the immortal sea or with the eternal female. The two reveal themselves to Monsieur George in *The Arrow of Gold* (1919) as twin "mistresses of life's values. The illimitable greatness of the one, the unfathomable seduction of the other working their immemorial spells from generation to generation fell upon my heart at last; a common fortune, an unforgettable memory of the sea's formless might and of the sovereign charm in that woman's form wherein there seemed to beat the pulse of divinity rather than blood" (I.88).

This is not to say that any one Conradian heroine is a Dantean Beatrice. Even if the critic overlooks Edith Travers and Rita de Lastaola of *The Arrow of Gold* and confines his analysis to Jewel, Emilia, Winnie, Natalia, and Lena, he has to admit they are subjected to gentle irony. Like men, they have their illusions, although their belief that the men will discover themselves in love is far more beneficial than the male's pursuit of his ideal conception of himself. Neither is the heroine conscious that she is the hero's experience of timelessness. But she is the guiding power on his quest. Awakening him to the life from which he has isolated himself, she is his experience of love. "Charity," Conrad wrote to Marguerite Poradowska, "is eternal and universal Love, the divine virtue, the sole manifestation of the Almighty which may in some manner justify the act of creation." [37]

Thus although not a Dantean Beatrice in any one story, by the end of the collected fiction the Conradian heroine becomes a nineteenth-century Beatrice who inspires the Conradian hero with more awe than sexual desire, inevitably so because of Conrad's method. Reworking the doubling technique over a constantly magnified feminine landscape creates a heroine as the hero's double. Since the paradox is concretized in her and since she is his double, the paradox is concretized in him. If he accepts her as a woman bounded by life and death whose person embodies a mystery, he discovers she may be a vessel of divinity. If he then accepts himself as a man bounded by life and death whose person embodies a mystery, he discovers it is this mystery that makes redemption possible. The hero who responds to the heroine, who initially received him as a saviour by ascribing 'wholly other' qualities to him, discovers the existence of 'wholly other' life: he discovers the saviour within himself.

Even though this transformed experience is qualified by the language of analogy because the center is a mystery, Conrad's method moves toward revealing the light at the heart of darkness. Just as the reworked image moves toward symbol, so too does the progression in the hero's experience with the heroine move toward a glimpse into the mythic suggestiveness of the mystery. By the time of the major novels, Mrs. Gould is positioned next to the statue of the Madonna, as in the following example: " 'Come to lunch, dear Dr. Monygham, and come early,' said Mrs. Gould, in her travelling dress and her veil down, turning to look at him at the foot of the stairs; while at the top of the flight the Madonna, in blue robes and the Child on her arm, seemed to welcome her with an aspect of pitying tenderness" (IX.505).[88] Charles Gould does not respond to his wife, the donor of the picture of the Resurrection to the mine workers, but the doctor does and is reborn. To Razumov Natalia is a divinely appointed agent of redemption sent to betray him back into truth and peace. The concluding chapters of *Victory* suggest that Heyst, like Razumov, moves from atheism toward at least a disposition to believe. Such expressions as Lena's being under an influence "outside of her and more worthy" (XV.394) and Davidson's " 'Let Heaven look after what has been purified' " (XV.411) coupled with the role of the envoys as avengers suggest that for Conrad the denouement of Heyst's life unfolds in a cosmos in which the "comminatory voice of the storm" increases in its menacing quality until he surrenders to the "transfigured" Lena, triumphant in her "divine radiance," at which time the thunder ceases and the stars emerge (XV.401–7).

In Conrad's imaginative world the interior journey, a descent into darkness, becomes a journey toward light. The heroine becomes an agent of redemption while remaining a real woman. The hero discovers 'wholly other' life, making redemption possible, while remaining a man bounded by death. Together these paradoxes create the final paradox: Conrad demythicizes any one experience to extract its moral import, but the total body of experience, while retaining the moral import of the individual episodes, approaches the re-creation of the Christian myth. By the time of *Victory*, the heroine is at once the hero's conscience and elected destiny forcing him to take the interior journey, as well as a woman who wants to save her lover. Lena may be sent from a divine center, but Heyst must discover the potential within himself. He must redeem himself while he is being redeemed through her intercession. There is the germ of this paradox in "Heart of Darkness." Discovering that he is free to be moral or immoral in an indifferent universe, Marlow elects to turn about while he is being " 'permitted to draw back' " his hesitating foot (XVI.151).

Conrad's letter to Edward Noble, advising him how to cultivate his poetic faculty, marks his contribution to the re-creation of the Christian myth: "You must squeeze out of yourself every sensation, every thought, every image, —mercilessly, without reserve and without remorse: you must search the darkest corners of your heart, the most remote recesses of your brain,—you must search them for the image, for the glamour, for the right expression." [39] In Jung's depth psychology, behind each individual's unconscious lies the collective unconscious, the contents of which are the elemental symbols or images inherited in the structure of the brain. Jung gives the name archetypes or primordial images to these elemental symbols. When the hero descends into himself, he "finds himself apparently in deepest darkness, but then has unexpected visions of a world beyond. The 'mystery' he beholds represents the stock of primordial images which everybody brings with him as his human birthright, the sum total of inborn forms peculiar to the instincts. I have called this 'potential' psyche the collective unconscious. If this layer is activated by the regressive libido, there is a possibility of life being renewed, and also of its being destroyed." [40] Since these archetypes are the constituents of myth, the raw materials which form the narratives of myths, by descending into the region of fabulous forces within man himself, the repository of these primordial images, Conrad's fiction prepares the way for Ford's fiction.

The Secret Agent illustrates the archetypal pattern that moves toward the Christian myth without actually re-creating it. Opening the door of the "frightfully hot" parlor, Verloc "discloses the innocent Stevie, seated very good and quiet at a deal table, drawing circles, circles, circles; innumerable circles, concentric, eccentric; a coruscating whirl of circles that by their tangled multitude of repeated curves, uniformity of form, and confusion of intersecting lines suggested a rendering of cosmic chaos, the symbolism of a mad art attempting the inconceivable" (XIII.45). The inarticulate Stevie is his brother-in-law's salvation in the fallen world of London, for his circles represent the perfection of eternity, which makes time possible and which impinges on time. R. W. Stallman thinks the secret agent is time; J. Hillis Miller, death; Ted E. Boyle, love.[41] The three are fused in Stevie. He makes Verloc's life possible because he is the link between his brother-in-law and sister; without him Winnie would never have married Verloc. He is Verloc's experience of the unpredictable that breaks in on the routine of daily life; for example, his pouncing on the latter's hat and reverently carrying it away surprises the anarchist. He is Verloc's experience of the love offered by his wife. Winnie is pleased to think her husband responds to her brother's devotion. " 'Might be father and son,' she said to herself" (XIII.187). Had Verloc responded to his wife, he would have responded to Stevie. Had he responded to his potential son, he would not have betrayed him.

During their first interview scene, the one in which Winnie defends her brother to her husband, the "drowsy ticking of the old clock on the landing becomes distinctly audible in the bedroom" (XIII.57). During the second scene, in which Winnie pushes Stevie "to the front without loss of time," the "lonely clock on the landing counts off fifteen ticks into the abyss of eternity" (XIII.179–81). Ignoring the passage of time, Verloc forfeits his temporal life. Sending Stevie to bomb the Observatory where time is calculated, he forfeits the love offered him by Winnie.

In the third scene time ends for the anarchist, the martyred boy returning with a vengeance in his sister's person to kill him. In terms of the design of the novel, the betrayal of Stevie is the removal of love, compassion, and self-sacrifice from the world. The Professor, whose mission is to destroy everything, appears in Chapter IV, the chapter that chronologically follows the explosion, and then reappears in Chapter XIII, the chapter that follows Winnie's suicide.

Not only is Stevie seen pencilling circles that represent the perfection of eternity, he is also invested with provocative religious symbolism in Chapter VIII, the chapter that follows Chief Inspector Heat's collecting the pieces of the dismembered body and the Assistant Commissioner's quest for an explanation for the address on the collar. In this chapter Stevie rides with his mother and sister in an "apparatus like a mediaeval device for the punishment of crime" (XIII.163). The trip, in which time seems to stand still and motion becomes imperceptible, takes them past St. Stephen's, which should call to mind the first Christian martyr. The driver of the "Cab of Death" (XIII.170) is rewarded with "pieces of silver" (XIII.165) for delivering them to the Charity home. When the son overhears the anarchists talking about " 'eating people's flesh and drinking blood,' " he " 'gets into his passions' " (XIII.59). No matter what he is meant to suggest, though, Stevie remains the archetypal slain and resurrected god.

I do not think anyone would argue that the symbolic world of *The Secret Agent* is not ironic. Guerard writes that "this is not a tragic world of noble defeats and vast forces overthrown. *The Secret Agent's* vision is of 'a mediocre mankind' in an 'imperfect society': flabby, debased, eternally gullible. The Stevies and other weaklings are al-

ways available, to be used and abused by the Verlocs and
the Karl Yundts" because Stevie is "the very type for
Conrad of dumb, gullible, sentimental humanity." [42]
When compared with the traditional pattern of the hero
of myth, the pattern of Stevie's life is indeed ironic and
perverse as Miss Rosenfield demonstrates, although in the
society within this novel Stevie is both hero and scape-
goat. She sees in the image of cannibalism "a demonic
parody of the sacramental feast in which the hero's body is
eaten by his followers in order to revitalize the community.
The symbolic Christian phase of this rite, the Eucharist,
becomes a mockery here." [43] I am in agreement with these
two critics, but I contend that whereas Verloc and Ossipon
close off the possibility of redemption in the Christian
sense by rejecting the potential son, Razumov and Heyst
keep the possibility open by accepting their potential for
love and self-sacrifice. It is Verloc who, after the son has
been blown to bits, makes a mockery of the Eucharist by
devouring the roast beef, "laid out in the likeness of fune-
real baked meats for Stevie's obsequies" (XIII.253). It is
Verloc who, shortly thereafter, rips away Winnie's veil, un-
masking "a still unreadable face" (XIII.256). Her face
becomes readable as she approaches him in that she resembles her brother, but "lying on his back and staring
upwards" (XIII.262), he does not see her until it is too
late. Betraying his potential for life, he finds death at the
hands of his wife. Sitting "under her black veil, in her
own house, like a masked and mysterious visitor of impenetrable intentions" (XIII.256), she embodies the inscrutable intention of "Heart of Darkness" and the impenetrable mystery that sweeps away the Professor's tirade.
No matter what she is meant to suggest, though, Winnie remains the archetypal virgin-mother who offers her brother-
son to mankind.

I am not trying to make Conrad a Christian writer, but it would be a serious error to think of him as an anti-Christian.[44] His emphasis on the heroine as an agent of redemption, the hero's confession of guilt, discovery of his immortal soul, acceptance of his potential for love and self-sacrifice, and the epiphany that reveals the transcendent and immanent reality must be set against the attitude expressed in some of his letters that Christianity is an illusion, a fable satisfying man's need to give meaning to a beclouded existence.[45] And by insisting on the reality in time while revealing the reality outside time in which all patterns are reconciled, he suggests a sacramental experience, which is made possible by the Incarnation. Yet the critic cannot push this argument too far without destroying the suggestiveness of the experience. I think the soundest position is that Conrad is best appreciated as an artist whose intention is to awaken in us "that pagan residuum of awe and wonder which lurks still at the bottom of our old humanity" (XV.vii).

His artistic credo, expressed in the Preface to *The Nigger of the "Narcissus,"* is "to make you see." The artist snatches "a passing phase of life" and "by the power of the written word" shows "its vibration, its colour, its form," reveals the "substance of its truth—discloses its inspiring secret: the stress and passion within the core of each convincing moment." Making us see the truth, art awakens that capacity in us for awe and wonder, the only way we can respond to the truth because it is a mystery that recedes from us the closer we come to it. Although "art itself may be defined as a single-minded attempt to render the highest kind of justice to the visible universe, by bringing to light the truth, manifold and one, underlying its every aspect," it cannot possess the mystery. Just as the individual is swallowed up in the heart of darkness if he dares possess it, so art is no longer art the moment it stops rendering life's vibration, color, and form (XXIII.xi–xiv). "The world of the living contains enough marvels and mysteries as it is," he explains in the Preface to *The Shadow-Line* (1920), to keep him from turning to the "mere supernatural" (XVII.vii) beyond the horizon. He found the method congenial to his vision and his talent for creating suggestiveness without sacrificing surface reality. In fact, the archetypal pattern in his fiction approaches the re-creation of the myth only because he first demythicizes to draw the reader into the realm of supernatural wonder within man himself.

Conrad faces the same problem in his fiction that Eliot faces in *Four Quartets*. Since eternity is meaningful only in relation to time, the problem is to so fracture the tangible, visible world that it will reveal the timeless in time without sacrificing the tangible, visible world. The novelist's method is that of dislocating and relocating objects the reader takes for granted, of rendering impressions in a startling manner, of bringing multiple perspectives and shifting points of view to bear on a subject, of reorganizing chronology, of balancing ironic detachment and dramatic immediacy, of building up images with minute variations so they are constantly becoming symbols, of doubling characters and situations. His techniques enable the reader to glimpse the truth made manifest in this world. Since the truth is a mystery, Jim may not be " 'one of us' " because by deserting Jewel he becomes the slain god; Emilia Gould may be the dispenser of grace in Sulaco; Stevie may be more than Winnie's idiot brother; Natalia and Lena may be divinely appointed agents from a center that may be a loving God, sent to awaken Razumov and Heyst to their potential for love and self-sacrifice. For Conrad man can never totally know the truth so long as he is a self-conscious part of the tangible, visible world, but he can have the religious experience that makes the moral act possible and he can be reborn through the agency of the woman. I think it indisputable that Conrad is a religious writer, his art being grounded in the paradox of death in life—life in death, although I should like to add Rodolphe Mégroz's conclusion: "He is religious in his attitude to mere existence, but all his capacity for religious experience is identified with his creative effort." [46]

By disclosing, through the image, "the stress and passion within the core of each convincing moment," Conrad has taken us to the point where we are ready to ascend to the reality that may have been drawing the hero onward all the while he was descending. Although we cannot know the inscrutable intention, at least we know we have left the desolate world of *The Inheritors*. Conrad takes the first step necessary to re-create the Christian myth, restoring the Christian tradition. Not substituting a human center for a divine center but criticizing every quest that turns away from the human center, he affirms his faith in the one experience in which man can realize himself. Paradoxically, by renouncing the quest for redemption beyond the horizon to concentrate on the human concrete, he releases a reality that may be drawing man beyond the horizon. His imaginative world can take us no further; however, he prepares us for Ford's imaginative world.

2.

Ford Madox Ford

From the spate of novels Ford Madox Ford wrote during his period of apprenticeship, the years between the period of collaboration with Conrad and 1915, when *The Good Soldier* was published, I have selected one, a romance, *The Young Lovell* (1913), to illustrate the nature of the initiation the Fordian hero must pass before he can become a reintegrated man. It is this novel which Caroline Gordon feels is the key to Ford's life work: "Through all his works one thread runs. All his fictions seem to have been inspired by one vision. That goddess who is larger than life and even more terrible than she is beautiful. The Flower Goddess Olwen, Blodewedd, the Owl, lamp-eyed, Circe, the pitiless falcon, or Lamia with the serpent's flickering tongue. . . . Whatever name the goddess goes by, this poet has remained faithful to his first vision—a vision which comes to every man in youth. He has fought manfully in those ranks which, as Mr. Graves has pointed out, have numbered many a good poet, telling and re-tell-

ing, as long as he had the breath, that story which he, himself, called 'the saddest story I have ever heard.' He dis-
tinguished himself, certainly, in the telling of it and died
as he lived, a good soldier." [1]

Set in 1486, against the background of an uneasy peace
between barons, king, and church, the romance opens with
Young Lovell's breaking of his self-imposed vow to kneel
in a chapel till dawn on the day of the ceremony in which
he will be raised to the rank of "good knight and soldier
of Christ and Our Lady" (42).[2] Assailed during the night
by visions of Behemoth, Leviathan, Mahound, Helen of
Troy, and the Witch of Endor, he cannot pray: "These
were the old, ancient gods of a time unknown—the gods
to whom the baal fires were lit; gods of the giants and
heroes of whom even his confessor spoke with bated
breath. Angels, some said they were, not fallen, but indifferent. And some of the poor would have them to be little people that dwelt in bogs and raths, and others held
them for great and fair. He could not pray; he could not
cross himself; his tongue clove to his jaws; his limbs were
leaden. His mind was filled with curiosity, with desire,
with hope." When he sees a light, he staggers to his feet
in the darkness and steps out of the chapel, to encounter
an old witch who points toward a white horse moving
across the dunes. " 'And that shall be your bane,' " she says
to him. " 'Ah me, for the fine young lording.' " Mounting
his horse, Hamewarts, to pursue the white horse, Young
Lovell crosses the threshold of the first stage, the separation stage, of the tripartite archetypal pattern:

Slowly, with mincing and as if shy footsteps,
Hamewarts went down through the rushes from that
very real world. Young Lovell perceived that the
brown was a carpeting that fluttered, all of sparrows.

It had a pearly and restless border of blue doves, and in this carpet the white horse stepped ankle-deep without crushing one little fowl. He perceived the great-petalled flowers, scarlet and white and all golden. On a green hill there stood a pink temple, and the woman on the back of the white horse held a white falcon. She smiled at him with the mocking eyes of the naked woman that stood upon the shell in the picture he had seen in Italy.

"But for you," he heard himself think, "I might have been the prosperest knight of all this Northland and the world, for I have never met my match in the courteous arts, the chase or the practice and exercises of arms."

And he heard her answering thoughts:

"Save for that I had not called thee from the twilight" (4–12).

Upon his release, as if from "a deep dream" (47), Young Lovell thinks he stayed with the White Lady for less than an hour; actually, he has been gone from his estate for three months. In the interim the bastard son of Lord Lovell, Decies of the South, wearing his half brother's armor, has taken his place in the ceremony of knighthood and betrothal to Lady Margaret Glrorem. With his half sisters, Isopel and Douce, and their husbands, Sir Walter Limousin and Sir Symonde Vesey, he has seized control of Lovell Castle, imprisoned Young Lovell's mother, Lady Rohtraut, and had the Earl of Northumberland bring judgment for sorcery against him, dispossessing him of his property. This is the situation the hero faces when he returns. His immediate tasks therefore are regaining his legal inheritance, restoring order to his lands, and rejoining the woman to whom he should be affianced. To

accomplish these goals is to complete the archetypal pattern.

His immediate tasks are part of a much larger ordeal,
however: the regaining of his Christian heritage. " 'Even
let me go in Christ's name, for I have many businesses,' "
he beseeches the White Lady. Having "all the time of this
earth and beyond it" (47-8), she releases him because she
knows he will always be enchanted by her. She is right.
Despite his commitment to the Christian chivalric code,
he is immobilized by desire to rejoin his goddess. When
he learns he has been dispossessed, he knows "there could
be no doubt that the law would not help him to retake his
Castle; but he longed for her red, crooked, smiling lips.
He must therefore get together a band and besiege that
place; and at the thought of climbing through a breach in
great towers whilst the cannon spoke and the fascines fell
into the ditches, arrows clittered on harness, greek fire
rustled down, and the great banners dropped over the tu-
mult, his blood leapt for a moment. But her hair he remembered in its filaments and it blotted out the blue sea
that lay below his feet and was more golden than the gold
of the broom flowers and the gorse that surrounded him.
He thought that, first, he must have the sanction of the
Bishop Palatine and his absolution from any magic he
might in innocence have witnessed; but, in longing for her
queer smile, he could scarcely keep from springing to his
feet. He knew he must be moving over the hills, but the
remembrance of her breasts crossed with her girdle kept
him languishing there in the hot sun as if his limbs had
lost their young strength" (79-80). Despite his commitment to the Christian heroine, her image wearies him
when he compares it with that of the pagan heroine.

The reader is introduced to the conflict between
paganism and Christianity before the hero leaves on his

quest. Young Lovell takes the visions "to be in the nature of the very old chapel, since it had stood there over the tiresome and northern sea ever since Christendom had come to the land, and it was proper to think that, just as those walls had seen the murdering of blessed saint Oddry by heathens and Scots whilst he sang mass, and even as pagans and sorcerers had in the old times contended for that ground, now, having done it in the body, in their souls they should still haunt that spot and contend for the soul of a young lording that should be made a knight upon the morrow" (2–3). As the story unfolds, the novel uncovers the roots of this conflict in the hero's dual heritage. Young Lovell is the son of Lord Lovell, one of the Ruthvens, descendants of a Welsh brigand, and Lady Rohtraut, one of the Dacres of the North. His half brother, Decies of the South, who "followed him like his shadow" (31) before he disappeared from the estate and who grins at Lady Margaret with "lascivious lips" (43) as he pushes up his visor after the betrothal, is the son of Lord Lovell and a witch. Whereas Lady Rohtraut, who approves of both her son's vigil as proper preparation for the solemn ceremony and his betrothal to Lady Margaret, is outraged by his half brother's deception, her husband, who favors Decies, dies in a paroxysm of laughter when he realizes the extent of his bastard son's impudence. Later, Young Lovell's mother's servant tells him even though the members of the family call themselves Lovells, " 'Ruthvens ye will remain, and ye are never of this countryside but of the Red Welsh or the Black Welsh or of some heathen countryside. And always ye have had truck with witches and warlocks' " (81). The Fordian hero's dilemma, then, is how to reconcile his pagan and Christian heritage, how to integrate his sexual and religious impulses in the service of

Christ and Our Lady, for the Bishop identifies the White
Lady, who by awakening Young Lovell has charmed him,
as " 'the spirit that most snareth men to carnal desires. So
doth she show herself to each man in the image that should
snare him to sin, with a face, kind, virtuous and alluring
after each man's tastes. That is the nature of such false
gods' " (238).

"Will he come again?" is a question asked during
Young Lovell's three-month absence. He does return from
his initiation and he does score a decisive victory over the
forces who have dispossessed him of his lands, but he
never scores a decisive victory over the fabulous forces
within himself. He is a hero with divided allegiance.
Though knighted, absolved, and betrothed, he cannot rid
his mind of the memory of the White Lady's crooked
smile. After rejoining Lady Margaret, routing the enemy
from his castle, and restoring order to his lands, he renounces the world to enter an anchorite's cell to do pen-
ance for his sins until he dies. Yet in what surely must be
one of the strangest resolutions to a divided self in twentieth-century fiction, he is also reunited with his goddess
in his dreams. The closing section of the romance moves
to "a very high valley of Corsica," where "the mistress of
the world" sits upon "a throne of white marble in a little
round temple. . . ." In front of the temple a young knight
and a warrior engage in combat, at the conclusion of which
the women of the goddess anoint "the limbs of those com-
batants with juices and oils" which heal their wounds. "So,
courteously, they devised upon all things, and that knight
thought never upon the weariness of Northumberland or
upon how his mortal body lived in the little hermitage not
much bigger than a hound's kennel that was builded
against the wall of the church. . . ."

No, there they lay or walked in lemon groves devising of this or that whilst the butterflies settled upon their arms. And when they would have it night, so there was the cool of the evening and a great moon and huge stars and dimness fit for the gentle pleasures of love (306–10).

In *The Young Lovell* the Fordian hero does not pass his ordeal; he does not regain his Christian heritage. The fault is not his, however. He accepts the White Lady's guidance to discover the center of his pagan heritage within himself, but he remains a slain and resurrected god in her service. He does not become a good knight and soldier of Christ and Our Lady, since there is no figure of Our Lady in the novel who is able to guide him to the center of his Christian heritage: the slain and resurrected Christ within himself. The doubling technique makes Lady Margaret the Christian counterpart to the pagan heroine, but she is no match for the White Goddess. That there is really no contest between the two antagonists is demonstrated just prior to the attack on the castle. Lady Margaret and the monk Francis, Young Lovell's spiritual adviser, clasp each other's hands for comfort while praying fiercely for the success of their champion in the battle. Above them, on the tower, the young knight is watching the approaching waterspouts, the form the White Lady assumes to protect her lover, which she does by inundating the battlefield, ensuring his defeat of Decies.

The Bishop's explanation to Francis in Part Two that the nature of the apparition of the White Lady corresponds to the spiritual state of the beholder provides the reader with a clue to Lady Margaret's inability to guide the hero. She recounts to Sir Bertram of Lyonesse how on three occasions " 'Saint Katharine, whom I love above

other saints, appeared to me in a gown of gold and damask
and leaning upon her wheel. She looked upon me sorrow-
fully, as who should say my true love—for whom I had
besought that saint many times—was dead to me' " (180).
If the Bride of Christ appeared to her three times to tell
her that her true love was dead, he must be literally dead.
She cannot understand in what other way he could be dead
to her. When Sir Bertram, a cunning man who marries
the wealthy Lady Rohtraut, expresses his opinion that
Young Lovell cannot be dead but must be a captive of the
White Lady, whom he has seen and who appeared to him
to be " 'a vampire, a courtesan or a demon from the East,' "
she is shocked. Not only does she understand the apparitions of Saint Katharine to mean he is dead, but she too
has encountered the White Lady, who appeared to her
to have " 'the kindest face' " of any woman she has ever
seen (182). For her Sir Bertram is a liar, especially since
she hears Young Lovell's voice and foot on the stairs. Over-
joyed at his return while apprehensive about the meaning
of the apparitions of Saint Katharine, she wants to embrace him. "But that she might not do for fear of her manners. For she had been well schooled, and, whereas, she
might well, if she would, give him her towers and lands
and men and bondsmen, still she could not go against the
ban of the Church; for the ladies of her house of Eure
were very proud ladies. Neither, for pride, though the
tears were wet upon her cheeks, would she ask him what
ban it was that he lay under" (220). Although "gallant and
fair and loving," Lady Margaret is unable to combat her
antagonist because she has not descended into the region
of fabulous forces within herself. The thought of marrying
her is "an intolerable weariness" to Young Lovell (287),
who must journey beyond the horizon to his White God-

dess to have his wound healed, to experience the gentle pleasures of love.

Young Lovell does not become a good soldier of Christ. Neither does Edward Ashburnham in *The Good Soldier,* despite a title which implies the archetypal pattern is completed and the heritage regained in this novel. But not only is the pattern not completed, it does not even shape the novel. What does is a quest by the narrator, John Dowell, through a maze. Why Dowell makes Edward the good soldier is a consideration that must be held in abeyance until the critic finds his path through the maze, for this novel, the first work from the period of Ford's maturity as an artist, is a more deceptive fiction than *The Young Lovell,* requiring a more subtle reading than does the romance.

In a recent article Brother Joseph Wiesenfarth, after summarizing the diversity of interpretations of *The Good Soldier,* suggests examining "a different dimension" of the novel "in an attempt to elucidate some facet of structure or meaning that is more likely to yield a more satisfying degree of probability or perhaps certainty itself." [3] His examination, which compares the novel to James's *The Sacred Fount,* offers an excellent starting point, since each novel is a first-person narrative, related after the events, by a man who tells more about himself than about the events. And, as in the case of *The Sacred Fount* and "Amy Foster," the way to find one's path through the labyrinth of *The Good Soldier* to determine the meaning of the story is through Dowell's mental processes and emotional attitudes as they are made manifest in his narration. One must begin here, for all efforts to discuss the events of the novel apart from the consciousness of the man who is the sole reporter of them end in confusion and disagreement. If the other approach leaves much to be desired, the critic should be willing to try this one, particularly because he is dependent on what the narrator tells him.

At the opening of Part Four, Dowell reminds the reader he is telling his story "in a very rambling way so that it may be difficult for anyone to find his path through what may be a sort of maze. I cannot help it. I have stuck to my idea of being in a country cottage with a silent listener, hearing between the gusts of the wind and amidst the noises of the distant sea the story as it comes. And, when one discusses an affair—a long, sad affair—one goes back, one goes forward. One remembers points that one has forgotten and one explains them all the more minutely since one recognizes that one has forgotten to mention them in their proper places and that one may have given, by omitting them, a false impression" (183). Although much of Dowell's analysis of the characters' motives, passions, and involvements is based on conjecture, the events can be put in chronological sequence. On August 4, 1904, three years after they were married, John and Florence Dowell, leisured Americans living on the Continent, meet a retired British army officer and his wife, Edward and Leonora Ashburnham, at Bad Nauheim, a health resort in the Taunus Mountains where the Dowells spend their summers because Florence has duped her husband into believing she has a weak heart. With the Ashburnhams is a young woman, Mrs. Maisie Maidan, whom they have brought to the resort because she is a heart patient. She dies on the day the two couples take a trip to a Prussian castle. Nine years from the date of the meeting, on August 4, 1913, Florence commits suicide when she realizes her husband has learned of her sexual intimacy with a man named Jimmy before their marriage. While in America, seeing to the settlement of her estate, Dowell receives cables from the Ashburnhams asking him to come to their home at Branshaw Teleragh in England. Shortly after his arrival, Edward confides in him that he is in love with Nancy Rufford, the daughter of Leonora's friend, a girl who has lived with them for years and whom he has just sent to India to rejoin her father. After Edward commits suicide, Leonora divulges the information to Dowell that Nancy was one of many women her husband was in love with, but the blow that hits him "full in the face" (104) is the revelation that Florence was Edward's mistress.

Since Dowell's reliability is a matter of dispute among critics, I want to establish four facts about him. One, he demands answers to the questions, "What does one know and why is one here?" not merely for his own peace of mind, although that is his immediate goal, but because the future of civilization is in jeopardy: "I don't know. And there is nothing to guide us. And if everything is so nebulous about a matter so elementary as the morals of sex, what is there to guide us in the more subtle morality of all other personal contacts, associations, and activities? Or are we meant to act on impulse alone? It is all a darkness" (10–2). It is possible to see in the frequent use of "heart" and "darkness" an allusion to "Heart of Darkness," a narrative re-creating the interior journey to the center, just as it is possible to see in Dowell's imagining himself with a "sympathetic soul" (12) listening to the sea and wind and looking at the moon an allusion to Arnold's "Dover Beach," a poem urging that lovers "be true / To one another" [4] in a spiritless modern world witnessing the breakup of the old order with its traditional values and virtues. If these are allusions in Part One of his narrative, then from the opening of the novel the discrepancy between what he sees and what the reader perceives begins to appear.

Two, he does not understand the persons he knew and the events he witnessed. "Who knows?" "God knows," and "Who the Devil knows?" are expressions which punctuate his narrative as does some variation of "I don't know": for example, "I know nothing—nothing in the world—of the hearts of men" (7); "You ask how it feels to be a deceived husband. Just heavens, I do not know" (70); and "I don't know. I know nothing. I am very tired" (245). His wife is "a riddle" (23), "a problem in Algebra" (120). His convoluted narrative is an attempt "to puzzle out what I know of this sad affair" (3).

Three, he consistently contradicts himself when giving the dates of the events. The confusion of dates cannot be the novelist's error. From Ford's comments on translating the novel into French, we know he was pleased with "the intricate tangle of references and cross-references" in it.[5] We also know he revised the work between its partial appearance in *Blast* and the book publication. We cannot be certain about the time of the events, but we can be certain of what the contradictions reveal about the narrator. They are "part of Dowell's personality."[6] His statement that Maisie died on August 4, 1904, the same day he and Florence met the Ashburnhams, which is contradicted by other statements, indicates his need to simplify the complexities he does not understand. This need is best illustrated in his yearning for the "permanence" and "stability" of an uncomplicated past: "I can't believe that that long, tranquil life, which was just stepping a minuet, vanished in four crashing days at the end of nine years and six weeks. . . . No, indeed, it can't be gone" (6).

Four, since in his quest for an interpretation he seeks a pattern in what he does not comprehend, his "attitude toward the characters and events with which he deals is in constant evolution as the novel progresses." [7] He will continue to test theories until he finds a satisfying one.

Now we can pursue Brother Wiesenfarth's suggestion that we study a different dimension. We have a narrator who searches for an explanation in what he does not understand. As a result he distorts the time to make the past more manageable, and he applies tentative explanations in the hope that one will make sense of the events. We will read *The Good Soldier* as the ironic narrative of a man who wants to find some cause for the collapse of his world or some structure as a defense against the "falling to pieces of a people" (5).

The first bulwark against chaos to which Dowell turns is manners. The Ashburnhams, " 'quite good people,' " and the Dowells knew how to behave in public. This section, Part One, deals with genealogy and pseudo-cultural pursuits. Yet it is clear from the first chapter on that manners cannot provide the permanence he seeks, for Leonora, "extraordinarily fair and so extraordinarily the real thing that she seemed too good to be true," may have been a harlot and Edward, "the cleanest-looking sort of chap; an excellent magistrate, a first-rate soldier, one of the best landlords, so they said, in Hampshire, England," was not the man to be trusted with another's wife. "The model couple," the Ashburnhams, "never spoke a word to each other in private." Dowell, whose life was spent in hearth and smoking-room and who can "vouch for the cleanness of my thoughts and the absolute chastity of my life," even questions himself (4–12).

His groping for an explanation permits the reader to apprehend the irony in the novel. His values are superficial. His sense of order is summed up in the passage in which he lists the "carefully arranged" items in the resort hotel (21). His sense of stability is a careful arrangement of the details of the Hotel Excelsior dining-room and the colors of the countryside scene. His sense of belonging is a desire to return to cities he and Florence visited so that he "should have something to catch hold of now" (14). His sense of purpose is being a nurse to an unfaithful wife: "my occupation, my career, my ambition" (49). His selection of " 'good people' " is the result of knowing "whether they will go rigidly through with the whole programme from the underdone beef to the Anglicanism" (37).

At this point Dowell realizes that reviewing the manners of his group does not help him "get an inch deeper" into the meaning of the past. In giving "a rather extraordinary instance" of this failure to "get an inch deeper" (37) —their visit to the Prussian castle where the Protestant document, the Protest, is displayed in one of the chambers (this scene is designated the Protest scene)—he moves to another bulwark, religion. In relating the events leading up to and including this scene, he unconsciously turns to the principals' religious training, in the process blurring the time between the events. Florence's stumbling upon Leonora and Maisie in the hotel corridor outside of Edward's room brought about the meeting of the two couples, which led to the trip to the Prussian castle where Florence began her annexation of Edward by laying her finger on his wrist. Her aggressiveness precipitated Maisie's death because upon their return to the hotel the young woman overheard Florence questioning Edward about their relationship. Since Dowell was willing to accept Leonora's explanation for the frightening scene in the chamber—that Florence and Edward were speaking disparagingly of her religion, Roman Catholicism—the final third of Part One begins his quest for permanence in religion.

His narration reveals his mental processes. Each attempt on his part to discern a pattern leads him to another tentative bulwark or cause, which is subsequently rejected, with the matter of the attempt forming the basis for the next possible bulwark or cause. While detailing the events surrounding the Protest scene, he summarizes the cause of Edward's passionate involvements, the role of Leonora in these involvements, and the role of Florence in effecting the initial meeting. For him Leonora was the victim of her convent-school education, which brings him back to the Protest scene and his willingness to accept her explanation for her fury in the castle. Since Florence's overture to Edward was the essence of this scene, precipitating Maisie's death, he merges her death with this scene and his meeting the Ashburnhams, contradicting himself on the dates.

Having mentioned Leonora's background and having accepted her explanation, Dowell turns to religion as a possible pattern. It is during the last third of Part One and all of Part Two that we encounter a cluster of expressions such as "God knows," "by God," and "by the grace of God." This section contains the Protest scene, the vision of Judgment Day, and references to "Providence."

Relinquishing religion as a possible pattern, he reveals another side of himself which contributes to the developing irony. His religious sense is superficial also. His expressions are perfunctory expletives. His remark, " 'On Corpus Christi'—or it may have been some other saint's day, I cannot keep these things in my head" (124), betrays an ignorance of Christ and saints' days. The comment, "He was not a Catholic; but that was the way it took him" (134), on what must have been an agonizing experience for Edward, sobbing before the image of the Virgin Mary after letting Leonora know he would not try to corrupt Nancy, is so prosaic as to be incredible. At no point in the narra-

tive does he indicate any spiritual awareness or growth;
at most his response is empty and mechanical: "It is not
my business to think about it [God's compassion]. It is
simply my business to say, as Leonora's people say: '*Re-
quiem aeternam dona eis, domine, et lux perpetua luceat
per eis. In memoriam aeternam erit. . . .*' "(70)

We can demonstrate the failure of religion for Dowell
from another direction. "This is the saddest story I have
ever heard" is the opening sentence of *The Good Soldier*.
The events of the past constitute the saddest story because
he can neither discern a pattern in them nor find a protec-
tion against their repetition. The suffering, agony, and
death he records lack a meaning: "And why? For what
purpose? To point what lesson? It is all a darkness" (164).
Whenever he fails to find an explanation, he repeats the
motif, "the saddest story." This first occurs during the
recounting of Maisie's death, which combines manners (the
befriending of the young woman by the Ashburnhams)
and religion (Leonora's background, the Protest scene,
and the final scene of Part One): "Yes, this is the saddest
story . . ." (51).

He next turns to a third possibility, passion, because
his investigation of Edward's involvements leads him to
seek out the cause of "the importunities . . . the tempes-
tuous forces that pushed that miserable fellow on to ruin"
(51-2). But he cannot assign the cause to "inscrutable destiny" (49), "coincidence" (77), or "some curse" (79) any
more than he can to Providence so that in rejecting "the
permanence of any early passion," he repeats "the saddest
story" motif (114-5). Yet he persists in the hope that he
can decipher the past. The quest continues.

His method betrays his lack of understanding. Unable
to pierce through to the center, he becomes hopelessly
enmeshed in minutiae. Unlike the speaker of *Four Quar-*

tets, whose method is to return to the beginning so that he can redeem the past, by encircling the event until it bursts open revealing the Word, Dowell recounts the events over and over again because he does not know what else to do, thereby creating the very circularity he hopes to escape.

That Dowell has not deciphered the past is evident in the account of his trip to America. Like the narrator of *The Sacred Fount,* he sees, not objective reality, but an extension of his own mental processes and attitudes. Specifically, all he remembers is that persons complained to him about "mysterious movements" and "influences" (154). What really happened we have no way of knowing, but since he is obsessed with mysterious movements and influences as the cause of the events he witnessed in Europe, we have reason to suspect he is writing more about himself than about events in Philadelphia. After all, he remembers that Leonora was engaged in "fighting a long duel with unseen weapons against silent adversaries" (129), which I take to be another allusion to "Dover Beach." [8] His parting comment to his second-nephew, Carter, and his fiancée is interesting: "May Fate deal very kindly with them" (155). Unable to discover an explanation, he blames the past on Fate or mysterious movements and influences.

The opening of Part Four returns to the Protest scene, the allusion to "Dover Beach," and "the saddest story" motif. After relating the effect of Florence's meddling, in the first two-thirds of Part Four, he is still unsuccessful; the page before the break in the writing of the narrative repeats the motif. He is desperate for an answer: "It is this part of the story that makes me saddest of all. For I ask myself unceasingly, my mind going round and round in a weary, baffled space of pain—what should these people have done? What, in the name of God, should they have done?" (233)

Conscious their lives were false but unable to understand why, he can neither recapture his lost "terrestrial paradise" (237) nor free himself from the circularity. He therefore arrives at a solution by simply summarizing the final events of the nine-year history: Edward's suicide after receiving a telegram from Nancy, " 'Having rattling good time' " (255); Nancy's madness after learning of Edward's suicide; and Leonora's remarriage to a very ordinary man, Rodney Bayham. Given his lack of perception, his cataloguing of details, this is all he can do. At last he has a satisfactory interpretation. Neither manners nor religion nor passion can cause or prevent adultery, madness, suicide. The two finest persons he knew, Edward and Nancy, were destroyed while Leonora achieved happiness. The answer is obvious: society eliminates the abnormal and accepts the normal. The concluding sections of Part Four are devoted to the castigation of the male by the two females, acting to preserve "the feminine commonweal" (245), the normal society: Leonora insisting to Nancy that although her husband was a dissolute man not worthy of a woman's love, she must give herself to him to save him, and Nancy insisting to Edward that although she could not love him, she was willing to give herself to save him. He has reached the "end of the story" (252). And since "society must go on, I suppose," he continues, "and society can only exist if the normal, if the virtuous, and the slightly deceitful flourish, and if the passionate, the headstrong, and the too truthful are condemned to suicide and to madness," he can, in the crowning irony of the novel, explain himself. Because he failed to win the love of Florence or Leonora or Nancy, because he was neglected and misunderstood, he must, in his "fainter way, come into the category of the passionate, of the headstrong, and the too-truthful" (253).[9]

The picture in *The Good Soldier* is that of a chivalrous knight, Edward, bedeviled by women he sought to comfort because it is given to us by a narrator who, seeing himself as a chivalrous knight bedeviled by women in a faint way, identifies with Edward and blames Florence and Leonora. The picture therefore is no more Ford's than Kennedy's in "Amy Foster" is Conrad's, but whereas the latter modifies the doctor's tale by using a double narrator technique, the former so weighs down his single narrator's tale with image, allusion, and situation charged with a suggestiveness Dowell misses that this single narrator unknowingly facilitates our quest. By retelling the events because he cannot discern a pattern, he invites us to reexamine the past until we perceive the explanation for the adultery, madness, and suicide. We must penetrate the maze, a projection of Dowell's bewilderment, to see the figure in the carpet. As we do we unmask the deluded Edward and his disciple.[10]

Although I agree with Samuel Hynes's comments, in one of the best essays on the novel, on the epistemological problem in limited narration and especially with his argument that "the real events of the novel are Dowell's thoughts about what has happened, and not the happenings themselves," I disagree with his conclusion that "the narrator's fallibility is the norm," that we have no other authority within the novel against which we can judge Dowell's interpretation.[11] The novel's primary frame of reference is religious.[12] Dowell returns to the Protest scene or its consequences at the end of each of the first three parts. We have his vision of Judgment Day, his consideration of a possible Providence, and his allusion to Philippians iv.7 (251). Much of his narrative is given over to Leonora's religious upbringing. The "first real trouble" between the Ashburnhams came from her refusal to allow

Edward to have a Roman Catholic chapel built, even though "he was quite ready to become an emotional Catholic" (142). Nancy saw herself as "some Deborah, some mediaeval saint" (225). There are Dowell's outbursts such as "God knows," Edward's prostration before the image of the Virgin, his quotation from Swinburne (251), Nancy's " 'Credo in unum Deum Omnipotentem' " (234), the epigraph, and discussions of marriage and divorce, Roman Catholicism and Protestantism. Further, there is the peculiarly religious imagery in his language, despite his declared hostility to religion. To give but three instances: Leonora's pimping was "the cross that she had to take up during her long Calvary of a life" (70); the "sacrilege" of "burgling a church" would have been easier than entering Florence's locked bedroom unannounced (89); and Edward's praise for Nancy "atoned for" the bitterness of her childhood (112).

Because the narrator does not comprehend the import of what he says, we realize the relevance of the epigraph, from Psalm 118 (119): "Blessed are the undefiled in the way, who walk in the law of the Lord." [13] The psalmist is conscious that the Lord brought men "out of darkness, and the shadow of death; and broke their bonds in sunder," in Psalm 106 (107), that in Psalm 111 (112) for the just man "a light is risen up in darkness. . . ." Dowell is aware that "it is all a darkness" (12), but for him as for the others there is no ray of light. On the contrary, they were over whelmed by the darkness. He brought Nancy from "a darkened room" (234) in Ceylon to a life of mental darkness in Branshaw Manor, "rendered darker by the fact that it lay in a hollow crowned by fir trees with their black shadows" (223). Here is his gloss on the Psalm: "But what were they? The just? The unjust? God knows!" (70). The one insight he has is there will be no illumination, no transfiguration, no breaking of the bonds: "So life peters out" (254).

In spite of his many references to light, Dowell is blind to its source. Not knowing himself, he identifies with Edward, who, not knowing himself, fancied himself a redeemer whose mission was to extend solace to mournful females, a delusion that set in motion a series of disasters. In her naïveté Leonora followed Edward about "full of trustfulness, of admiration, of gratitude, and of love. He was also, in a great sense, her pastor and guide—and he guided her into what, for a girl straight out of a convent, was almost heaven" (141). For a wife living with a husband forever comforting other women, though, he guided her into hell. Together he and his wife acted as "saviours to the poor, dark-eyed, dying" Maisie (64), bringing her with them to Nauheim, where they hastened her death. When Edward praised Nancy "it must have been as if a god had approved her handiwork or a king her loyalty" (112). When he arranged for her to rejoin her father in India so that she would not feel compelled to rescue her mother, a vicious woman who had taken to the streets in Glasgow, she "sat there in a blissful dream," for her Lohengrin was "saving the world and her, in the black darkness" (231), only to drop her into the darkness of insanity. As a statement of faith, her " '*Credo,*' " uttered by a girl bereft of reason, is as vacuous as her other remark, " 'Shuttlecocks,' " is pathetic, uttered by a girl "tossed backwards and forwards between the violent personalities" of Edward and Leonora (253).

The women must assume their share of responsibility for what happened, since they accepted Edward as their Saviour, but the disasters must be traced back to his failure to know himself. While Dowell is recounting the events, image, allusion, and repeated situation combine to expose

Edward's self-deception. The Kilsyte case should have awakened Edward to his human nature. In the witness box, on trial for comforting a nursemaid on a train, "there came suddenly into his mind the recollection of the softness of the girl's body as he had pressed her to him" (156)—the recollection of a man, not a god. It did not awaken him any more than did his affairs with La Dolciquita, a Spanish dancer whom he wanted to acquaint with salvation because she surrendered her virtue to him at Monte Carlo; or Mrs. Basil, the wife of a fellow officer in India; or Maisie; or Florence. Whether or not he consummated the affairs is irrelevant (the source of the information is Leonora); the fact is they constituted more than enough experience to awaken him to his sexual nature. Years later, however, still unconscious of any "physical motive" (111), he declared his love to Nancy, deluding himself that his interest in her was fatherly concern. When he learned he could not command her love, he killed himself after "looking up to the roof of the stable, as if he were looking to heaven" (256). By having him commit suicide in a stable, Ford "concludes his novel with the reminder that the real source of the passion that ironically leads man to the worshipful idealizations of romantic love is after all only the needs of the animal." [14]

To maintain, as some critics do, that Edward is a good knight and soldier of whom Ford approves is to minimize the epistemological problem in first-person narration and to ignore the dedicatory letter to Stella in which Ford relates how the novel, originally *The Saddest Story*, came to receive by accident its present title. Dowell's consciousness shapes the narrative, confuses the dates, and seeks a pattern. The repetition of "the saddest story," Ford's choice of title, is Dowell's admission that the past is inexplicable. The interpretation constructed in the concluding section is Dowell's, not Ford's, because it fulfills his psychological need to defend himself. If we argue it is Ford's, we are in the extremely awkward position of holding that Dowell is Ford's spokesman at the end of the novel but not in the confusion of dates and not in such statements as that about Corpus Christi. It is Dowell, not Ford, who is blind to the religious frame of reference. It is Dowell, not Ford, who cannot see that the others made a god of man—obviously, for Dowell himself idolizes Edward.

While discussing Ford's novels of social satire, *The Inheritors* through *Mr. Fleight* (1913), John A. Meixner correctly notes that "the satiric tone is adopted only occasionally, and it is not Ford's method to set up targets to be exposed as the climax and point of a scene, as in Swift or Thackeray." [15] One way to demonstrate the novelist's artistry in his later novels is to analyze his ability to set up a target and demolish it, not only as the climax of the scene but also of the novel. In the one instance I intend to examine, he does it exactly as Swift does it, using the language Swift uses in *Gulliver's Travels*.[16]

I do not contend in what follows that *Gulliver's Travels* is an intentional source for *The Good Soldier*, although there are interesting parallels between the two tales. Each is a first-person narrative, told by a man who misunderstands the meaning of his experience because he fails to know himself. Each narrator creates a false god to worship, eventually being sickened by his wife. Each narrator concludes his narrative with a sweeping condemnation of society, from which, in his role as disciple of his ideal, he is estranged. Each work ends in a stable, an ironic reminder to males who deny their nature. Rather, I want to show that a single sentence in the last chapter of *The Good Soldier* can illuminate the entire novel if when we read this sentence we relate it to a passage in the eighteenth-century satire on the nature of man.

In Part Four of *Gulliver's Travels,* Gulliver lives among the Houyhnhnms, where he comes to denounce his Yahoo nature and revere the Houyhnhnms, a race of horses who act strictly in accordance with the dictates of reason. The high point of this voyage is Chapter X. Gulliver writes, "When I happened to behold the Reflection of my own Form in a Lake or Fountain, I turned away my Face in Horror and detestation of my self; and could better endure the Sight of a common *Yahoo,* than of my own Person. By conversing with the *Houyhnhnms,* and looking upon them with Delight, I fell to imitate their Gait and Gesture, which is now grown into a Habit; and my Friends often tell me in a blunt Way, that *I trot like a Horse;* which, however, I take for a great Compliment." [17] The next chapter begins his journey home to England. It is in Chapter XI and the final one that his pride is evinced in his condescending attitude to Don Pedro, the ship captain who brings him home; in his contempt for his wife, children, and all mankind; and in the purchase of two horses with which he spends his time in a stable. In five words Swift reveals a man whose reaction to the brutality of passion divorced from reason propels him to the simplicity of reason divorced from passion, from that which is inhuman to that which is nonhuman. In his pride Gulliver wants to emulate the Houyhnhnms, whose unnatural lack of emotions—unnatural if taken as a standard for man—is seen in their attitude toward courtship, marriage, procreation, and death. A man should not "trot like a horse," Swift is saying, because he belongs to a different order; he is not a horse. He should try to be a rational animal, accepting his Yahoo nature but controlling it with his reason and his conscience guided by religion.

Gulliver's blindness is a moral catastrophe for Swift as is Dowell's for Ford, culminating in the penultimate sentence of the novel.[18] Having read the telegram from Nancy, which he then handed to Dowell to give to Leonora, Edward decided to commit suicide. Dowell wanted to say, " 'God bless you,' " because he too is a sentimentalist. He explains why he did not speak: "But I thought that perhaps that would not be quite English good form, so I trotted off with the telegram to Leonora" (256).

Disgusted by the Yahoo part of man, Gulliver embraces its opposite because he fails to know himself. When he "intreats those who have any Tincture" of pride "that they will not presume to appear" in his sight, he is unaware his self-esteem in being able to trot like a horse is the measure of his own pride. Dowell suffers from a want of understanding, a failure of sensibility, a deficiency of judgment. He is unaware he is trotting like a horse. He idolizes Edward, whom he linked early in the narrative with "a raging stallion" (12), because the latter fulfilled his romantic image of what he wishes he could be: a feudal lord benevolent to servants, faithful to principles, attractive to women. Dowell's verdict, that society eliminates the passionate, the headstrong, and the too-truthful, is his construction of an interpretation that will explain both the events of the past and his isolation, since he likes to think of himself as a passionate follower of Edward. He can rationalize about his rejection by society by convincing himself that society eschews those who are passionate.

At the end of his narrative, he apotheosizes Edward: "I seem to see poor Edward, naked and reclining amidst darkness, upon cold rocks, like one of the ancient Greek damned, in Tartarus or wherever it was" (252). His deification of Edward is the result of intellectual and emotional myopia so that when he leaves his master in the stable he blindly "trots off with the telegram to Leonora." He will be his lord's disciple, caring for Edward's beloved Nancy

in Edward's estate. As he says, "I can't conceal from myself
the fact that I loved Edward Ashburnham—and that I love
him because he was just myself. If I had had the courage
and the virility and possibly also the physique of Edward
Ashburnham I should, I fancy, have done much what he
did" (253). He cannot see that in confusing man and God,
human passion and Christ's Passion, the others were responsible for their misery and the distortion of the values
built upon the distinction. He does not understand, since
Edward is his god also. But Ford, like Swift, does understand. By placing the final scene in a stable, he makes us
see that the raging Edward was a human animal, not a
Saviour, and the trotting Dowell a less than human animal,
not an intelligent interpreter of the past. In a single sentence he recalls Swift's satire at the same time that he
crystallizes his satire on the absence of moral knowledge
in the contemporary world.

Thus Dowell's picture of a fragmented modern world,
the spiritual and moral consequence of confusing man
and God,[19] of substituting a human center for a divine
center, is juxtaposed with a picture suggesting a unified
world with traditional values and virtues receiving its sus-
tenance from a center which Dowell cannot discover because he has already committed himself to Edward as his
good knight and soldier. He applies the Jesuit motto, *ad
majorem Dei gloriam* (186), to the patience of women waiting for their husbands to return from their rutting seasons,
but the Jesuits, in the tradition of their founder, for whom
Christ is the Good Soldier, dedicate their lives to the military ideal of service and self-sacrifice for their Knight.

The Good Soldier is an ironic narrative for two
reasons. There is a discrepancy between Dowell's understanding of a situation and our understanding of it based
on his report, which reveals more than he comprehends.

The best example is the Protest scene. Leonora's explanation, which he accepts, is neither consistent with her behavior—she is more the jealous wife than the religious fanatic—nor substantial enough to explain her reaction. She must be adopting a pose because she realizes he is blind to the significance of Florence's laying her finger on Edward's wrist while they look at the document. We also learn from such statements as that about Edward sobbing before the image of the Virgin that Dowell is so emotionally barren his responses are deficient.[20] Two, I think Ford takes for granted that his readers know the difference between Edward and the Saviour. I do not mean to imply, however, that the novelist puts the whole burden of critical intelligence on us. I believe there is sufficient evidence in the novel to warrant the judgment that the hell of their lives followed from their mistaking the human for the divine. Dowell cannot grasp this because his lack of critical intelligence prevents him from understanding. All he can do is report what he saw. His lack of understanding, his worship of Edward, enable us to evaluate the past, Edward, and him.

If Edward was a sentimentalist, at least he tried to live according to a feudal code. If Leonora and Nancy saw him as their Saviour, at least they were passionate about it. If Florence was a villainess because she was motivated by a desire for material gain, at least she was motivated. Dowell, who remains alive to tell their tale, to wring from it its meaning, does not know what to tell and instead constructs an explanation to justify his role. His interpretation satisfies as both cause and defense. Society's crushing of the passionate, the headstrong, and the too-truthful explains his loneliness, since he includes himself in this category, and by including himself as a faint member, he does not have to fear that society will concern itself enough to want to destroy him. The literal-minded, alienated, rootless creature of the modern age, he replaces Edward as the owner of Branshaw Manor, where, morally and spiritually defective, he sits in darkness next to an insane girl. He is the twentieth-century's absolute zero, an elevator operator (71) between the sacred and the profane, running errands to each but partaking of neither.

Although Young Lovell does not resolve the Fordian hero's dilemma, he does journey to the center of his pagan heritage by accepting the White Lady's guidance. Dowell does not even begin the archetypal journey, even though he has numerous opportunities. Florence would look invitingly over her shoulder as she entered the bathing place at Nauheim as if to say to her husband, " 'I am going in here. I am going to stand so stripped and white and straight —and you are a man . . .' " (88). Every morning she would come out of her locked bedroom during the two years Jimmy lived with them in Paris "as fresh as Venus rising from any of the couches that are mentioned in Greek legends" (89).[21] Instead, he deceives himself into believing he has resolved the dilemma by identifying with Edward, whom he makes both pagan god and good soldier of Christ.

Into a world of moral chaos and social decay, Ford places a man who cannot comprehend, but the longer Dowell retells the events the more we descry a standard against which we must judge his picture, which enables us to discover the cause of the "falling to pieces of a people" and which allows us a glimpse into the center which gives this standard its life. Ford's masterstroke, having a bewildered narrator so repeat the events that they yield an interpretation he cannot perceive, is itself the limitation of the novel. By constructing a psychologically satisfying permanence and stability, Dowell removes the necessity for journeying to the center, and since he does not cross the threshold, we are left with only a suggestion or a glimpse into it. It remains for *Parade's End* (first published as a tetralogy in a single volume in 1950) to create the journey from death to life, taking Conrad's world one more step, completing the archetypal pattern, re-creating the myth, and restoring the Christian tradition. Before the immense novel takes this step, though, the shorter novel eliminates any confusion about the direction to take to right the inverted world of *The Inheritors*. Following Conrad's lead, Ford criticizes the quest for redemption beyond the horizon that renounces the human concrete, but even more so than his collaborator, he attacks the deification of the human concrete as a substitute for a traditional divine center. Ford does not turn away from the hell on earth, pretending it does not exist; on the contrary, by accepting it as the hell within man, he pushes through it to emerge on the other side in the paradise within man. It is from this new vantage point that the reader can look back on the desolate landscape of *The Inheritors* and ahead to the paradise beyond the horizon.

As deceptive a novel as *The Good Soldier* is, it stands in the same relation to *Parade's End* as *A Portrait of the Artist as a Young Man* to *Ulysses*. Since *Parade's End* is considerably more dense than *The Good Soldier*, we cannot appreciate Ford's immense novel unless we recognize the allusions in Part One of *Some Do Not . . .* (1924). If we pursue them they will uncover the basic antagonism in the tetralogy: the conflict between two conceptions of reality, two archetypal experiences, two myths, two traditions that finally erupts on the battlefield of France in 1914–18.

In the first chapter of the first volume, in the year 1912, two young men, civil servants in the Imperial Department of Statistics, are traveling from London to Rye

so that Vincent Macmaster can call on the Reverend
Duchemin, a parson who has helped him in the writing of
a monograph on Dante Rossetti. That morning the hero
of the novel, Christopher Tietjens, received a letter from
his wife, Sylvia, asking him to take her back because she
is bored with the man with whom she had run away four
months earlier. So distracted by what he takes to be his
friend's state of shock that he cannot correct the proofs for
his monograph, Macmaster blurts out, " 'You can't say the
man wasn't a poet!' " Tietjens counters by arguing that
his poetry is disguised eroticism, an attempt " 'to justify
fornication.' " As the argument proceeds, Tietjens makes
it clear that he understands why Macmaster would claim
greatness for Rossetti. Since he, Macmaster, stands for
" 'lachrymose polygamy,' " he feels Rossetti's poetry embodies his own values. But Tietjens does not want to listen
to his companion's preaching. Since he stands for " 'monogamy and chastity,' " he feels Dante Alighieri's poetry
embodies his own values: " 'Your Paolo and Francesca—
and Dante's—went, very properly, to Hell, and no bones
about it,' " he reminds Macmaster. " 'You don't get Dante
justifying them. But your fellow whines about creeping
into Heaven' " (16–8).

By contrasting the two poets' treatments of the lovers
condemned to hell, Tietjens contrasts the attitude toward
passion in each poet's work. On the second circle of the
inferno, Dante encounters the whirling souls of Paolo and
Francesca, blown about by their passion. In answer to his
question about the circumstances which lured them into
their illicit affair, Francesca relates how she and Paolo, her
brother-in-law, fell in love while reading a courtly romance.
" 'A Galeotto [synonymous with 'pander'] was the book
and he that wrote it' " (*Inf*. V.137), she says as Paolo weeps.
Although the Pre-Raphaelite poet was named for the

medieval poet and in addition to translating the *Vita Nuova* and passages from the *Commedia* took much of his subject matter from the earlier poet's work, his treatment of the lovers is very different from Dante's. Tietjens's judgment is a rewriting, for fictional purposes, of Ford's own judgment published in 1902: "Dante's story of Paolo and Francesca da Rimini holds all the world to-day because, without allusion to anything, it is a clear, keen, cold, and yet sympathetic, human rendering of passion, sin and retribution. Rossetti's picture of the same title appeals to us not as a picture of Dante's rendering of that incident, but as a picture of immense, vibrating passion that Rossetti had observed for himself." [22]

Macmaster defends Rossetti's poetry because he idealizes passion. In fact, there is the suggestion that by reading Rossetti, not Dante, he becomes a modern Paolo with the parson's wife, Edith Ethel Duchemin, a modern Francesca who reads Ruskin, not Dante. Macmaster dreams of meeting "the type of woman" he needs: she will be "tall, graceful, dark, loose-gowned, passionate yet circumspect, oval-featured, deliberate, gracious to everyone around her" (13). For him " 'the circumspect—yes, the circumspect classes, will pilot the nation through the tight places' " (20). Tietjens, who knows the ruling class is so shot through with corruption that it is leading England to war, quotes (or misquotes) lines from Alice Meynell's "The Shepherdess" to ridicule his companion's romanticism:

> She walks, the lady of my delight,
>   A shepherdess of sheep;
> She is so circumspect and right:
> She has her thoughts to keep (19).

This stanza has a greater impact when we see some of the ruling-class women on the next page. "In lovely sable cloaks, with purple or red jewel cases, with diaphanous silky scarves flying from motor hoods," they are "drifting towards the branch train for Rye, under the shepherding of erect, burdened footmen" (21). The process of exposing Macmaster's lachrymose polygamy continues in the opening chapters of this volume. In Chapter V when Macmaster visualizes his return to the circumspect woman, Mrs. Duchemin, Ford repeats the jewel image used in the description of the women on the railway platform (and, as we shall see below, the mirror image used in Tietjens's impression of the " 'obese, oily man,' " Rossetti) to disclose the real goal of their rendezvous: "in the tall room, with the long curtains: a round, eagle mirror reflected them gleaming: like a bejewelled picture with great depths: the entwined figures." Edith Ethel's circumspection amounts to concealing her illicit relationship and, later, the abortion; Macmaster's idealization of his passion is undercut by his leaving her side "with the hard tread of a conqueror" (103–4).

Despite Ford's thoughts about Rossetti as a man and a poet,[23] in *Parade's End* the glorification of human passion in his paintings and poems represents the culmination, in Edwardian England, of the displacement of the Christian tradition. When Tietjens tells Macmaster he does not want to listen to his preaching, he explains that it revolts him " 'to think of that obese, oily man who never took a bath, in a grease-spotted dressing-gown and the underclothes he's slept in, standing beside a five-shilling model with crimped hair, or some Mrs. W. Three Stars, gazing into a mirror that reflects their fetid selves and gilt sunfish and drop chandeliers and plates sickening with cold bacon fat and gurgling about passion' " (17). Tietjens's impression of Rossetti's inspiration for "The Blessed Damozel" should be compared with Dante's testimony to his inspiration for the *Commedia*. The concluding section of the *Vita Nuova* is Dante's statement of his dawning recognition of the role of Beatrice as a mediatrix sent by "Him through whom all things live":

> After this sonnet a miraculous vision appeared to me, in which I beheld things which made me determine never to speak of that blessed lady until I could write worthily of her. To attain this end I study as hard as I can, as she knows in all truth. Therefore if it pleases Him through whom all things live that my life may continue for a few years, I hope to write of her what has never been said of any woman.
>
> Then may it please God who is the Lord of Grace that my soul may rise to see the glory of its lady, who gazes in rapture on the face of Him "who is blessed throughout all ages." [24]

In the Paolo and Francesca paragraph, Tietjens refers to himself as a Jeremiah. This is the second major allusion that must be clarified. The prophet received his divine commission in the thirteenth year of Josiah's reign. Instead of observing the Book of the Law discovered in the Temple, the Jewish people were reverting to an earlier worship, that of the moon goddess, the idolatry outlawed by the Book of the Law, whose central demand was the cleansing of the country from idolatrous worship. Since sexual immorality was a feature of astral worship, the Book of Jeremiah uses the metaphor of the faithless wife for the faithlessness of Judah. The prophet warned Judah that unless she harkened to the word of the Lord Jerusalem would be destroyed by the coming war. His warning was not heeded. Bewailing his nation's doom, he was imprisoned by his own people, who hated him.

Tietjens obeys the Lord's commandments. He consents to take back his faithless wife, but he knows " 'war is as inevitable as divorce' " (21). As a civil servant and heir to his family's estate at Groby (since his older brother, Mark, plans not to marry) he knows his country is governed by Sylvia's deceit and promiscuity; the romanticism of Macmaster; the hypocrisy of Mrs. Duchemin; the stubbornness of General Campion; the jealousy of Campion's sister, Lady Claudine; the stupidity of her husband, the Hon. Paul Sandbach; the obtuseness of the Liberal Cabinet Minister, the Rt. Hon. Edward Waterhouse; the absenteeism of the bank director, Lord Port Scatho; and the cowardice of Port Scatho's nephew, Brownlie. At this time he has only two alternatives: to betray everything he believes in to live their kind of life or to maintain his principles in isolation. Hated, mistrusted, maligned by the members of his class because they cannot tolerate a moral man in their circle, he is driven "outside the herd" (128) and into his lonely self.

In *The Good Soldier* we have to penetrate the surface of Dowell's narrative before we can perceive an explanation diametrically opposed to the one he accepts. The happenings yield two interpretations, but, identifying with Edward, Dowell can see only the one. Hence the deceptiveness of the novel. The situation is altered in *Parade's End,* but Ford's method is the same. We are given two attitudes which we must penetrate. As we do we see them forming two diametrically opposed conceptions of reality. Tietjens takes his stand on a tradition discredited in the modern world, yet there would be no contest if it were merely that poets such as Rossetti have displaced Dante. Tietjens traces his heritage back to Dante and the Book of Jeremiah, but he does not understand that for the tradition to come to life in the modern world he must rediscover its roots in himself. The Book of Jeremiah is Dante's source for the beasts which attack the pilgrim-poet in the forest, making him realize he cannot climb the slope but must descend, with reason's assistance, into hell, at the second circle of which he confronts himself in Paolo. Macmaster, on the other hand, does not know the tradition on which he takes his stand because he idealizes passion. If he knew it he could trace it back to a radically different experience from Dante's, given ritual form in the myth of Ishtar and Tammuz, Venus and Adonis. Image and allusion in the next chapter link with image and illusion in the first chapter, uncovering the center of the tradition represented by Rossetti's poetry, the deadly antagonist of the center of the tradition represented by Dante's poetry.

Chapter II of *Some Do Not . . .* is a dialogue between Sylvia (of the forest) and Father Consett, at Lobscheid (in praise of divorce, separation, the vagina), a resort in the pine woods of the Taunus Mountains to which she has come to be with her mother, Mrs. Satterthwaite, before rejoining her husband. Agreeing to return to Tietjens now that she has left her lover, Perowne, Sylvia declares her intention to " 'torment that man. And I'll do it. Do you understand how I'll do it? There are many ways. But if the worst comes to the worst, I can always drive him silly . . . by corrupting the child,' " the son about whom he is " 'perfectly soppy . . . though he half knows it isn't his own.' " She ensnared him by luring him into sexual intimacy because she was convinced that she was pregnant by a married man named Drake. When the priest threatens to sprinkle holy water on her, chanting the words, " '*Exorciso te Ashtaroth in nomine,*' " she "erects her body above her skirts on the sofa, stiffened like a snake's neck above its coils." Not sure whether the " 'very powerful devil,' " Astarte Syriaca, is dead, he reminds her that " 'devils *are* always trying to get in. And there are especial spots. These deep forests are noted among others' " (38–41).

Perhaps the easiest way to indicate the pagan myth alluded to in *Parade's End* is to quote two passages from Joseph Campbell:

> Indeed, I believe that we may claim with a very high degree of certainty that in this Halafian symbology of the bull and goddess, the dove, and the double ax, we have the earliest evidence yet discovered anywhere of the prodigiously influential mythology associated for us with the great names of Ishtar and Tammuz, Venus and Adonis, Isis and Osiris, Mary and Jesus. From the Taurus Mountains, the mountains of the bull-god, who may already have been identified with the horned moon, which dies and is resurrected three days later, the cult was diffused, with the art of cattle-breeding itself, practically to the ends of the earth; and we celebrate the mystery of that mythological death and resurrection to this day, as a promise of our own eternity.[25]

> Now the dying and resurrected god of the archaic high civilizations of the Near East, Tammuz-Adonis, for whom the women wept in the Temple of Jerusalem (Ezekiel 8:14) and whose Egyptian counterpart was Osiris, was actually out hunting a wild boar when he was gored in the loin and rendered impotent; he descended in death then to the lower world, and was resurrected only when the goddess, Ishtar-Aphrodite, whose animal is not indeed the civet cat but the lion, descended to the underworld and released him.[26]

The Astarte-Ashtoreth moon goddess cult was the one out-lawed during Josiah's reign to which the Jews reverted during the time of Jeremiah. Rossetti wrote a poem, "Astarte Syriaca," to accompany his painting of that title. The poem commemorates "That face, of Love's all-penetrative spell / Amulet, talisman, and oracle,— / Betwixt the sun and moon a mystery." [27]

By forging image and allusion, Ford moves from a contest between two myths in a remote time to an argument between two men on a train in the year 1912. Bombarding the surface, he progressively localizes the contest until the centers of the two myths are revealed within Tietjens. The center of the pagan myth is initially figured in Sylvia, high priestess of a modern satanism that demands brutality in its sexual life, this life to include adultery as well as marriage. The dialogue takes place at Lobscheid, " 'the last place in Europe to be christianised' " (29), in a room the walls of which are decorated "with pictures of animals in death agonies: capercailzies giving up the ghost with gouts of scarlet blood on the snow; deer dying with their heads back and eyes glazing, gouts of red blood on their necks; foxes dying with scarlet blood on green grass" (26). Sylvia has recently given up her association with a group that plays at Black Masses, a ritual that involves " 'cutting the throat of a white kid and splashing its blood about' " (42). A bitch, she delights in arousing males so they will then idolize her, only to discard them after she has aroused them. For her Christopher is impotent, even though he appeared to be her votary by having sexual relations with her before their marriage, in the sense that he will neither debauch himself by throwing himself into her orgiastic rites nor revenge himself by seeking consolation with a mistress. A man of principle, he believes in monogamy and chastity.

Sylvia demands frenzied worship of the female; Christopher believes in life organized around reason. She is an agent of death because she insists on passion without commitment; he wants to preserve life. At the opening of *Some Do Not* . . . , he remarks to the cabman that the mare's condition is improved since he, the cabman, started putting less licorice in her mash. Part One of this novel ends with his saving the life of the horse hit by Campion's automobile. " 'You know, Chris,' the General said, 'you're the most wonderful hand with a horse . . .' " (142). But with him and men like him "outside the herd" and unable to stand up effectively against Sylvia's circle because they do not know themselves, World War I becomes a slaughter of the oxen of the sun.

If *Parade's End* were a good man's attempt to resist an evil woman's influence, it would be much less complex. Its complexity is the result of the complexity of the characters. Macmaster dreams of finding his circumspect woman yet is attracted to "girls of the most giggling, behind-the-counter order, big-bosomed, scarlet-cheeked" (13). Sylvia looks like " 'a picture of Our Lady by Fra Angelico' " (28), yet her "black figure shows in silhouette against the open doorway" (41). She loathes her husband since he refuses to worship her yet is fascinated by his resistance. Tietjens seems "to have no feelings" (8) about his wife's letter, yet when he receives it he is so "staring with the intentness of a maddened horse" Macmaster thinks he is "going mad" (15).

At Rye, Tietjens, Macmaster, Campion, Sandbach, and Waterhouse play a round of golf. During the game a young woman appears beside Tietjens to ask him to rescue her companion, a Gertie Wilson, who is being chased by drunken golfers who want to have some sport with the two demonstrating suffragettes. By tripping the local constable who has come upon the scene, he enables the two young women to get away, but in so doing he infuriates Sandbach, who wants him arrested for obstructing the course of justice. At the time of the incident, he does not realize that the young woman who appeared beside him is Valentine Wannop, the daughter of the late Professor Wannop, his father's close friend. He learns her identity from his godfather, Campion, who takes him aside in the locker room to admonish him about his scandalous behavior. The incident on the links, which for the general was prearranged, confirms the stories he has been hearing from his sister and brother-in-law that his godson is spending Sylvia's money on a mistress, which accounts for the rupture between the young man and his splendid wife.

Although he is a good man, Tietjens is guilty for not being honest about himself and Sylvia. He justifies his silence with his godfather by telling himself a gentleman does not complain publicly that his wife is a bitch and it is better for his son "to have a rip of a father than a whore for mother" (77). This is self-deception. In his disgust with himself for giving in to passion before his marriage, he now denies any passion in himself. In his refusal to worship Sylvia, who demands the male allow himself to be rescued by her, he has made a deity of reason. His sin is pride, his belief that by sheer force of reason he can pretend Sylvia's influence does not affect him, that by sheer force of will he can ignore her presence, that by sheer force of character he can maintain his principles in the midst of moral decadence. That he cannot resist his wife's influence is apparent early in the tetralogy: getting drunk, he knows he has "carried the suppression of thought in his conscious mind so far that his unconscious self had taken command and had, for the time, paralysed both his body and his mind" (80). Later Valentine tells him his principles are repressive if he insists on them at the expense of life when she accuses him of being heartless. Therefore not only will the tetralogy expose the causes of the 1914–18 holocaust by exposing such characters as Sylvia, Macmaster, Mrs. Duchemin, and the Rev. Duchemin, who has to be physically restrained from shouting obscenities at breakfast parties, it will also chart the journey Tietjens must make into himself before he can dispense with the mask he assumes to conceal the truth from himself. By refusing to confront his wife, he is denying his pagan heritage.

The polarity that operates within *Parade's End* is established in the first paragraph in the counterpoising of "virgin" and "immaculate" with "scarlet" and "yellow." " 'I might come across another woman' " (11), Tietjens remarks to Macmaster as they approach the portal. Father Consett warns Mrs. Satterthwaite that Sylvia's " 'hell on earth will come when her husband goes running, blind, head down, mad after another woman' " (42). " 'I'm not one to cry for the moon,' " the mother's spiritual adviser rebukes the daughter (33); " 'Go away, I bid you, and say a Hail Mary or two' " (41).

Sylvia Tietjens is a twentieth-century Astarte; Valentine Wannop, a twentieth-century Diana and a twentieth-century Beatrice. Just as image and allusion link to uncover the center of the pagan myth, so too do they link to uncover the center of the Christian myth. The Book of Jeremiah is so important a text that I want to quote the verse from it that contains the Lord's promise of redemption and then a commentary on the verse: "How long wilt thou be dissolute in deliciousness, O wandering daughter? for the Lord hath created a new thing upon the earth: A WOMAN SHALL COMPASS A MAN" (xxxi.22). The commentary reads as follows:

And then a great sign is promised, so great that it is even called a creation. The verb is in the perfect tense ("hath created"), but it is generally admitted that this is merely another example of the well-known idiom, the "prophetic perfect", a vivid manner of representing a prophecy as already fulfilled. . . . Instead of the initiative being taken by the man, as is usual in human generation, the physical process on the purely human side will be set on foot by the woman, who will *"press round"* a man. . . . The miracle is emphasized by the word used for "woman" being an unusual one, which stresses the sexual character. The word for "man" (that found in *Gabri-el* "man of God") is also an unusual one, implying strength and power; a cognate word (a fact significant in the present context) is applied as a name to the Messias in Is 9:6 ("God the Mighty"), and directly to God himself in Ps 23:8 (twice); Deut 10:17; etc.[28]

Valentine, whose masculine name means health or strength, is *Parade's End* redemptive agent, the antithesis of the wandering, dissolute daughter and faithless wife, who will exert pressure on Tietjens, forcing him to take the interior journey. The antagonism, the polarity within the novel, is within him: "Kill or cure! The two functions of man. If you wanted something killed you'd go to Sylvia Tietjens in the sure faith that she would kill it: emotion, hope, ideal; kill it quick and sure. If you wanted something kept alive you'd go to Valentine: she'd find something to do for it. . . . The two types of mind: remorseless enemy, sure screen, dagger . . . sheath!" (128) Confronting the one function, he will discover the other.

Prior to Valentine's entry into his life, Tietjens faces two equally ruinous alternatives: to betray his principles

for Sylvia and her circle or to maintain them in sterile
isolation. As a married man unable to fulfill himself sexually with his wife, he will experience a widening split between his religious and sexual impulses; or to put it in
other words, before Valentine's entry the only alternative
to Sylvia's Astarte cult is sexual abstinence. Valentine can
cooperate with him to heal his disintegration by reuniting
these impulses. As he takes her home after the Duchemins'
breakfast party, they walk through a literal and symbolic
field. "Marguerites," or pearls, is the first item in the order
of plant life surrounding them. "Coltsfoot" has heart-
shaped leaves; it may also suggest the young male horse on
whom Valentine's redemptive powers operate to save it
from becoming a "maddened horse." "Wild white clover"
is a trifoliolate herb with white flowers. "Sainfoin" means
healthy or holy hay, and "Italian rye grass" is used to make
hay. "Our Lady's bedstraw" requires no comment. "Dead-
nettle" suggests the death that precedes resurrection. Following "dead-nettle" comes "bachelor's button," or "rag-
ged robin"; the rebirth of the single man is being indicated. Ford tells us the meaning of "cowslip": "paigle, you
know, from old French *pasque,* meaning Easter." Marriage
and procreation are communicated in the next item—
"burr, burdock (farmer that thy wife may thrive . . .)"—
so long as the burr and burdock do not "wive," perhaps
because a burr is also a circular boss at the base of a horn,
a halo round the moon. "Violet leaves . . . over black
briony," or bryony, comes from the Greek and Latin meaning to swell; black bryony is a name given to an endog-
enous climbing plant, lady's seal. "Wild clematis: later
it's old man's beard" suggests the flowering vines to complete the leaves over briony, a fulfillment which completes
an earthly cycle and which points ahead to the next and
last item; one species of clematis is popularly called vir-

gin's bower. The last item is "purple loose-strife," which combines the Passion with the end of strife or deliverance from strife (105).

A paradigm of death and rebirth, a fusion of religious and sexual imagery, this series points the way to Tietjens's redemption if he will open his heart to Valentine. He feels trapped, though. He feels he cannot be sexually intimate with her because for him that would be the equivalent of his wife's running off with Perowne. He rejects divorce on principle, yet to continue seeing Valentine as a friend, not a woman, is to deny any fulfillment to her. His inability to act decisively is rendered imaginatively in the movements within this chapter. As he crosses the field, trying to decide whose reputation must be sacrificed, he "kills" the flowers with his stick, just as he figuratively " 'deflowers' " his walking partner when he chooses to use her as a screen to protect his wife's reputation (107–8). At the sound of an approaching dog-cart, he, with Valentine, races blindly into the V gate where he is then stuck, "trying to push through like a mad bullock" (109), until Mrs. Wannop's voice assures them it is not the police who her daughter fears are scouring the countryside for her and Gertie Wilson. At Mrs. Wannop's cottage he sits immobile, wavering between the pain induced by thoughts of Sylvia and the pleasure induced by thoughts of her counterpart. " 'Valentine! Valentine!' " her mother calls; " 'Go to Christopher in the study' " (124).

In its symbolic import Chapter VII of Part One of *Some Do Not . . .* is as rich as the first two chapters. Riding home with Valentine after taking Gertie to her uncle's house, Tietjens responds to her physical presence: he "moons along under the absurd moon that had accompanied them down the heaven." As chaste Diana she can keep her silhouette "between him and the moon"; as a healthy, attractive young woman she can arouse him sexually. When he begins to tease her, they enter "a bank of solid fog that seems to encounter them with a soft, ubiquitous blow." The fog becomes symbolic of the blurring of their moral perception, for the silver mist increases as they are agreeing they "have no responsibilities."

Valentine's plunging into the silver lake is both excruciating temptation—it is very easy for him to jump in after her—and recall to responsibility—if he goes after her he will lose the horse and what little sense of direction he has left. Forced to pay attention to the road while conscious of her presence nearby, he is under a strain so acute he has to struggle against his desire to have a "holiday," in a contest between his principles and the lure of an "immense, improbably brilliant horn of a moon, [which] sends a trail as if down the sea, straight to his neck," almost engulfing him. The mist "appears to spread from his neck, absolutely level, absolutely silver, to infinity on each side of him." He is saved from going under by his recognition that the girl walking alongside the cart is " 'the only intelligent living soul' " he has met in years, someone he can talk to, and by her scrambling up beside him, her hair "darkened by the wetness of the mist, but . . . golden in the sudden moonlight." By rejoining him, she eliminates any temptation to abandon the cart, but by reappearing next to him, she brings the temptation closer. Their night reaches its climax when, looking into her eyes, he sees his "destiny" and naturally leans forward to kiss her. His conscience, however, reminds him, " 'Gentlemen don't. . . .' " They have recovered the way home. " 'It's the day! . . . The longest day's begun . . . ,' " she says to him while ahead of them a church "rises out of the mist." They have not surrendered themselves to the Astarte-Ashtaroth-Venus rites (125–39).

Although this section of the tetralogy ends with Tietjens reaffirming his belief in principles as his sole guide in life, there is hope for him. Campion's crashing into the cart with his automobile brings Tietjens back to the impossibility of his present situation with Valentine. He has yet to enter the inferno, but her last words to him before the accident are, " 'You will get through . . .' " (139). He must admit he is not so "spotless" (76) as he thinks. He must learn not to "care more for his wife's reputation than for any other factor in a complicated world" (117). He must adjust his principles to accommodate the truth of Valentine. In short, he must take the archetypal journey with Valentine as his guiding power to confront the death within himself before he can become a whole man.

The extent of his journey can be measured by two allusions to Dante in Part Two of *Some Do Not. . . .* Before we look at these, I want to indicate two techniques Ford uses to great advantage in this section. Part One utilizes the time-shift indirectly. When the scene shifts from the train to Lobscheid, image and allusion expose veins beneath the surface, whose roots extend into antiquity, but since the scene returns to the present in Chapter III and each chapter thereafter in Part One follows in chronological order, the action is fixed on the surface. Tietjens does not begin his interior journey until in Part Two five years after his ride with Valentine, he is home recuperating from shell shock. The gradual return of his memory, which takes him back into the past to the events surrounding the outbreak of war and which culminates in his ability to recollect the first stanza of Christina Rossetti's poem, "Somewhere or Other," is dramatic proof he is making the journey.

The "tide" begins to "turn" (185) for him when he begins to remember the details of Macmaster's and Mrs.

Duchemin's illicit affair: how they kept the affair secret; how the Port Scatho group chanced upon them while they were gurgling Rossetti poems in Scotland; how he screened for them, damaging his reputation by accompanying Edith Ethel to London as if she were his mistress. Valentine undergoes a comparable experience. She remembers the "turning-point" in her life occurred on the day she learned the details of this same affair: how Macmaster and Mrs. Duchemin disguised their lust; how Edith Ethel raged when she realized she was pregnant; how she demanded Valentine answer her question, " 'How do you get rid of a baby?' " (229). Journeying into themselves, Christopher and Valentine confront their doubles, Macmaster and Mrs. Duchemin, on an intermediate circle of hell, for the modern Paolo and Francesca belong in Sylvia's camp, the camp of death. " 'And I warn you,' " Edith Ethel sums up their position to Valentine, " 'if the split comes—as it must, for what woman could stand it!—it is Mrs. Tietjens we shall support. She will always find a home here' " (260).

Ford's craftmanship is superb in this section. By combining the time-shift with the doubling technique, he makes Christopher and Valentine, independent of each other, unearth the buried past. They too were part of the affair, regardless of how much or how little they were willing to see at the time. They too secretly desire each other, and by not being honest in their relationship, they have created conflicts within themselves. The extension of their self-deception is the illicit affair of Macmaster and Mrs. Duchemin. Since war broke out the day after the parson's wife returned to London, World War I is the inevitable result of sexual immorality, faithlessness, deception, betrayal, and abortion.

Now we can examine the progress Tietjens has made since Chapter VII of Part One. He has been to war and he has lost his memory. The first of the two Dante allusions appears here, when he tries to explain to his wife the effect of the explosion which hospitalized him. He relates to her a strange experience he had in the hospital. Orderlies carried past his bed the body of a nurse, Beatrice Carmichael. " 'That seemed to wake up a fellow on the other side of the room with a lot of blood coming through the bandages on his head. . . . He rolled out of his bed and, without a word, walked across the hut and began to strangle me. . . . Then he began to shout *"Faith!"* He shouted "Faith! . . . Faith! . . . Faith! . . ." at intervals of two seconds, as far as I could tell by my pulse, until four in the morning, when he died. . . . I don't know whether it was a religious exhortation or a woman's name, but I disliked him a good deal because he started my tortures, such as they were. . . .' " He does not fully understand his experience, but he cannot forget it: " 'I don't know, I don't know to this day. . . . The point is that when I knew that I didn't know *that* name, I was as ignorant, as *uninstructed*, as a new-born babe and much more worried about it. . . . The Koran says—I've got as far as K in my reading of the Encyclopaedia Britannica every afternoon at Mrs. Wannop's—"The strong man when smitten is smitten in his pride!" ' " (169–70).[29]

In order for him to be shell-shocked, he had to go to war; in order to go to war, he had to quit the Department of Statistics because he was "sick and tired of faking" figures (236). Between the time of his separation from the Civil Service and his decision to return to the Continent, he must listen in anguish to Sylvia's denunciation that he has " 'foully used' " her: " 'Well, be proud when you die because of your honour. But, God, you be humble about . . . your errors in judgment' " (172–3). Confessing he is " 'not a whole man any more' " (176) enables him to re-

gain his memory. As he does he closes his account with
Port Scatho's bank, resigns from the club, admits his civilization is doomed, dispels the rumor that Valentine has had
a child by him, and asks her to be his mistress his last
night in England.

The second time he senses the "tide is turning" (200)
is just after he has been reminded of Valentine clearing
the table in her mother's cottage. Minutes later he remembers the first two lines of "Somewhere or Other," which
he was unable to identify in the previous chapter. He adds
the third and fourth lines, although he does not quote
them correctly, when, reacting to his brother's comment
that Sylvia loves him, he becomes determined to "have his
night" with Valentine (224). In this Christina Rossetti
poem "the face not seen, the voice not heard, / The heart
that not yet . . . / Made answer to my word" waits "beyond the wandering moon," on the other side of "the last
leaves of the dying year / Fallen on a turf grown green." [30]
As Christopher leaves for the Western Front, Valentine
commits her heart to him, offering him a life beyond the
death that is Sylvia, a life on the other side of their
doomed civilization that has "contrived a state of things
in which leaves rotted by August" (217).

Tietjens is moving away from Sylvia toward Valentine.
One of the few scenes in the tetralogy in which husband
and wife show any trace of tenderness toward each other
is blasted when he tries to remember the name of the priest
who, unknown to him, warned her what to expect if she
did not change her attitude toward her husband and marriage. She "stands up, her eyes blazing out of a pallid face
of stone" and then "screams piercingly" at him that his
father's heart was broken by the lies about him that Mark's
friend, Ruggles, passed on to the old man: " 'You were a
squit who lived on women's money and had got the

daughter of his oldest friend with child . . .' " (177–8).
Shortly thereafter Tietjens begins to regain his memory.
The more he does the more he is "completely swallowed
up in the endeavour to imagine the embraces of Valentine
Wannop" (216), whose image starts to replace that of her
antagonist in his mind.

Valentine was not able to help Christopher until she
became more a real woman than an idealized Diana, since
he needs a woman with whom he can redeem his blighted
life. In this section Valentine, like Christopher, journeys
into her past to confront the truth of her desire for him.
Between the time of the turning point in her life and her
acceptance of his proposal that they spend their last night
together, she must relive in her memory Edith Ethel's denunciation of her, for Edith Ethel believes the rumor that
she has had a child by her lover. Admitting she is merely
"a little nobody" (274) who has prepared the sofa in case
he does ask to spend the night frees her from self-deception. Knowing herself, she begins to fight for the man she
loves. Paradoxically, the more she becomes a woman the
more she becomes a figure as well. Having already decided
" 'she's got enormous eyes; a good neck; good shoulders;
good breasts; clean hips; small hands . . . neat ankles' "
and that since " 'she stands well on her feet' " and her
feet are " 'not too large,' " she is " 'a real good filly' "
(227), Mark Tietjens tells Valentine what she must be for
his brother: " 'You were made for him. . . . You can't
blame people for coupling you. . . . They're forced to it.
. . . If you hadn't existed they'd have had to invent you.
. . . Like Dante for . . . who was it? . . . Beatrice?
There *are* couples like that' " (278). This second allusion
to Dante in Part Two returns to Tietjens's hospital experience. Since Beatrice Carmichael is dead, Valentine will be

his Beatrice. Her commitment makes it possible for him to have faith on the next stage of his journey, which he must take alone. So that he does not lose faith she gives him a talisman on which are written the words, " 'God bless you and keep you: God watch over you at your goings out and at . . .' " (284).

The end of *Some Do Not . . .* gathers up the motifs and allusions of the first volume, deepening the symbolic dimension beneath the surface realism. In the final chapter of Part One, Tietjens faced his first temptation. It would have been easy for him to take advantage of a sexually unawakened girl responding to his attention, and given the state of his marriage and the pressures pulling him apart, it would have been understandable. A man of principle, he overcame that temptation. The second temptation is more enticing: since Valentine loves him and knows he loves her and since she may never see him again, she wants a child by him. He also overcomes this one, for a reason the opposite of the one usually given by frustrated lovers: it would be " 'too . . . oh . . . *private*' " (283). The experience would be robbed of naturalness, love, and beauty. It would be the secret, ugly affair of Macmaster and Mrs. Duchemin, fornicating under the sanction of the book of Dante Gabriel Rossetti, the line of whose poem, " 'Since when we stand side by side,' " Tietjens quotes in this chapter. Instead, they elect to remain faithful to the Lord's commandments, for while pledging themselves to each other, they see in their imagination "landscapes . . . sand dunes, close-cropped. . . . Some negligible shipping; a stump-masted brig from Archangel . . ." (285). Despite the "gaping, splintered hole" (70) in her side, the brig from Archangel, which he saw following the rescue of the suffragettes, is a better vessel than the glistening modern fishing boat from Lowestoft.

The end of *Some Do Not . . .* also prepares the reader for the opening of *No More Parades* (1925). Reviewing his evening, Christopher, on the verge of total collapse, listens to the debate between his conscious and subconscious selves, one voice urging him to kiss the girl, the other soliciting him to restrain himself. Even though he overcame the two temptations, he has not yet faced the test he must pass before his two selves can be reconciled. Christopher and Valentine can be glad they do not attend the Friday salon presided over by Edith Ethel Macmaster and her second husband, they can share a memory, they can whisper their love to each other, but they cannot be man and wife until he confronts the White Goddess in her bower at the bottom of hell. Sitting in his room, he remembers the last detail of his evening with Valentine— "he had caught, outside the gates of his old office, a transport-lorry that had given him a lift to Holborn" (288)—at the same time that, his memory still impaired, he is not sure what it is about their evening she will not forget. But by accepting " 'the talismanic passage' " (284), he accepts her guidance on his descent.

We have already seen how chapters in Part Two of *Some Do Not . . .* repeat images and allusions from chapters in Part One to carry the novel forward in such a way as to intensify the drama and open up levels of meaning. If Vincent Macmaster is what Christopher might have become, Captain McKechnie is what he will become unless he faces his problem. Captain Tietjens's double in *No More Parades* is mad, the result of his failure to act decisively with his wife. Instead of divorcing her as he was given leave to do, he slept with her and her lover, an Egyptologist, an expert in Egyptian antiquities, which, I assume, includes astral worship. Tietjens's refusal to confront Sylvia has so paralyzed him that he rationalizes his refusal to grant leave to a Welsh miner, 09 Morgan, deceiving himself into believing he fears the soldier's faithless wife's lover will kill him. His sigh, " 'Thank God, Sylvia can't get here!' " (311) is the extremity of self-delusion. She can go anywhere he goes because he fell the day he allowed her to lure him into sexual intimacy and he confirmed their union the day he married her. Since they are married both literally and symbolically, she is his hell. Attempting to flee from her only drives him deeper into himself and therefore closer to her. As soon as McKechnie mentions her, Tietjens sees her "in a sheath gown of gold tissue, all illuminated, and her mass of hair, like gold tissue too, coiled round and round in plaits over her ears" (299). This is followed by an image of her "standing at attention, her mouth working a little" (300) while he was saving their son's life by placing his feverish body in icy water, reducing his temperature.

Rebirth through immersion into oneself is the controlling metaphor of *Parade's End*. "Kill or cure! The two functions of man" begins a passage quoted above to indicate the polarity within the tetralogy. For Conrad every man must take the archetypal journey into the mud to discover the truth of himself mirrored in the woman who reigns in the heart of darkness. Since the Conradian heroine is a bearer of death and life, two aspects of a single center within the human concrete, the Conradian hero can discover the life within himself only if he first accepts the death within himself. The two aspects of the single center are in the Fordian hero also, but there is no redemption in *The Good Soldier* because, seeing through a distorted lens, Dowell deifies the human concrete. In *Parade's End* Ford splits reality into two centers, embodying each in a different heroine while keeping the battleground for their activities within the hero. Since he dei-

fies reason much as Macmaster deifies passion, Tietjens
cannot form a union with Valentine until, journeying
through the mud, he accepts his union with Sylvia. When
he does he will move to a new vantage point, from which
he will discover the single center that reconciles his dual
heritage.

Employing various techniques, alone or in conjunc-
tion with one another, Ford defines the paralysis that renders Tietjens increasingly vulnerable to the pressures cracking him apart. In terms of surface realism, Tietjens wants
to remain where he is. Stationed at a camp for new drafts
near Rouen, he rejects any offer to be relocated in England yet swears he is unfit for front-line duty. Almost the
whole of Chapter III of Part One is an interior monologue
within a time-shift, with Tietjens "setting himself coolly
to recapitulate every aspect of his separation from his wife"
(341–2). Sweating profusely, he tries desperately but un-
successfully to concentrate on his marriage, for the idea
"suddenly occurs to him that his parting from his wife
had set him free for his girl" (345). To deceive himself he
is free, he must force his mind to keep one pace ahead of
the nagging doubt about Sylvia's departure for Birkenhead
severing their marriage bonds. Unsuccessful in this mental
gymnastic, he finds himself spilling his drink. "What in the
world was he doing? Now? With all this introspection?
. . . Hang it all, he was not justifying himself. . . . He
had acted perfectly correctly as far as Sylvia was concerned.
Not perhaps to Miss Wannop. . . . Why, if he, Christopher Tietjens of Groby, had the need to justify himself,
what did it stand for to be Christopher Tietjens of Groby?
That was the unthinkable thought" (350).

An allusion can expose the falsity of his position. Trying to convince himself that Sylvia's departure severed
their union, he hums "*'Che faro senz' Eurydice? . . .'*"

(316) from Act IV of Gluck's opera. He stops because he realizes he is absurd. In the next scene of the opera, the God of Love restores his wife to Orpheus. "Far from being faint and pale" (316), Sylvia may be very much alive. Or an image can clarify the conflict within him. No matter how hard he resists thinking about his wife, he constantly sees her "coiled up on a convent bed. . . . Hating . . . Her certainly glorious hair all round her. . . . Hating . . . Slowly and coldly . . . Like the head of a snake when you examined it . . ." (339). He cannot stall off the thought of Valentine either; she comes "wriggling in. At all hours of the day and night. It was an obsession. A madness . . ." (338). Anxious to get a grip on himself, Tietjens challenges his double to a contest. He will supply the rhyme scheme for a sonnet, McKechnie the rhymes, he the lines, and McKechnie a translation into Latin. Together they compose an " 'undertaker's mortuary ode' " (318).

The event that initiates the movement within this second volume is 09 Morgan's death, preceded by the image of the cruel Sylvia and immediately followed by Tietjens remembering "a horse from a cut on whose chest the blood had streamed down over the foreleg like a stocking. A girl had lent him her petticoat to bandage it." He lifts the dead soldier's body and as the blood smears his hands, the image of the girl whom he never expected to see again becomes more vivid to him. "Gratified" that he does have strong feelings, he thinks "deliberately" about her. "His heart missed a beat. Obedient heart! Like the first primrose. Not *any* primrose. The *first* primrose. Under a bank with the hounds breaking through the underwood. . . . It was sentimental to say *Du bist wie eine Blume.* . . . Damn the German language! But that fellow was a Jew. . . . One should not say that one's young woman was like a flower, *any* flower. Not even to oneself. That was sentimental. But one might say one special flower. A *man* could say that. A man's job. She smelt like a primrose when you kissed her. But, damn it, he had never kissed her" (308–9). His inner conflict remains unresolved, however. Although he considers the possibility that he caused the Welshman's death by refusing him leave, he continues to deceive himself that Sylvia's influence cannot touch him. We know better: outside the moon rises "begumboiled, jocular, and grotesque" (312).

In keeping with the moon goddess myth, Ford has Sylvia come to her husband's assistance. According to the summary from Campbell quoted above, the goddess descends into the underworld to rescue her impotent lover. The time of *No More Parades* covers a three-day period, three months after husband and wife parted, he for France, she for Birkenhead, with each of the three parts of the volume covering a section of one of the three days. Since *Parade's End* was originally intended to be a trilogy,[31] this volume is the climax of the hero's ordeal with the White Goddess.

It is one thing to allude to a myth and another thing to bring it to life in fiction. As a novelist Ford must ground the myth in real people in real situations. He must make Sylvia's motivation credible. There is a validity to Caroline Gordon's comment that Sylvia so "towers above all the other" characters that "at times we are tempted to wonder whether she is human," [32] but it should also be stressed that her attitude toward her husband is perfectly understandable. She is a female who demands recognition, for her experience has been with men who fawn over her. A fantastically beautiful woman, she is accustomed to men reacting to her presence. A faithless woman who travels in a group for whom sexual immorality is the norm, she is baffled by a man who belongs to the same group and who acted like other men before their marriage but who is neither sexually aroused by her any longer nor willing to divorce her. She cannot comprehend how he can live with her without exhibiting sexual desire. "Obviously sometimes, at night, with a little whiskey taken he must want to!" (156) she muses in *Some Do Not. . . .* If he does he never indicates it to her. Since he is impotent with her, she arranges a meeting between him and the girl he loves, confident that under the circumstances they will have an affair. She hopes to capitalize on this, dragging him down to the level of the importunate male she can dominate. If she cannot do this she figures at least she will have the pleasure of knowing he betrayed his principles with Valentine. Her strategy fails: he does not take a mistress.

Sylvia offers him life but life that would destroy him as a man. "At the end of her tether," she comes to Rouen, supposedly to effect a reconcilation but actually to bring him " 'to heel' " (384). Quickly sensing he is not corresponding with Valentine because he does not look "alive" (385), she plans to whip his emotions into a frenzy, to inject her conception of life into him. Her motivation is hatred. Her husband's tired, sagging form walking away from her resembles that of a white bulldog she whipped to death. " 'There's a pleasure in lashing into a naked white beast. . . . Obese and silent, like Christopher . . .' " (417). Described in the images of snake, ice, and statue, she manifests her hatred in slander, torture, and blasphemy— " 'By the immortal saints,' she exclaims, 'I swear I'll make his wooden face wince yet' " (381)—even taunting him about not seeing his son again. Whatever sympathy we might feel for her when she confides in Major Perowne that she wishes to be reunited with Christopher is smothered when she gives her ex-lover permission to come to her room that night, knowing her husband will be there. " 'She wanted some fun' " (462), is the latter's lame explanation for her perversion.

While here we should remark a connection Ford makes between Sylvia and the war. She is friendly to the Germans and the civilians who profit from their control of the military, twin forces of folly, stupidity, and insanity, the consequences of hatred and perversion. Significantly, war started the day the German army overran the Belgian frontier near Gemmenich, which name suggests the men being emasculated by Sylvia and the human community being demolished by the war. The individual soldiers, herded together like animals, " 'stampeding' " like " 'cattle' " during an air raid (312), are the confused victims of these intriguing civilians and unfaithful women. Neither civilian nor combatant, Tietjens wards off the "immense cat . . . parading, fascinated and fatal," round his hut (315) yet "gets cattle into condition for the slaughterhouse" (362). By refusing to surrender, he can properly equip his drafts for battle in spite of the chaos around him, yet by refusing to fight, he must watch helplessly as they move to the front, "unknotting themselves like snakes, coiling out of inextricable bunches, sliding vertebrately over the mud to dip into their bowls" (331). Thus the appointment of a single command of the allied armies will be literally the turning point of the war in that it will free the officer staff from interfering civilians and neurotic bitches so that it can concentrate its energy on the enemy and it will permit the individual armies and soldiers to function as disciplined units within the military hierarchy. Symbolically, it will be the reintegration of the divided self, the whole man standing erect in his freedom.

Sylvia was doomed the minute Christopher began to remember the poem "Somewhere or Other." The echo of the words of this poem, which she had heard at a "charity concert," stayed with her "like something terrible and alluring: like a knife she would some day take out and with which she would stab herself" (201). " 'Don't' " remember! (163) she screamed at him in *Some Do Not. . . .* He does, because he has been making the interior journey. Her hatred alienates him, driving him to another woman, but he has been moving toward Valentine ever since that scene. Ford has not simply given a modern idiom and setting to a pagan myth. Rather, he captures its rhythm, its appeal, and its fury when locked in deadly combat with the only life in his imaginative world that can defeat it. Faithful to his vision, the author maintains a delicate balance between Sylvia as a goddess who descends to rescue her lover, forcing him to come to her, and Christopher as a hero whose descent into himself, protected by Valentine's guiding power, brings him to the death concealed at the heart of his interior and the life awaiting him.

As in previous sections, allusion, image, and motif are our guides through *No More Parades*. Midway in Part One of this volume, while walking with a colonel from Campion's headquarters who has driven out to the camp with a woman, Tietjens speculates about being ordered to the front lines: "Back to the Angel with the Flaming Sword. The wrong side of him!" (331). In Genesis when the Lord expels Adam and Eve from the garden of Eden, He places an angel with a flaming sword to guard the tree of life. Since sin is the death of the soul, the *Inferno* is the first stage of a long, arduous journey through death to the triumph of life in the transformed garden. In Canto IX of the *Purgatorio*, the poet-pilgrim must prostrate himself at the feet of the angel who guards the entrance to purgatory. His confession completed, he must submit to the angel's incising seven P's into his forehead with his gleaming sword to mark the sins he must expiate on his ascent. Only then can he enter the gates, eventually to pass through the wall of fire, on the other side of which lies the earthly paradise, where he is reunited with Beatrice. Tietjens cannot go forward because he has not confessed. When Colonel Levin questions him about applying for front-line duty, he replies, " 'Why? Because I've had a man killed on me? . . . There must have been a dozen killed to-night' " (331). Yet his predicament on this dark, frozen landscape is no more hopeless than Dante's in the dark words. Dante has his Beatrice; Tietjens, his Valentine. He would be condemned forever to the no man's land he inhabits were it not for her image, which keeps wriggling into his consciousness. Declaring his desire to talk to her, for he concludes she is the woman at the camp gates, he submits to his ordeal: "But, damn it, he, he himself, would make a pact with Destiny, at that moment, willingly, to pass thirty months in the frozen circle of hell, for the chance of thirty seconds in which to tell Valentine Wannop what he had answered back . . . to Destiny!" Levin corrects him: " 'Damn you, you ass! It's your wife who's waiting for you at the bottom there' " (339–40).

Having elected to go to the gates, only to be informed that Sylvia has returned to Rouen to wait for him there, Tietjens must answer "O Nine Morgan's eyes, looking at him with a sort of wonder." The downward journey to "the end of the earth" is about to come to rest in the sleeping bag in which he has been reviewing the events of the past three months. "And at the thought of the man as he was alive and of him now, dead, an immense blackness descended all over Tietjens. . . . Suddenly the light goes out. . . . In this case it was because of one fellow, a dirty enough man, not even very willing, not in the least endearing, certainly contemplating desertion. . . . But your dead . . . *yours* . . . your own. As if joined to your own identity by a black cord. . . ." Abruptly the images change, the tempo increases, and the direction reverses. Awakened from his slumber by the cries of the living soldiers, he "thrusts one of his legs cumbrously out of the top of his flea-bag" (355-7). He drinks cocoa with McKechnie, rejoices that England will not betray her commitment to fight Germany, laughs "good-humoredly at his projection of a hereafter" as imagined by the modern world—hoping to "be just in time for the last train to the old heaven . . ." (366)—and once again saves the life of a horse "for which he is responsible" (378). Mounted on Schomburg, with the lark's song in his ears, he "drops down a mud lane" on a cold December day to ride into Rouen (378).

Parade's End is so finely structured a novel that the middle section, Part Two, of the middle volume of what was originally a three-volume work is literally and symbolically the dead center of the book because the point of view is that of Sylvia, the dead center of the world of the novel.[38] We are inside her looking at her husband moving away from her; we are with her in the pit watching him ascend. In effect the novel has turned upside down for them. Whereas she pursued him in order to torment him, he has come to her kingdom, hell, the "be-mirrored lounge of the best hotel" in Rouen (379). Just as his movement reverses, so does hers, her deadly influence now reflected onto herself from the mirrors. Compelled to listen to him converse with Second-Lieutenant Cowley, she is powerless before his suffering and the realization of her defeat. Trying to impress the captain's wife while replying to the captain's question whether he, Tietjens, had saved 09 Morgan's life at Noircourt two years earlier, the subaltern tells her how on the preceding day her husband held the dead body in his arms " 'as if he'd been a baby.' "

" 'No, . . . I don't remember' " whether Morgan was the
man given another chance on the frozen, moonlit battlefield of Noircourt, Cowley answers Tietjens, who cries out,
" 'Supposing I let him off one life to get him killed two
years after. My God! That would be too beastly!' " Sylvia
then has a vision of Christopher lowering their son into
icy water. The shock lies not in the content, the same as his
in Part One, but in understanding the significance of that
act, for which he assumed responsibility: "Something had
said to her, just in between two crashes of the gun: 'It's his
own child. He went as you might say down to hell to bring
it back to life. . . .' She knew it was Father Consett saying
that. She knew it was true: Christopher had been down to
hell to bring the child back. . . ." Sealed in hatred and
despair, she has been defeated by love, compassion, and
pity: "It gave her a sense of despair: the engrossment of
Tietjens, in common with the engrossment of this dis-
reputable toper. She had never seen Tietjens put his
head together with any soul before; he was the lonely
buffalo. . . . Now! Anyone, any fatuous staff-officer, whom
at home he would never so much as have spoken to; any
trustworthy, beer-sodden sergeant, any street-urchin dressed
up as orderly . . ." (433–8).

The contrasts continue in Part Three: an unofficial
investigation by Colonel Levin and General Campion of
the events of the preceding night. Tietjens is under arrest
for throwing Major Perowne out of his wife's bedroom and
for barring entrance to the room to the provost marshal, a
General O'Hara. Awakening in the morning, he interprets
the shadow falling across the sunlight to be a sign, "a slight
intervention of Providence" (444); Sylvia feels deserted.
He is in "purgatory" (447); she knows she is in hell. To
Levin he defends the allied action against Germany as
" 'the one decent action that humanity has to its credit in

the whole of recorded history' " (453–4); for her war is men's excuse to "indulge themselves in orgies of promiscuity" (438). Ford's switching the point of view in this section to Tietjens's consciousness is another stroke of genius because it emphasizes the reversal that has taken place. Tietjens can look back on the preceding night. Death is behind him. When Campion quotes the lines, " 'The grave's a fine and secret place / But none I think do there embrace,' " from Marvell's "To His Coy Mistress" (475), Tietjens understands that succumbing to Sylvia's temptation in her bedroom would have been his death. He has successfully overcome his third temptation, the deadliest of the three. Understanding this, he knows he must separate from his wife, a decision he wishes to communicate to Valentine, to whom he talks in his sleep (" 'almost ghost-like' " alluding to Tannhäuser kneeling by Elisabeth's bier) and with whom he associates his vision of paradise. There being no reason to " 'shield that whore' " (495), he tells his godfather, who has learned from another officer of Sylvia's affair with Perowne in 1912, the truth about his father's not speaking to her. Campion's commentary, " 'He knows he's given his wife away!' " (497) is a beautiful example of the economy of Ford's later style, for in one sentence he crystallizes a whole volume. With the general inspecting the cathedral-like cook-house, Tietjens has his last sense of a parade, "as after a funeral" (500). Although by no means whole, he has scored a decisive victory over the White Goddess. Released from arrest, he accepts his orders for the front.

I will have to rearrange into correct chronology the time of Chapter I of Part Two of *A Man Could Stand Up–* (1926) to indicate the correspondence between the *Purgatorio* and this volume. One night a few months before the April morning of the present, Major Tietjens, who

prior to that night had sat ignominiously as an idle battalion second-in-command, was driven from the dug-out,
his nerves wracked by the supernatural sounds of the underground picking. Ford's rendering is a typical passage that
communicates on two levels—the second, a twentieth-
century counterpart to the beginning of Dante's ascent:
"After a perfect hell of noise; after so much of noise that
he had been forced to ascend the slippery clay stairs of the
dug-out. . . . And heaven knew if there was one thing
that on account of his heavy-breathing chest he loathed, it
was slippery clay . . . he had been forced to pant up
those slippery stairs. . . ." Becoming second-in-command
of his "own soul," checking on the men in the trenches, he
chanced upon "a tiny subaltern, gazing upwards at a
Verey illumination, with an elbow on an inequality of the
trench and the forearm pointing upwards." His "rapt face
suggested The Soul's Awakening!" (556–8) The subaltern
is Second-Lieutenant Aranjuez, the young officer whose
life he will save. Two nights before the April morning,
with the Commanding Officer in no condition to lead the
men, he took full command of the battalion during a battle
in which German soldiers, resembling hooded Misericordia
brothers and appearing as if with supernatural silence,
attacked the British lines.

The present time is dawn of a day in April. Standing
in mud, midway between the frozen landscape of *No More
Parades* and the spring at the base of the mound above
him, Tietjens comes to the "conviction that, if his head—
and of course the rest of his trunk and lower limbs—were
suspended by a process of levitation to that distance above
the duckboard on which, now, his feet were, he would be
in an inviolable sphere. These waves of conviction re-
curred continually: he was constantly glancing aside and
upwards at that splash; it was in the shape of the comb of

a healthy rooster; it gleamed, with five serrations, in the just-beginning light that shone along the thin, unroofed channel in the gravel slope" (543). Though not in Dante, the cock is appropriate in Part Two, since it is traditionally a figure of the priest calling his parishioners to the Mass, and since Christ is the great high priest, it is a figure of the Saviour.[34] Herald of the dawn that calls the faithful to the ascent of mount purgatory—the Sacrifice of the Mass—it is Tietjens's goal. He does not grasp its significance, but we should, for when he peers out of the trenches, ahead he sees three wheels, three frosty erections, and, suspended in the latter, "three bundles of rags and what appeared to be a very large, squashed crow. How the devil had that fellow managed to get smashed into that shape? It was improbable. There was also—suspended, too, a tall melodramatic object, the head cast back to the sky. One arm raised in the attitude of, say, a Walter Scott Highland officer waving his men on" (552).

The time-shift in this chapter is as important as that of *Under Western Eyes*. By having Tietjens remember the ascent of the slippery dug-out stairs and the attack of the hooded soldiers, Ford can create the sense that these incidents occur during the day as Tietjens relives them in his mind. They are behind him in time, but his remembering them in the present proves that at this stage they are as real for him as his desire to reach the cock, thoughts of which alternate with his recollections. They do not fade until his thoughts converge on the future with Valentine. By having him remember these incidents, Ford can also position two impressions next to each other in his memory —"Valen . . . Valen . . ." and the voice in his nightmare saying, " *'Bringt dem Hauptmann eine Kerze,'* " at the end of this chapter—preparing for the opening scene of Chapter II and ultimately the scene in the sunlight on the mound. Thinking of "Valen . . ." and the voice, Tietjens listens to the notes of the cornet, which are "as efficient working beneath the soul as the picks of miners in the dark," because he hears the lyric, attributed to Thomas Ford, entitled "There is a lady sweet and kind" (563–4). He admits it cannot refer to Sylvia. We know it must refer to Valentine. The third stanza contains the lines, "I touched her not, alas! not I, / And yet I love her till I die," and the fourth stanza:

> Had I her fast betwixt mine arms,
> Judge you that think such sports were harms,
> Were't any harm? no, no, fie, fie,
> For I will love her till I die [35]

foreshadows Part Three of *A Man Could Stand Up—*, where he and his "lady sweet and kind" realize that even though they cannot marry love has made inevitable their union. The underground picking drove him from the dugout; the lyric propels him toward the earthly paradise.

Hearing the lyric, representative of the seventeenth century, the "only satisfactory age in England" (566), Tietjens remembers Herbert's "Virtue," a poem in which the virtuous soul, unlike the day, the rose, and the spring, "never gives; / But though the whole world turn to coal, / Then chiefly lives." [36] Recalling the poet's cloistered life at Bemerton, he imagines "himself standing up on a little hill, a lean contemplative parson, looking at the land sloping down to Salisbury spire" (567). To stand up on a hill, he must accept the consequences of such an action. As soon as he does, his ascent is rapid. Atoning for his part in 09 Morgan's death, he accepts command of the Ninth Glamorganshires, thereby accepting the responsibility of saving as many men as possible. As an officer he must evaluate the deployment of the enemy troops as well as his own. In so doing he experiences compassion for all soldiers, German as well as British and Welsh, "sacrificed for the stupid sort of fun called Strategy" (562). As battalion commander he must give orders or his unit cannot function. When he does he achieves single command of himself, dismissing his other self, McKechnie, with the words, " 'I'm commanding here' " (575), shortly before being informed that Campion is taking over single command of the allied armies. To Tietjens "it means that the end of the war is in sight" (594).

He arrives at the mound. "Honeycombed with springs," it is a "miniature Primrose Hill" (626), the spot for him "to be alone with Heaven" (633) and while reclining in the sun to commune with the young woman whose image in *No More Parades* made him think of the first primrose. "His whole being . . . overwhelmed by her" (604), he renounces Bemerton and Groby because he wants "to live . . . in a four-room attic flat, on the top of one of the Inns of Court. With Valentine Wannop. *Because of Valentine Wannop!*" (633)

Strengthened by Virgil's urging, in Canto XXVII of the *Purgatorio*, that he shall see Beatrice when he passes through the wall, Dante hurries through the fire, the last barrier separating him from the earthly paradise. The following morning, Wednesday after Easter, he has such yearning for her sweeping his soul onward that he feels his "feathers grow for flight" (123). Allegorically, Virgil, who guided him this far, has served his purpose. His sinful nature purged, his sensual desire purified, Dante is crowned lord of his soul by his reason, which takes its rightful place as the poet-pilgrim enters the garden of Eden. Inside he meets Beatrice, who appears "within a cloud of flowers" and who so reprimands him he must make a final confession of his sins before he is allowed to join her on the opposite bank of Lethe. She has replaced Virgil as his guide. Reunited with her, he witnesses the masque of the heavenly pageant. " 'Adam,' " the figures murmur as she descends from her car. Then they encircle "a tree stripped of its flowers and all its foliage in every branch" (XXXII. 37–9). This is the tree of good and evil associated with the fallen Adam, since Dante writes in Canto IX, "I, who had with me something of Adam, lay down, overcome with sleep . . ." (10–1). When the Griffin binds the Cross to the tree, the boughs bloom:

> As our plants, when the great light falls on them mingled with that which shines behind the celestial Carp, begin to swell and then each is renewed in its own colour before the sun yokes his steeds under other stars, so, showing colour less than of the rose and more than of the violet, the tree was renewed which before had its branches so bare (XXXII.52–60).

The Incarnation, with Its extension, the Passion and the Redemption, grafts grace onto man's nature, transforming the old Adam into the new Adam. Awakened by the voice crying, " 'Arise' " (XXXII.72), Dante is summoned to Beatrice, who directs him to drink from the waters of Eunoe. "Remade, even as new plants renewed with new leaves" (XXXIII.143–4), he is ready for his ascent to the stars.

As the new Adam replaces the old, so Beatrice replaces Eve. She cooperates to restore Dante to the garden of Eden, lost by "Eve's boldness" (XXIX.24), because she has guided his entire journey by commissioning Virgil to show him the way out of the dark woods. " '*Benedictus qui venis*' " (XXX.19), the angels sing to announce her, for she leads him to Christ, the source of grace, Whose two natures he sees on the top of mount purgatory only as reflected in her eyes. The more he responds to her love, the more he receives her love and the more his soul is flooded with grace until, through Mary's intercession in Canto XXXIII of the *Paradiso*, he is allowed to gaze into the "Light Supreme" (67). A real woman and a figure of Mary, the second Eve and Mother of Redemption who sent her to Virgil, Beatrice is Dante's experience of grace on earth.

Since the *Purgatorio* is the Sacrifice of the Mass, " '*Benedictus qui venis*' " signals not only the coming of Beatrice but the advent of the Saviour in the Eucharist. While Dante beholds the two natures of the Griffin as reflected in Beatrice's eyes, his soul, "full of amazement and gladness, tasted of that food which, satisfying with itself, for itself makes appetite" (XXXI.127–9). Early in the tetralogy Father Consett warned Mrs. Satterthwaite Sylvia's hell would come when her husband ran after another woman. To the mother's question whether he would do that, the priest replied, " 'What's to stop it? . . . *What* in the world but the grace of our blessed Lord, which he hasn't got and doesn't ask for?' " (42). Christopher has never prayed for grace—at best, he knows he wants to reach the rooster—but he has fallen in love with Valentine, his Beatrice. She is his experience of grace. His longing for reunion to engage in "the intimate conversation that means the final communion" (629) of their souls will be delayed until later in *Parade's End*. However, Lance-Corporal Duckett, who resembles her, serves him "three heaps of ethereal sandwiches" (631–2) and coffee, which comes from the Arabic word for wine, in a scene that can only be read as an imitation of the Communion feast.

Since the *Commedia* is the imitation of Christ, at each stage of which Dante is lifted higher onto the Cross, he is reborn as the new Adam after he partakes of the Eucharist. *A Man Could Stand Up—* follows the same pattern. Tietjens ascends the Primrose Hill, thinks of Valentine, and confesses to himself he has been "loafing, contemptuous, . . . a sort of eternal Second-in-Command" (629–30). His pride broken, he admits he needs her. After drinking the coffee, he chooses not to write her that he loves her because if he is subsequently killed in action it would not be fair to her. In his situation this is an act of genuine self-sacrifice. Described as Michelangelo's *Adam,* who is then blown upside down by a shell from a Bloody Mary, he is reborn in grace. He is "suspended in space. As if he were suspended as he had wanted to be in front of that cockscomb in whitewash" (637). The descent into hell taught him that hatred and death were within himself; the ascent of mount purgatory teaches him that love and life are "capable of existing within" himself (629).

The weight of an inescapable past, the hope of a new future, the passing of the test in the initiation stage coalesce to create the movements within the two novelists' works. The movement of a Conrad story is down and then up for Marlow, who returns to life a new man after the descent into his heart of darkness. It may be that this movement is a movement toward grace. I do not know because Conrad does not know. At most, we can say that for him life is mysterious, pregnant with suggestiveness, its heart of darkness a mute, inscrutable presence that cannot be denied. Since the mystery is initially experienced in the woman, the movement is circular for Lord Jim, who, by deserting Jewel because he is determined to redeem himself, reenacts his desertion of the *Patna;* but first circular and then linear for Razumov, who, by responding to the unveiled Natalia, discovers he is potentially both betrayer and redeemer. Even Dowell asks himself unceasingly, his mind "going round and round in a weary, baffled space of pain—what should these people have done?" *Parade's End* supplies the answer.

The failure of the characters in *The Good Soldier* to know themselves causes their misery. Although Ashburnham and Tietjens are men of principle, the latter is saved from the folly of the former because by making the interior journey, he accepts his marriage to Sylvia and his desire for Valentine. Step by step his self-image is deflated: he loses his memory; he realizes he is responsible for 09 Morgan's death; he admits he should have confronted his wife years ago; he confesses he needs Valentine. He discovers his human, that is, fallen, nature. "You may expel Nature by pleading," but it does no good, he learns; *"tamen usque recur"* (665), he muses while speaking on the telephone to Mrs. Wannop in Part Three of the third volume.

Throughout the first two volumes Tietjens is accused of acting as if he were Christ. Sylvia mocks him with the gibe used to mock Christ, in Mark xv.31: " 'He saved others; himself he could not save' " (404). " 'He wants . . . to play the part of Jesus Christ' " (379), she tells Perowne in the hotel lounge in Rouen. Her husband does play at being Christ. Hence the complexity of the tetralogy. He refuses to have any sexual intercourse with his wife because to do so would be taking his cue from her: it would divorce the act from any commitment. Knowing she is unfaithful, he does not love her. A man of principle, he will not take a mistress either. No wonder Sylvia accuses him of self-deception!

He is not Christ. His playing at being Christ is an excuse for not being honest. By denying his sexual nature,

he is a dead man, but he cannot know this until he probes
the abyss in the be-mirrored lounge in Rouen, which in-
cites him to attain reunion with the girl he loves, with
whom he can reconcile reason and passion. Journeying
through the brutality of passion divorced from reason and
the simplicity of reason divorced from passion, the inhuman and the nonhuman, he reaches the rooster, a perfect
figure to symbolize the reintegration of his religious and
sexual impulses. Once Tietjens sheds his illusion about
himself, he can discard the notion that he is suffering the
Passion and accept his "passion for the girl" (349). Once he
admits, " 'I've got to save myself first!' " (637) refuting
Sylvia's charge that he is still playing at being Christ, he
can "save others." Literally blown upside down by the explosion and buried in the mud, he is metaphorically blown
upside down so that he reverses roles with Valentine-
Beatrice. Feeling "tender, like a mother," after being
pulled out by two of his men, he pulls Aranjuez out of the
mud. The boy unable to stand, "drooping like a flower
done in slime," Tietjens carries him to safety (639). This
accomplished, he returns to dig out Valentine's surrogate,
Duckett. He is not Christ—he botches the rescue of Aranjuez, who loses an eye—but Christ-like. Penetrating the
realm of supernatural wonder, he discovers Christ in himself, enabling him to be the redeemer Ashburnham fancied
himself to be. He becomes the good soldier: Christ-opher
(Christ-bearer), who will rescue Valentine.

Ford carefully sketches in the coming of Valentine's
redeemer in Part One of *A Man Could Stand Up—*. Hidden
in the depths of her memory, he must be brought forth
gradually until the mention of his name on Armistice Day
by her headmistress, Miss Wanostrocht, releases her from
a " 'state of suspended animation' " (519). The "tantalis-
ingly half-remembered voice" of Edith Ethel on the tele-

phone, "as if from caverns" (504), quoting Carlyle—" 'And
then I remembered that it was the birthday of their Redeemer!' " (508)—recalls to Valentine the Sage of Chelsea's
affected superiority and Edith Ethel's conceit when inton-
ing that quotation. Remembering her past with Mrs. Macmaster, she begins to recollect experiences with Christopher
such as their moonlit ride that she has been repressing.
The sarcastic reference to Christmas is replaced in her mind
by her remembrance of "one immense star, though, histor-
ically, there had been also a dilapidated sort of moon"
(524). Since he wanted to kiss her that night, she asks herself
why he has not written to her. She believes him "Godlike,
Jesus Christ-like" (527), but his silence has left her in hell.
Now that he is back in England, she wonders whether
Sylvia will keep them apart. "What *should* keep them
apart? . . . Middle Class Morality? A pretty gory carnival
that had been for the last four years! Was this then Lent,
pressing hard on the heels of Saturnalia?" (534) As I read
this passage, Lent has a double meaning. It is the season
from Ash Wednesday to Easter, the penitential season preceding Valentine's rebirth, and the season, called St. Martin's Lent in the Middle Ages, from November 11 to
Christmas. Later we learn on this night, November 11,
1918, Christopher and Valentine stand "on the top step of
St. Martin's Church" (777). Read this way, it balances the
Christian feast against the pagan December feast, Saturnalia, pointing ahead in Part Two to the birth of Valentine's redeemer.

Christopher is Valentine's redeemer in that he saves
her from two disastrous alternatives. She can remain a
repressed physical instructress in a girls' school, with an
anemic spinster for a headmistress; or, what is more likely,
she can break loose from her repression to be another
Sylvia. A normal female with normal feminine desires, she

is afraid she will "never marry. And never be seduced!" Tired of being "nunlike," she wants "some fun! Now!" (513) As a single girl in love with a man who has been ignoring her, her fun would consist of promiscuous affairs with other men: a divorcing of the sexual act from the engagement of the couple performing the act.

What sets Valentine off from the women in *The Young Lovell* and *The Good Soldier* is that she is making the interior journey. Lady Margaret, Leonora, and Nancy do not know themselves, but she admits she is no Beatrice. Rather, she is an "oversexed ass" (527), an Eve tempting Adam-Christopher who has to consider the possibility that since he "didn't quite eat" the apple he may have been indifferent to her charms (525). Because this descent into herself is a turning upside down, Valentine "in Hell" (527) is the novel's third reversal. But just as Christopher is redeemed by her image guiding him to the top of the mound, so she is redeemed by his image "continually forcing" itself into her consciousness (518). This scene, then, corresponds to the scene in *No More Parades* where he leaves to confront the woman waiting for him at the camp gates, for she leaves the school to go to the man "calling for her" (518).

Since the movement of the *Commedia,* the basic structure of *Parade's End,* is downward, then upward, with reversals at the bottom of hell and the top of purgatory, we can predict Valentine's reversal or rebirth in this volume. The movement of Part Three is communicated through allusion and statement, Valentine's changing self-image marking the descent, her changing direction, the ascent. In Part One she sees herself as the faithful Penelope and the speaker of Christina Rossetti's poem, "Hoping against Hope," who hopes her lover will return before she

dies; in Part Three she sees herself as Barbara Allen, who
will die for the lover who dies for her on Martinmas
(November 11), and Alcestis, who dies to spare her husband's life. Feeling "death in her heart" (645), she is
frightened by the silence in the square, the empty house,
and Christopher's sudden appearance. At the base of the
staircase, she stands irresolute in the nadir of her descent,
unable to go forward or backward. Her ascent begins when,
deciding she will not be harmed, she mounts "the great
stone staircase" (649), resolved to stand with the man who
needs her.

Just as Tietjens has to renounce his illusion of himself as Christ before he can become Christ-like, so Valentine has to renounce her illusion of herself as Beatrice in
Part One before she can become Beatrice-like in Part
Three. Once she admits she needs Christopher, she can go
to him. She knows with her he can talk, purging himself of
the "grey spectral shapes" that haunt him (657). Loving
him, she wants to "atone" (659) for his blighted years with
Sylvia, making him a whole man again. Once she realizes
that since he needs her she does not have to feel humiliated
coming to him, she can tell her mother she has " 'got to' "
stay with him (653). Her mother's voice on the telephone,
"turned by the means of its conveyance into the voice of a
machine of Destiny," speaking in turn to her " 'little
child' " and her " 'dear boy' " (654–7), completes a movement started in *Some Do Not . . .* , cementing the overall
Dantean structure of the tetralogy. " 'Valentine! Valentine!
Go to Christopher in the study. At once . . . ,' " Mrs.
Wannop called to her daughter in Part One of the first
volume. By sending Valentine to Christopher and by speaking "between them," the mother "makes their union" in
their earthly paradise (669). Mediating "in God's name"
(654), she begs them to let their consciences be their guide.

Since their consciences tell them their love is free from hypocrisy, they commit themselves to each other.

Their decision to live together as husband and wife, although they cannot legally marry, is itself a reversal of their decision in *Some Do Not. . . .* Their journey to self-knowledge having taught them they love each other, they understand that not to live together would be a greater immorality than separating, for disengaging themselves would violate their need for each other. Together they can experience the love, the beauty, the intelligent conversation Tietjens believes constitutes the good life. As if "bathed in soothing fluid" (669), they can look into each other's eyes; no longer will they have to avert their glances. Making their choice according to the guidance of their consciences, not the approved morality of a promiscuous, scheming, hypocritical society, is, like Marlow's lie in "Heart of Darkness," a more moral act than the deception of Vincent Macmaster and Edith Ethel Duchemin. The repeated allusion to the Canticle of Canticles as Valentine ascends the stairs leaves no doubt about Ford's attitude. A song praising mutual love, it extols the real union of man and woman in the sanctity of marriage, which in its sacramental quality is a figure of Christ's union with the redeemed soul. " '*Veni, sponsa, de Libano,*' " the angels sing, alluding to the Canticle of Canticles, when Beatrice comes to Dante in the earthly paradise (*Purg.* XXX.11).

Ford's artistry in *Parade's End* is so superior to that of his other fiction, except possibly *The Good Soldier,* and to that of twentieth-century fiction in general, that by repeating the movement, initiating the second descent after the first descent has reached the bottom of hell and intersecting the two by means of a time-shift, he can create a new pattern, reversing the novel's direction.[37] Temporally, the movements follow this order: Tietjens's descent, reversal, ascent, and rebirth; Valentine's descent, reversal, ascent, and rebirth. Spatially, they follow this order: Tietjens's descent and reversal (*No More Parades*), Valentine's descent and beginning of reversal (Part One of *A Man Could Stand Up—*), Tietjens's ascent and rebirth (Part Two of *A Man Could Stand Up—*), and Valentine's reversal, ascent, and rebirth (Part Three of *A Man Could Stand Up—*). By interrupting the temporal order with a spatial order, Ford can reverse each character's role as the other's rescuer. When Tietjens is at the bottom of hell, Valentine's image impinging on his consciousness guides him to the top of purgatory. When she is at the bottom of hell, his image impinging on her consciousness guides her to the top of purgatory: while descending in Part One of *A Man Could Stand Up—*, she prepares for her redeemer's rebirth, which occurred earlier but which we do not read about until Part Two. At the end of Part Two, Tietjens is reborn as Christopher and Valentine is at the bottom of hell, about to ascend toward him as he descends toward her. In fact, he descends twice in Part Three, the first time to let her in the house, the second time to bring her upstairs to the celebration. "On a level," the two of them "look at each other for a long time." Then, united at last, "alone together," they ascend the stairway to commence their honeymoon (669).

Christopher's return to Valentine produces the only bulwark strong enough to prevail over the impetus out of which sprang the first half of the tetralogy. In Ford's imaginative world only the Christian union can withstand the lure of Venus worship, and the Christian union is possible in the novel only because Christopher assumes his role as head and Valentine her role as helpmate in their marriage. Sylvia increases "her hold over men" (145) by scorning their sexual overtures. Valentine worships Christopher for uniting himself with her. Sylvia has "to have men at her feet; that is, as it were, the price of her—purely social —daily bread . . ." (150). Knowing Christopher has come for her, Valentine wants to say, " 'I am falling at your feet. My arms are embracing your knees!' " (669).

Perhaps the most dramatic contrast involves two scenes, each toward the end of its respective half of the novel. When Campion quoted from Marvell's "To His Coy Mistress,"

> it came to Tietjens suddenly to think of Sylvia, with the merest film of clothing on her long, shining limbs. . . . She was working a powder-puff under her armpits in a brilliant illumination from two electric lights, one on each side of her dressing table. She was looking at him in the glass with the corners of her lips just moving. A little curled. . . . He said to himself:
> "One is going to that fine and secret place. . . . Why not have?" She had emanated a perfume founded on sandalwood. As she worked her swansdown powder-puff over those intimate regions he could hear her humming. Maliciously! It was then that he had observed the handle of the door moving minutely. She had incredible arms, stretched out amongst a wilderness of be-silvered cosmetics. Extraordinarily lascivious! Yet clean! Her gilded sheath gown was about her hips on the chair . . . (476).[38]

The pregnant Valentine wishes she could "deluge herself with a perfume called Houbigant and wear pink silk next the skin"; she would enjoy lying "between lavendered linen sheets with little Chrissie on soft, pink silk, air-cushionish bosoms" (811-2). But her reason quickly reasserts the primacy of fruitful love over extravagant desires:

It was queer that her heart was nearly as much in Christopher's game as was his own. As house-mother she ought to have grabbed after the last penny—and goodness knew the life was strain enough. Why do women back their men in unreasonable romanticisms? You might say that it was because if their men had their masculinities abated—like defeated roosters!— the women would suffer in intimacies. . . . Ah, but it wasn't that! Nor was it merely that they wanted the buffaloes to which they were attached to charge.

It was really that she had followed the convolutions of her man's mind. And ardently approved. She disapproved with him of riches, of the rich, of the frame of mind that riches confer. If the war had done nothing else for them— for those two of them—it had induced them at least to install Frugality as a deity (817–8).

Choosing to be a helpmate, she obeys the New Law, given definitive statement as it applies to marriage by St. Paul (Eph. v.21–33).

Although Christopher's descent to rescue Valentine emphasizes his role as redeemer and head of the family, we should not forget that her image guides him through death to rebirth. What the intersecting movements actually reveal is the interdependence of Christopher's and Valentine's growth. They rescue each other, creating a new future for themselves. Calling her, he leads her out of a girls' school; in union with him, she fulfills herself as a woman. Reconciling his religious and sexual impulses, she presents him with a new life; their child will be named Chrissie. Unlike Part Two of *No More Parades*, which concludes with the estranged couple ascending to Venusberg, the point of view Sylvia's as she watches her husband move away from her, *A Man Could Stand Up—* concludes with the two lovers ascending together to their earthly paradise to celebrate their reunion.

"I think it could be argued that *Last Post* was more than a mistake—it was a disaster, a disaster which has delayed a full critical appreciation of *Parade's End*," Graham Greene writes in his introduction to *The Bodley Head Ford Madox Ford,* which omits the fourth volume.[39] It is impossible, however, to render a full critical appreciation without *The Last Post* (1928). Although at times the style is diffuse and the tone sentimental, this volume delimits Mark Tietjens's defense against Sylvia. Since this was Christopher's defense before his descent, by alternating the point of view in Part One between Mark and his mistress, a Frenchwoman, Marie Léonie, Ford can show what would have become of Christopher and Valentine had they not taken the interior journey and what would become of the civilized world were it not for them, for Mark and Marie are their doubles.

Her mind cluttered with "débris" (682), Marie wants to decorate their home with Casimir-Bar's statuary, her idea of classical art. Her aesthetic taste governed by her acquisitive nature, she desires a more expensive home, fearful that when she is left alone Christopher and Valentine will despoil her. Like Mark, she conceives of life in terms of material comforts. One reason her mind is cluttered is that Mark has rarely spoken to her. "Amused" by her (683), he favors her with an "indulgent smile" or an occasional opulent gift (687) rather than with intelligent conversation that would sweep away the débris. Yet he believes theirs is the only satisfactory relationship in the Tietjens family. *The Last Post* demonstrates how wrong he is. "Their single topic of communion" horse racing (690), he marries her primarily to protect her holdings and only as a concession to his brother. They have no children.

Mark and Marie are good people, but never having descended, they cannot ascend to rebirth. Christopher had to pass his initiation in Sylvia's bower before he could surmount the hill, where he is reborn as the new man who reaches the rooster. Conversely, Mark thinks of himself as "being dead—or being a God" (728). One half of this thought is correct: he is dead to himself and to Marie because his failure to descend to rescue her has made it doubly difficult for her to fulfill herself. She knew practically nothing about him before his illness; he did not even allow her to use her own name before their marriage. Never having descended to her heart of darkness, she confuses God and man. Never having discovered herself, never having shared the truth of the man with whom she lives, who is neither God nor new Adam, she sees him, like Rodin but "different indeed from that Monsieur Christopher," as the rooster (701). For her he can "perform the feats of strength of a Hercules" (688). He can, but he does not because according to the pattern established by Christopher-Hercules with Valentine-Alcestis, he would have to move through death to rebirth first, and he is a "man who never moved" (677).

Since Christopher will not live at Groby, preferring to give it to Sylvia and his son, Mark does nothing to prevent Sylvia's decision to rent Groby to an American and to have Groby Great Tree uprooted. He will not even betray any emotion when she, in a final desperate attempt to torment the two brothers, comes to the cottage in West Sussex where the two couples are living. What Mark does have is indomitable will power. He is capable of opposing Sylvia but at the price of his and Marie's growth. His brother's descent began when, admitting his responsibility for 09 Morgan's death, he realized he would have to ex-

piate his guilt by assuming responsibility for all men before he could talk to Valentine again. As late as the day
he dies, Mark is given an opportunity to act. Admitting he
is "absolutely to blame" (739) for his father's death is a
beginning in that he admits he should not have asked Ruggles to check on Christopher for the father. During the
afternoon, however, he convinces himself the death was an
accident. In view of his need for "a pattern to interpret
things by" (832), his explanation has the ring of a Dowell
interpretation to it, a psychologically satisfying one that
eliminates the interior journey. Mark's rationalization,
even if sound, is not important. What is, is his refusal to
recognize that no man can stand alone, a truth his brother
discovered by following the image that led him to the top
of the hill. Always regarding "himself as master of his
fate" (739), he will not humble himself to confess he needs
Marie, which would mean giving himself. Since he has
never suffered the terrible agony of being responsible to
another person, he demands retribution on Armistice Day.
Ford metes it out to him with beautiful irony. When England does not humiliate her enemy by occupying the defeated Germany, he resolves "to withdraw himself for ever
from all human contacts" (689) by lying on his bed, frozen
in immobility.

Mark's and Marie's failure to grow is one future for
the civilized world. Marie has "an invincible scorn for
both language and people of her adopted country" (681);
"born tired" (737), Mark does not care for the land or
Groby Great Tree. The playing of the last post signifies
the end of the England he knows. Unwilling to change
with the changing times, he absents himself from a world
he refuses to understand. There is another future, though,
a hopeful one. As much as they love Groby Great Tree,
the "tallest cedar in Yorkshire; in England; in the Em-

pire" (732), Christopher and Valentine will not contest its removal. Neither will they despair for England. Christopher does not have to occupy his ancestral home any more than he has to punish Sylvia because he and Valentine have rediscovered their roots. In the novel these are the roots that clutch, the branches that grow. Mark's will can keep Sylvia on the defensive, but the fruit of Christopher's and Valentine's union drives her out of the country.

Early in *Parade's End* allusions and images start to point toward the commitment which banishes Venus worship. With Christopher and Valentine moving toward rebirth, these allusions and images, reverberating backward and forward, are paring the scope of influence of the original impetus while converging toward the new center of the tetralogy. By the time they form their union, the allusions and images have defined the new experience which replaces the old. I would like to begin with an allusion in *No More Parades* to *Tannhäuser,* which localizes "the face not seen, the voice not heard" in "Somewhere or Other," itself a narrowing of the allusion to the sign promised in the Book of Jeremiah. As Sylvia climbs the stairway to her bedroom in Rouen, she sees herself as Venus trying to seduce her husband away from Valentine-Elisabeth. In Act I of the Wagner opera, Tannhäuser wins his freedom from the Hörselberg by resting his hope "in Mary," at the mention of whose name Venus *"shrinks away and vanishes."* [40] In Act III, despondent because Rome will not grant him absolution, he is saved from surrendering to the goddess by Wolfram's invoking Elisabeth's intervention on his behalf. A figure of Mary, she has consecrated herself to the Virgin so that "heavenly grace on him may fall," and Venus, knowing she has lost Tannhäuser, *"sinks into the earth"* when she hears Wolfram cry out Elisabeth's name.

Valentine's reference to Malachi in the opening of *A Man Could Stand Up—* measures Christopher's progress since the reference to Jeremiah in the opening of *Some Do Not. . . .* The Book of Jeremiah calls the unfaithful wife, the astral worshipper, the follower of strange gods to repentance. The Book of Malachi cuts off Judah, for Judah "hath profaned the holiness of the Lord, which he loved, and hath married the daughter of a strange God" (ii.11). It behooves the good man to put this daughter behind him, for Elijah is coming to prepare for "the coming of the great and dreadful day of the Lord" (iv.5). In this same section Valentine remembers the star outshining "a dilapidated sort of moon"; she asks herself whether Lent is "pressing hard on the heels of Saturnalia."

Part Two of *A Man Could Stand Up—* supplies the answer in Tietjens's ascent of mount purgatory. That this experience uncovers the new center supplanting the old one receives further support from the image of the officer on the barbed wire waving his men on. He is reputed to be Lieutenant Constantine. By following the shining cross in the sky to victory over Maxentius, Constantine embraced Christianity and so became the first Christian Emperor. Ford's method bears fruit in *The Last Post.* Approaching the Tietjens home, Sylvia has her vision, which appears beyond the horizon:

> But it was the finger of God—or of Father Consett, who as saint and martyr, was the agent of God. . . . Or, perhaps, God, Himself, was here really taking a hand for the protection of His Christopher, who was undoubtedly an Anglican saint. . . . The Almighty might well be dissatisfied with the other relatively amiable Catholic saint's conduct of the case in which the saint of the other persuasion was involved. For

surely Father Consett might be expected to have a sore spot for her whereas you could not expect the Almighty to be unfair even to Anglicans. . . . At any rate, up over the landscape, the hills, the sky, she felt the shadow of Father Consett, the arms extended as if in a gigantic cruciform—and then above and behind that an . . . an August Will! (806)

This scene should be read as the counterpart to the opening scene of *The Inheritors*. On the summit of a hill in Kent, the Fourth Dimensionist offers Granger a vision of the future in which the symbol of England's spiritual center is demolished, prophesying that he will enlist with her since his love is a disease. On the summit of a hill in West Sussex, Sylvia has a vision of the future in which the center of Granger's and Tietjens's tradition is restored. She knows she has lost her husband to Valentine because she knows their love has cured him of her influence.

It is inevitable that Sylvia and Valentine confront each other in the fourth volume, not because an abandoned wife is curious about her husband's mistress but because they are antagonists who must oppose each other in Ford's imaginative world if either is to guide the hero on his journey. A statue, an "It" (824), the former is a cold, aloof, hateful female whose proper domain is hell. A living woman, the latter is a female able to love whose proper domain is the earthly paradise. Sylvia cannot ascend to paradise since she scorns pity and will not repent, although she knows that until she does purgatory is "closed to her by the angel with the flaming sword" (793). Typical of the novel's structure is the reversal of positioning of the heroines. On Armistice Day Sylvia simulates a fall from the top of the stairway to keep her husband from the woman he loves. In *The Last Post* Valentine descends from her bedroom to stand up against her adversary. Sylvia demands male slavery. Incapable of love, she cannot understand the nature of her husband's union with the other woman. To her they are running an Agapemone, a kind of free-love house. What she cannot grasp is that by giving themselves freely in love, Christopher and Valentine are participating in a love feast. And the fruit of their union is a new life in Christ. It is this new life which banishes Sylvia. Her world "waning" (808), she decides to divorce her husband so that she can marry Campion and leave England for India.

" 'C'est lamentable qu'un seul homme puisse inspirer deux passions pareilles dans deux femmes. . . . C'est le martyre de notre vie!' " (827) Marie says as she looks at the two women confronting each other. Initially, the two heroines are necessary to awaken Tietjens because it is only when they enter the novel that the archetypal pattern begins to shape the tetralogy. As soon as Tietjens accepts his " 'resumption yoke' " (30) with Sylvia, he meets the militant suffragette. His wife is the "thorn in his flesh" (788), who by pushing him toward Valentine goads him into accepting the younger woman's guiding power. This explains why Valentine finally sees Sylvia's "real features. There was about that figure something timid. And noble" (827). Her descent to him in Rouen spurs him to descend into hell, where he accepts his marriage to the female, death, his nature. Yet when he does accept, the emphasis shifts to him as a redeemer. Humbling himself in his nature, he discovers Christ in himself, enabling him to rescue Valentine, whose image spurs him to ascend mount purgatory. The great paradox in Ford's imaginative world is that by descending into hell Tietjens ascends mount purgatory, which is suffering the Passion on a human level, for this pattern is the imitation of Christ.

Christopher resolves the Fordian hero's dilemma as Young Lovell and Dowell do not. Just before he discovers the slain and resurrected god of the Christian heritage within himself by being buried in the mud, he remembers that years ago, descending a slope on the battlefield, "he had felt like a Greek God striding through the sea . . ." (631). Valentine also resolves the Fordian heroine's dilemma as Lady Margaret, Leonora, and Nancy do not. Tietjens first sees her in *Some Do Not* . . . appearing and disappearing "on the tops of the sandhills" (64) in much the same way that Young Lovell first sees the White Lady appearing and disappearing on the dunes. Tietjens's son even imagines her as the "Venus of Botti. . . . A crooked smile . . ." (715–6). That Valentine is able to reconcile her dual heritage explains why she is able to guide Christopher so he can reconcile his dual heritage, completing the archetypal quest.

Because Christ-opher brings a new life to Valentine by pursuing her image through death to rebirth, the movement of the immense novel is from adolescence to manhood, war to peace, slavery to freedom, paganism to Christianity, sin to redemptive grace, death to life. Thus the battlefield is not simply France during World War I but the symbolic landscape every man must cross on his journey from the dark woods to the sunlit garden.

The literature of our time may be sounding the death knell for our sick civilization, but Ford's immense novel gives an affirmative answer to the question posed in *The Waste Land:* "Shall I at least set my lands in order?" And since "Ford's art breathes life into the ancient political truth that the state is the soul writ large and the self is the republic in microcosm," [41] *Parade's End* shows the way to rebirth for a dying civilization. The Armistice is sounded when men, standing erect in their freedom, throw off the yoke of neurotic bitches and intriguing cowards, who, themselves emasculated, would emasculate those who still believe in responsibility to life. The political dimension cannot be divorced from the spiritual, for *Parade's End* also breathes life into the ancient spiritual truth that since the way down is the way up a man must descend into himself to rediscover his roots before he can stand up in harmony with his soul. "You must give up being a Christist," Ford wrote to Anthony Bertram in a letter of October 15, 1935, "and become a Christian or something else that is fierce and bitter as Christians have to be. Christianity isn't you know a Sunday supper with the maids given the evening off; it is eating flesh and drinking blood." [42]

Pursuing the image, which for Conrad reveals "the stress and passion within the core of each convincing moment" of life, Ford reveals the Passion. The single center that redeems in this imaginative world is the Incarnation, Which makes possible the sacramental experience. *Parade's End* can be divided into six units, the second three inverting and reversing the first three: the train ride between an originating station and a terminus; Tietjens's divorce from Sylvia, in the forest; the descent to dead center; the ascent to new center; Christopher's reunion with Valentine, in the garden; the revelation of God, eternity, infinity. Within this design antithetical allusions, images, and motifs such as Astarte and Alcestis, Venus and Mary, Saturnalia and Lent, the moon and the star, the positioning on stairways mark off the novel's movement. Ford's method is to penetrate the surface with narrative techniques, narrowing the range of the experience until it bursts open, revealing its core. At the novel's dead center, Sylvia remembers whipping a white bulldog in winter. Blood vessels exposed, it crawled under an euonymus bush to die. Since an euonymus bush bears crimson or rose-

colored capsules which on opening disclose the seed, we
have in this image, narrated from Sylvia's point of view,
the essence of the novel: from death emerges life.

The first half of the tetralogy, then, a movement
toward death, creates the second half, a movement toward
life. The counterpart to the whipping of the bulldog is the
sacramental union in *The Last Post*. "Like a dejected bulldog" (835), Christopher walks away from Valentine when
she starts to abuse him for failing to provide for his family.
Her concern, however, is for the child in her womb, and
her response to his turning away is to weep until Mark,
answering her sob—" 'How are we to live? How are we
ever to live?' "—elects to speak: " 'Did you ever hear tell o'
t' Yorkshireman. . . . On Mount Ara . . . Ara . . .' "
(835). Fittingly, it is Mark who, although refusing to move,
as a witness to the new life of his brother and Valentine
perceives that "the great night is itself eternity and the
Infinite. . . . The spirit of God walking on the firmament" (829). " ' 'Twas the mid o' the night and the barnies
grat / And the mither beneath the mauld heard that' "
(835), he whispers to her just after he alludes to Genesis
and just before he dies. Out of the crumbling of the values and virtues of the Christian tradition in *The Inheritors*
comes the rebirth of the Christian myth in *Parade's End*.

3.

The Old God in a New World

In the concluding chapter of her study of Conrad's political novels, Miss Rosenfield summarizes the society mirrored in twentieth-century fiction: "Cut off from the past, obsessed by the physical fact of time rather than comforted by the recognition of traditional values that are timeless, today's man lives in a secularized world which has lost its sense of community and identity. The growing desire for the analysis of experience, the emphasis on accumulation of wealth, the gradual diminution of the hierarchical structure of society—all these have augmented the oppressive senses of personal isolation. Even intense loneliness can no longer be shared. The hell described by religion has, indeed, become a hell within, a private inferno of titanic discontent." By means of allusions, images, and motifs from traditional myth, the twentieth-century novel reveals our society as a parody of "a stable and socially oriented past." By giving "our colossal nightmares ritual form by their narratives," twentieth-century novelists create the

" 'myths' of a profane civilization." [1] I agree with Miss Rosenfield—it would be difficult not to—yet I think Conrad's fiction also prepares the groundwork for the restoration of the tradition from which Western man derives his values by preparing the groundwork for the rebirth of the Christian myth in Ford's fiction, though a Christian myth made new for our profane civilization. [2]

The Christian tradition comes to a dead end in *The Inheritors* because Granger never descends into himself to discover the center of the tradition. He never discovers the slain and resurrected god within himself. Rather than sacrifice his hope of reward from his sister, he sacrifices "the institutions which hold us to the past, that are our guarantees for the future" (V.184). By severing himself from his heritage in an attempt to join her beyond the horizon of Canterbury Cathedral, he forfeits his future. Bracing himself to the shock of love he had known, "that all men had known; but greater, transcendental, almost terrible, a fit reward for the sacrifice of a whole past," he suddenly feels "the shock of an unknown emotion made up of fear and of enthusiasm, as though she had been not a woman but only a voice crying strange, unknown words in inspiring tones, promising and cruel, without any passion of love or hate. I listened. It was like the wind in the trees of a little wood. No hate . . . no love. No love" (V.192–3). The Fourth Dimensionist's prophecy is fulfilled: Western man's values and virtues have become diseases in the person of her brother, whose aspirations have so enervated him that he is "a ghost in a bottomless cleft between the past and the to come" (V.209). *The Inheritors* is truly circular, for the old God toppled in the opening scene and betrayed by Granger cannot come to life in the future until the Son is brought to life in the present.

Conrad and Ford share the same premise: the old God is dead and since science and materialism fail to give a satisfying new One, Western man, cut off from his past, is an abandoned derelict in a universe which, constantly stirring his surviving primitive religious instinct, invites him to uncover the mystery behind the veil of the visible world. Hence the archetypal pattern of the myth of the hero as organizing principle in their fiction serves a twofold purpose: it reveals, as Miss Rosenfield concludes, that our society is a parody of a stable and socially oriented past, but it also allows the hero to unearth the center of his tradition in the slain and resurrected god. By discovering the center, both novelists can then demonstrate that the archetypal pattern with its stages of separation, initiation and return mirrors the cycle by which a tradition no longer meaningful must be slain to be resurrected. That is, each novelist reworks the material of *The Inheritors* in his later fiction, utilizing the archetypal quest not only as an organizing principle upon which to structure his narratives but as a metaphor for the cultural quest that can revitalize the dead God, the tradition, by resurrecting the slain Son.

A fundamental difference between the two men is that although both begin with the premise that the tradition is moribund in the modern world, Conrad slays Christianity as a salvation scheme, Ford slays only a fixed form of Christianity. For Conrad the first stage of the tripartite archetypal quest is a separation from the dead tradition, a slaying of the old God as a divine plan in which man should place his hope for salvation. "The absurd oriental fable" from which Christianity starts "irritates me," Conrad wrote to Garnett. "Great, improving, softening, compassionate it may be but it has lent itself with amazing facility to cruel distortion and is the only religion which, with its impossible standards, has brought an infinity of

anguish to innumerable souls—on this earth." [3] It is only
when the Conradian hero renounces his hope for a paradise beyond the horizon that he can discover his roots on
earth. It is only when he sheds the illusion that he is destined for a supernatural end that he can discover himself
as a man. To Marguerite Poradowska Conrad wrote that
"one becomes useful only on realizing the utter insignifi-
cance of the individual in the scheme of the universe.
When one well understands that in oneself one is nothing
and that a man is worth neither more nor less than the
work he accomplishes with honesty of purpose and means,
and within the strict limits of his duty towards society,
only then is one the master of his conscience, with the
right to call himself a man." [4] It is only when he discards
"the ethical view of the universe," a view which, as the
novelist explains in *A Personal Record*, "involves us at
last in so many cruel and absurd contradictions . . . that
I have come to suspect that the aim of creation cannot be
ethical at all," that he can satisfy his surviving primitive
religious instinct. "I would fondly believe," Conrad continues in *A Personal Record*, that the object of creation is
"purely spectacular: a spectacle for awe, love, adoration,
or hate, if you like, but in this view—and in this view
alone—never for despair!" (VI.92) Never for despair because, even though disinherited, by accepting his roots as
a man on earth, he gains the knowledge with which he can
comfort his fears of death: all men are creatures of mud,
destined to live and die on earth.

Stripped of Western man's traditional supports, the
Conradian hero descends into the abyss of his interior, answering the invitation to confront the mystery behind the
veil within himself. The guiding power on the journey is
the heroine, before whose unveiled eyes he sees himself
in all his actuality and potentiality. Here we encounter the

first of many paradoxes in Conrad's imaginative world. The hero must journey into his heart of darkness, a journey which deflates his illusion that he is a supernatural being with nothing in common with the rest of mankind, before he can turn about to respond to another human being, but once he turns about he becomes a rescuer. Confronting the death within himself, one aspect of the concealed center, the common bond uniting mankind, he discovers the life within himself, the other aspect of the center. Accepting his marriage to death and his nature, he accepts his marriage to the female. In short, by accepting the knowledge that he is an abandoned derelict in what seems to be an indifferent universe, he can redeem his personal past by responding to another abandoned derelict on the terrain of Africa, Patusan, Costaguana, London, Geneva, or Samburan.

Just as Granger becomes the center of his world by betraying life, so do Lord Jim, Nostromo, Verloc, Razumov, and Heyst become the center of their world by either rejecting or accepting the life offered them. It may be that by passing their ordeals, Razumov and Heyst become Christ-like. Certainly there is the suggestion that the former is bathed in grace when, after being " 'washed clean,' " he goes to his public atonement and that the latter becomes a redeemer when he atones for Lena's deception, but Conrad does not pursue the suggestion. Nor does he pursue the suggestion that the heroine, a nineteenth-century Beatrice, is a figure of the Virgin Mary, since the intention of his art is to awaken in the reader "that pagan residuum of awe and wonder which lurks still at the bottom of our old humanity." What he does, however, is reestablish the basis for a myth grounded in the human concrete. It is the discovery of the region of timelessness within themselves which enable Razumov and Heyst to respond to Natalia and Lena in the world of time, thereby saving themselves as well as the heroines. Thus by renouncing the "mere supernatural" to concentrate on mere man, Conrad sounds the depths for the discovery of the supernatural in man's nature.

If the return stage does not reintegrate society, it does reintegrate the hero's divided self. If he does not bring the Son to life, Conrad does recover the primordial images, the archetypes, especially the slain and resurrected god, that are the necessary constituents of myth. If he does not restore the Christian tradition, he does prepare the soil for "the advent of loving concord" in which Natalia believes. It remains for Ford to dramatize the conflict "soaked in blood, torn by struggles, watered with tears," from which the "heavenly flower" will spring.

Conrad's fiction pellucidly mirrors the chasm in modern man's psyche, but although the novelist fissures the surface, he does not push through the center to emerge on the other side. The one character in his fiction who cracks the earth asunder dies with a cryptic smile on his lips. Lord Jim is an enigma to Marlow as he is to the author, whose ambivalence toward him is a commonplace of literary criticism. And as the novelist leaves his Malayan phase, his style becomes less oblique, his attitude less ambivalent, his characters more recognizable. Nowhere does he shatter the surface: neither in his most ambitious canvas, *Nostromo,* nor in his most tightly controlled narrative, *The Secret Agent.* Nowhere does he sunder before he reconciles.

Events in the second decade of the twentieth century were moving to a crisis that would shatter the civilized world. In his Preface to the first edition of *Victory,* Conrad admits his misgivings about the choice of title for a novel written in time of peace but published after the outbreak of hostilities. He did not want to deceive the public "into the belief that the book had something to do with war." At the opening of the novel, Heyst is perched on his island, remote from the affairs of men, with a smoking volcano as his nearest neighbor. As the novel unfolds the rumbling of an approaching storm increases. The thunder ceases, however, when he looks into Lena's eyes. The tremors did not subside on the Continent. In the late summer of 1914, the volcano erupted. By that time, though, Conrad was fifty-six years old with his creative energy almost exhausted. Ten years later he was dead. In 1914 his collaborator was only forty. Young enough to be a combatant, Ford returned from the nightmare of the cataclysm to write *Parade's End*.

Ford takes Conrad one more step, making explicit what he only suggests. Before he brings the Son to life, he uncovers man's roots in the struggle between two conceptions of reality, two archetypal experiences, two myths, two traditions: a struggle which erupts in the holocaust known as World War I. In *The Good Soldier* John Dowell, frightened and bewildered by the collapse of the old order, searches desperately for a sense of permanence and stability. Not knowing what else to do, he constructs a psychologically satisfying explanation to account for the suicide of his idol, the passionate Edward Ashburnham, who killed himself while looking "up to the roof of the stable, as if he were looking to heaven. . . ." On the eve of the upheaval, Christopher Tietjens insists to Vincent Macmaster, who has been defending Rossetti's poetry, that war is inevitable and with England in the middle of it: " 'Simply because you fellows are such damn hypocrites. There's not a country in the world that trusts us. We're always, as it were, committing adultery—like your fellow! —with the name of Heaven on our lips' " (20). It would seem, then, that the lachrymose polygamy of the Edward Ashburnhams and the Vincent Macmasters of Edwardian England causes World War I, were it not for the fact that Tietjens is very much like Dowell. He too fails to cross the threshold. Taking his stand on monogamy and chastity, he finds permanence and stability in the Christian tradition as it was given form and meaning and consciousness in Dante's poetry, even though this tradition has been displaced by the pagan tradition as it is given form and meaning and consciousness in Rossetti's poetry. The irony, however, is that he has contributed to the death of the tradition as a vital force by clinging to a fixed form of Christianity, refusing to acknowledge that the ritual in which he places his faith is itself a variation on a much older ritual. He is therefore deracinated in a double sense: he is cut off from both his Christian and his pagan heritage.

Tietjens " 'wants . . . to play the part of Jesus Christ,' " Sylvia tells Perowne, but the Fordian hero cannot regain his Christian heritage until he renounces the permanence and stability to which he clings because the tradition must be made new in the modern world. He cannot be restored to the old God until he brings the Son to life, and he cannot bring Christ to life until he accepts the matrix of his Christian heritage: his pagan heritage. In the terms of the novel, the male's marriage to the female is a marriage to passion with its roots in mankind's buried past. Tietjens's irresolution with Sylvia is a denial of his union with the female, his marriage to death, his nature. Yet at the same time he experiences a burgeoning desire for Valentine. He represses this desire, though, because to accept passion is to accept his nature. Hence the outbreak of the war on August 4, 1914, the day the German army overran the Belgian frontier near Gemmenich, signals not only the end of the tradition on which Tietjens takes his stand but the eruption of the conflict within the hero himself.

The bombardment of the Continent mirrors the bombardment within Tietjens. Ford sunders before he reconciles: for him disintegration is necessary before there can be reintegration. One of the pivotal scenes in *Parade's End* is Tietjens's description to Sylvia of the effect on him of the death of the nurse, Beatrice Carmichael. This scene marks the separation stage, for it marks a dawning recognition that his mind, his bulwark against his wife's influence, has been shattered by the explosion which hospitalized him. Regaining his memory, he confronts himself in Macmaster, the twentieth-century Paolo. As he allows the past to bloom in his memory, he begins to accept his passion for Valentine, the twentieth-century Beatrice, the girl who confronts herself in Edith Ethel Duchemin, the twentieth-century Francesca. Admitting his civilization is doomed, he closes his account with the bank, resigns from the club, and accepts the talismanic passage.

Guided on his initiation by Sylvia's image, which appears "before him so extraordinarily bright and clear in the brown darkness" that he shudders (299), and by Valentine's image, which comes wriggling into his consciousness, he descends into "the bottom of our old humanity," in Rouen, there to accept his roots. Confronting the death within himself on the Western Front, he ascends the battle-scarred mound, on the top of which he discovers the life within himself. Resurrected from the mud, he saves the lives of Aranjuez and Duckett and is even ready to challenge Campion if he tries to remove him from command. To the general he says, " 'I am in command of this Battalion, sir. I am Tietjens, second-in-command. Now in command temporarily. I could not be found because I was buried. Temporarily' " (643).

"We come, then," opens the section on Dante in *The March of Literature*, "to one of those stupendous mornings of human thought that, appearing from time to time and at great intervals, restore to us, in the general drabness and imbecility of the world, some of the respect for humanity that otherwise we must surely and definitely lose. The *Divine Comedy* of Dante stands out above the welter of sadism and ferocity of its era as the Cathedral of Chartres stands out and watches over all the plains of France and as the more gay Cathedral of Amiens dominates those terrible witnesses of human ferocity and madness—the fields behind the Somme. . . ." [5] I think *Parade's End* is one of the twentieth-century works that restore to us our respect for humanity because Ford completes the archetypal pattern, re-creating the myth and reaffirming the tradition. The ferocity and madness that sweep across the fields behind the Somme announce not only the end of a fixed form of belief but the beginning of the Christian tradition made new in our era. The return stage in Ford's tetralogy is possible only because Tietjens reconciles his dual heritage by discovering the slain and resurrected god of his Christian heritage within himself. Realizing "feudalism was finished; its last vestiges were gone" (668) and renouncing the cloistered life in the seventeenth-century parsonage at Bemerton since he wants to live with Valentine, he descends the staircase to bring upstairs the heroine whose image drew him to the summit of the twentieth-century's most recognizable landscape, the woman who had to descend into her own hell before she could reconcile her dual heritage. Their reunion, which reconciles the past and the future in the present, is a figure of Western man's reunion with the old God in a new world. Just before he dies Mark Tietjens perceives that "the great night was itself eternity and the Infinite. . . . The spirit of God

walking on the firmament." " 'Groby Great Tree is down
. . .' " (835), are his last words to Valentine. He knows
the war ended his world, but as he watches Sylvia depart
from the cottage, he also knows his brother's marriage will
produce descendants "to carry on the country without
swank" (831). The tradition will fructify in the union of
Christ-opher and Valentine, whose offspring will inherit
the earth.

Conrad and Ford, like Joyce and Eliot, are typical of
the authors in the first half of this century who redefine
Western man's values and virtues to make them meaningful today. By taking us from a moribund tradition to a
realm of archetypes to a re-created myth, the two novelists force us to reexamine the ways in which our traditions
can be infused with life in the twentieth century. If we
understand the continuity of the Christian tradition and
its viability in our literature, it is in large measure the result of our understanding the achievement of artists like
Joseph Conrad and Ford Madox Ford. Their works are
so rooted in the tradition from which they take their inspiration that they illuminate the origins of our heritage
and the possible avenues future artists might choose to give
flesh to their inspiration. Their fiction gives form and
meaning and consciousness to the human concrete as we
experience it in our age, for though there is no communal
experience in these novels comparable to that of the age
of feudalism, there is a new beginning, mined from the
depths of the lonely quests of Razumov, Heyst, Valentine,
and Tietjens.

Notes

INTRODUCTION

1. *Letters of Ford Madox Ford,* ed. Richard M. Ludwig (Princeton, 1965), pp. 156–157.
2. *The Nature of a Crime* (London, 1924), p. 7.
3. *Ibid.,* pp. 12–13.
4. Jocelyn Baines, *Joseph Conrad: A Critical Biography* (New York, 1960), p. 214.
5. Paul L. Wiley, *Novelist of Three Worlds* (Syracuse, 1962), p. 139.
6. *Joseph Conrad: A Personal Remembrance* (Boston, 1924), pp. 7–33.
7. *Ancient Lights and Certain New Reflections* (London, 1911), p. xi.
8. All quotations from *The Inheritors* and *Romance* are taken from Conrad's *Complete Works,* Canterbury Edition, 26 vols. (Garden City, New York, 1924). These two novels are included in the collected edition of Conrad's fiction as volumes V and VII. Hereafter quotations will be cited in the text with the volume and the page in ( ).
9. *Joseph Conrad,* p. 141.
10. *The Hero with a Thousand Faces* (New York, 1949), p. 30.
11. *Ford Madox Ford* (New York, 1967), p. 26. See Wiley, *Novelist of Three Worlds,* p. 141.

12. Ford Madox Ford, *Return to Yesterday* (London, 1931), p. 199.
13. *The Nature of a Crime*, pp. 105–106.
14. *Ford Madox Ford: From Apprentice to Craftsman* (Middletown, 1964), p. 18, n. 18.
15. All quotations from *Ulysses* are taken from the Modern Library Edition, new ed., corrected and reset (New York, 1961).
16. *A Reader's Guide to James Joyce* (New York, 1959), p. 124.
17. *Joseph Conrad: Achievement and Decline* (Cambridge, Mass., 1957), p. 69.
18. *Ibid.,* p. 99.
19. For those who share Moser's view, see Albert J. Guerard, *Conrad the Novelist* (Cambridge, Mass., 1958), pp. 54–55 and 254–255; J. Hillis Miller, *Poets of Reality* (Cambridge, Mass., 1965), p. 30; and Claire Rosenfield, *Paradise of Snakes* (Chicago, 1967), p. 58. For dissenting voices, see Ted E. Boyle, *Symbol and Meaning in the Fiction of Joseph Conrad* (The Hague, 1965), pp. 82–83; Adam Gillon, *The Eternal Solitary* (New York, 1960), pp. 85–98; Leo Gurko, *Joseph Conrad: Giant in Exile* (New York, 1962), pp. 201–202; and Donald C. Yelton, *Mimesis and Metaphor* (The Hague, 1967), pp. 220–225. Another reading of the later novels, and a very important one, is given in Paul L. Wiley, *Conrad's Measure of Man* (Madison, 1954), especially Chapter IV, "The Knight: Man in Eden," pp. 132–198.
20. *Joseph Conrad: A Psychoanalytic Biography* (Princeton, 1967), pp. 47, 109, 217 *et passim*.
21. *Conrad: A Reassessment* (Cambridge, 1952), p. 107.
22. See M. C. Bradbrook, *Joseph Conrad: Poland's English Genius* (New York, 1965), p. 66, n. 1; Guerard, pp. 257–258 and 274–275; and Moser, pp. 133, 140–143, and 163. Two recent studies which correct these misreadings are Sharon Kaehele and Howard German, "Conrad's *Victory:* A Reassessment," *MFS*, X (Spring 1964), 55–72 and George F. Reinecke, "Conrad's *Victory:* Psychomachy, Christian Symbols, and Theme," in *Explorations of Literature,* ed. Rima Drell Reck (Baton Rouge, 1966), pp. 70–80.
23. Although I am obviously in agreement with much that Miss Rosenfield writes in her archetypal analysis of Conrad's political novels, *Paradise of Snakes* (Chicago, 1967), there are differences in our approaches and conclusions. For example, I place greater emphasis than she on the role of the heroine.
24. Campbell, *The Hero with a Thousand Faces*, p. 71.
25. The *Vita Nuova*, trans. William Anderson (Baltimore, 1964), p. 39.

26. Dorothy L. Sayers, "The Greater Images," in the *Commedia*, 3 vols. (New York, 1962), I, 67.

27. All quotations from the *Commedia* are taken from the translation by John D. Sinclair, 3 vols. (New York, 1961).

28. Beatrice Corrigan, "Introduction," in *Italian Poets and English Critics, 1755–1859: A Collection of Critical Essays* (Chicago, 1969), pp. 27–28. See also Werner P. Friederich, *Dante's Fame Abroad: 1350–1850* (Rome, 1950), pp. 181–339 and Paget Toynbee, *Dante in English Literature: From Chaucer to Cary*, 2 vols. (London, 1909).

29. *The March of Literature* (New York, 1938), p. 355.

30. *Ibid.,* pp. 358–360.

31. For the wearing of a veil as an act signifying incorporation into the sacred world, see Arnold van Gennep, *The Rites of Passage,* trans. Monika B. Vizedom and Gabrielle L. Caffee (Chicago, 1960), p. 168.

32. Ambrose Gordon, Jr., *The Invisible Tent* (Austin, 1964), p. 20.

33. John A. Meixner, *Ford Madox Ford's Novels* (Minneapolis, 1962), p. 121.

34. Richard A. Cassell, *Ford Madox Ford: A Study of His Novels* (Baltimore, 1962), p. 265. Cassell goes on to insist, though, that "Christopher cannot be divorced from the Christian tradition."

35. All quotations from Eliot's poems are taken from *Collected Poems: 1909–1962* (New York, 1963).

36. *Selected Essays,* 3rd ed., enl. (London, 1951), p. 430.

JOSEPH CONRAD

1. See Baines, p. 267; Richard Herndon, "The Genesis of Conrad's 'Amy Foster,' " *SP*, LVII (July 1960), 549–566; Gustav Morf, *The Polish Heritage of Joseph Conrad* (London, 1930), pp. 89–91; and Oliver Warner, *Joseph Conrad* (London, 1951), p. 147.

2. All quotations from Conrad's fiction are taken from the *Complete Works,* Canterbury Edition, 26 vols. (Garden City, New York, 1924). Hereafter quotations will be cited in the text with the volume and the page in ( ).

3. *A Reader's Guide to Joseph Conrad* (New York, 1960), p. 142.

4. Herndon, p. 550.

5. See Osborn Andreas, *Joseph Conrad: A Study in Non-Conformity* (New York, 1959), pp. 70–72; Gurko, pp. 210–212; Moser, pp. 86–87; and Walter F. Wright, *Romance and Tragedy in Joseph Conrad* (Lincoln, 1949), pp. 165–166.

6. Although he does not study the narrators, Guerard, pp. 49–50, reads the story as "a generalized comment on the lonely, uncomprehended, absurd human destiny. . . . Thus it is the human condition to be caught in a snare. . . ."

7. Letter of February 8, 1899, in Georges Jean Aubry, *Joseph Conrad: Life and Letters,* 2 vols. (Garden City, New York, 1927), I, 268.

8. Ford, *Joseph Conrad,* p. 140.

9. See letter of November 5, 1912, in *Letters from Joseph Conrad: 1895–1924,* ed. Edward Garnett (Indianapolis, 1928), p. 243.

10. See Introduction, n. 18.

11. Gurko, p. 67.

12. See Jerome Thale, "Marlow's Quest," *UTQ,* XXIV (July 1955), 351–358. Reprinted in *The Art of Joseph Conrad,* ed. R. W. Stallman (East Lansing, 1960), pp. 154–161.

13. See Stephen A. Reid, "The 'Unspeakable Rites' in *Heart of Darkness,*" *MFS,* IX (Winter 1963–1964), 347–356.

14. *Conrad's "Heart of Darkness" and the Critics,* ed. Bruce Harkness (Belmont, 1960), p. 163.

15. It is here that I part company with Donald C. Yelton, pp. 273–274, who writes that "there are many passages in Conrad in which this fissiparous quality of the self is hinted at by the device of the man who confronts his image in a mirror." I see in the twin-hills image a feminine landscape. For Yelton's analysis of *Lord Jim,* see n. 19.

16. According to Ford, *Joseph Conrad,* p. 213, Conrad tried for a short time to run into decasyllabic lines the paragraph containing Marlow's impression of the Negress' entrance—surely some indication of the vividness and concreteness of the passage for him.

17. Letter of May 31, 1902, in *Joseph Conrad: Letters to William Blackwood and David S. Meldrum,* ed. William Blackburn (Durham, 1958), p. 154.

18. See letter of May 19, 1900, in *Joseph Conrad: Letters to William Blackwood and David S. Meldrum,* p. 94.

19. For analyses of the image of the cleft mountain in *Lord Jim,* see Dorothy Van Ghent, *The English Novel* (New York, 1953), pp. 229–244 and Yelton, pp. 225–239.

20. Elliott B. Gose, Jr., "Pure Exercise of Imagination: Archetypal Symbolism in *Lord Jim,*" *PMLA,* LXXIX (March 1964), 146, writes, "Even at the end he could still admit his responsibility by affirming his love for Jewel as a human being."

21. See Tony Tanner, *Conrad: "Lord Jim,"* Studies in English Literature, No. 12 (London, 1963), p. 55.
22. For the Biblical reference implicit in the phrase, see Dudley Flamm, "The Ambiguous Nazarene in *Lord Jim,*" *ELT*, XI (1968), 35–37.
23. For the original name, see the letter of July 10, 1896, in *Letters from Joseph Conrad: 1895–1924*, p. 61.
24. Of the works not analyzed in this study, there are allusions to Dante or the *Inferno* in "Autocracy and War" (III.87), "To-morrow" (XX.276), and "The Warrior's Soul" (XXVI.1). Baines, pp. 19–20, cites a letter from Apollo Korzeniowski to his cousins, in which he alludes to what Dante did not describe, as an instance of Conrad's father's morbid religiosity. For Conrad's debt to the *Inferno* in "Heart of Darkness," see Robert O. Evans, "Conrad's Underworld," *MFS*, II (May 1956), 56–62, reprinted in *The Art of Joseph Conrad*, pp. 171–178. But see E. H. Visiak, *The Mirror of Conrad* (London, 1955), p. 129: "This is not to say, however, that Doña Rita [the original of Rita de Lastaola of *The Arrow of Gold*] inspired Conrad's work in the manner that Beatrice inspired Dante."
25. Letter of March 7, 1923, to Ernst Bendz, in Aubry, *Joseph Conrad: Life and Letters*, II, 296.
26. Jackson W. Heimer, "Betrayal, Confession, Attempted Redemption, and Punishment in *Nostromo,*" *TSLL*, VIII (Winter 1967), 561–579, sees Dr. Monygham redeeming himself through his love for Emilia.
27. *Craft and Character* (New York, 1957), p. 166.
28. *Politics and the Novel* (New York, 1957), p. 111.
29. For the best single statement of Conrad's method, see Marvin Mudrick, "The Originality of Conrad," *HR*, XI (Winter 1958–1959), 545–553. Reprinted in *Conrad: A Collection of Critical Essays*, ed. Marvin Mudrick (Englewood Cliffs, 1966), pp. 37–44.
30. For the importance of the interview scenes in the structure of the novel, see John Hagan, Jr., "The Design of Conrad's *The Secret Agent,*" *ELH*, XXII (June 1955), 148–164.
31. Rosenfield, p. 156.
32. *Conrad's Politics* (Baltimore, 1967), p. 240.
33. Sharon Kachele and Howard German, "Conrad's *Victory*: A Reassessment," *MFS*, X (Spring 1964), p. 55. See also Karl, pp. 246–267.
34. Meyer, p. 352.
35. Karl, p. 88.

36. Letter of March 23, 1896, in *Letters from Joseph Conrad: 1895–1924*, p. 46.

37. Letter of March 5, 1892, in *Letters of Joseph Conrad to Marguerite Poradowska: 1890–1920*, trans. and ed. John A. Gee and Paul J. Sturm (New Haven, 1940), p. 42.

38. Miss Rosenfield, p. 55, sees an identification between Emilia's benevolence and "that of the mother of Christ."

39. Letter of October 28, 1895, in Aubry, *Joseph Conrad: Life and Letters*, I, 183.

40. C. G. Jung, *Symbols of Transformation*, trans. R. F. C. Hull, 2 vols. (New York, 1962), II, 408.

41. R. W. Stallman, "Time and *The Secret Agent*," *TSLL*, I (Spring 1959), 101–122, reprinted in *The Art of Joseph Conrad*, pp. 234–254; Miller, pp. 13–67; Boyle, pp. 186–194.

42. Guerard, pp. 225–229.

43. Rosenfield, pp. 103–107.

44. Any attempt to make Conrad a Christian writer should first take into account the Oriental influence on him. See William Bysshe Stein, "*Heart of Darkness*: Bodhisattva Scenario," *Orient / West*, IX (September–October 1964), 37–46; "Conrad's East: Time, History, Action, and *Maya*," *TSLL*, VII (Autumn 1965), 265–283; "*Almayer's Folly*: The Terrors of Time." *Conradiana*, I (Summer 1968), 27–34; and "The Eastern Matrix of Conrad's Art," *Conradiana*, I (Fall 1968), 1–14. Analyzing "Heart of Darkness," Robert F. Haugh, *Joseph Conrad: Discovery in Design* (Norman, 1957), pp. 38 and 55, writes that "Kurtz has become pre-Christian, primal energy, demiurge," that the knowledge gained in the interior is "a pre-Christian knowledge." Of all the critics Wright, p. 50, gives what is perhaps the most reasonable evaluation: "Conrad objected to Tolstoy for making the Christian religion his basis; yet he himself not infrequently arrived at a resolution of a paradox in accord with Christian sentiments."

45. The well-known letters of December 22, 1902, and February 23, 1914, in *Letters from Joseph Conrad: 1895–1924*, pp. 185 and 245 must be set against such lesser known ones as that of March 5, 1892, in *Letters of Joseph Conrad to Marguerite Poradowska: 1890–1920*, p. 42 and that of October 8, 1923, quoted in Eloise Knapp Hay, *The Political Novels of Joseph Conrad* (Chicago, 1963), pp. 192–193, n. 79. For Meyer, p. 351, Conrad's statement in his letter of February 23, 1914, "was but one side of a coin, for in his fictional writings it requires little discernment to discover powerful and poignant overtones of a deep and abiding devotion to that early Catholic faith." In his study of the re-

lationship between Conrad's letters and short fiction, Edward W. Said, *Joseph Conrad and the Fiction of Autobiography* (Cambridge, Mass., 1966), p. 15, finds that World War I marks in both letters and fiction a "general shift in attitude—from an outright belief in hell to a willing faith in purgatory."

46. *Joseph Conrad's Mind and Method* (New York, 1964), p. 246.

FORD MADOX FORD

1. *A Good Soldier* (Davis, 1963), p. 23.
2. All quotations from Ford's fiction are taken from *The Young Lovell* (London, 1913), *The Good Soldier* (New York, 1951), and *Parade's End* (New York, 1961). Hereafter quotations will be cited in the text with the page in (   ).
3. "Criticism and the Semiosis of *The Good Soldier*," *MFS*, IX (Spring 1963), 48.
4. *The Poems*, ed. Kenneth Allott (New York, 1965).
5. Dedicatory letter to Stella Ford, in *The Good Soldier*, p. xx.
6. Patricia McFate and Bruce Golden, "*The Good Soldier*: A Tragedy of Self-Deception," *MFS*, IX (Spring 1963), 58. They discuss Ford's revisions, 55–57, as does Charles G. Hoffmann, "Ford's Manuscript Revisions of *The Good Soldier*," *ELT*, IX (1966), 145–152.
7. Elliott B. Gose, Jr., "The Strange Irregular Rhythm: An Analysis of *The Good Soldier*," *PMLA*, LXXII (June 1957), 495.
8. Cf. the concluding three lines of "Dover Beach": "And we are here as on a darkling plain / Swept with confused alarms of struggle and flight / Where ignorant armies clash by night."
9. For Mark Schorer, "An Interpretation," in *The Good Soldier*, p. xi, this is Dowell's "weirdest absurdity, the final, total blindness of infatuation, and self-infatuation."
10. For a very thorough analysis of the dual function of the animal imagery in the novel, see Jo-Ann Baernstein, "Image, Identity, and Insight in *The Good Soldier*," *Critique*, IX, 1, 19–42.
11. "The Epistemology of *The Good Soldier*," *SR*, LXIX (Spring 1961), 225–235.
12. See James Hafley, "The Moral Structure of 'The Good Soldier,'" *MFS*, V (Summer 1959), 121–128 and Wiley, *Novelist of Three Worlds*, p. 200.
13. All quotations from the Bible are taken from the Douay Version of the Old Testament; the Confraternity Edition of the New Testament (New York, 1950).

14. James Trammell Cox, "The Finest French Novel in the English Language," *MFS*, IX (Spring 1963), 82.
15. Meixner, p. 85.
16. There are allusions to *Gulliver's Travels* in *Parade's End*, pp. 574 and 620. For Ford's opinion of Swift, see *The English Novel* (Philadelphia, 1929), pp. 91–93 and 107–108 and *The March of Literature*, pp. 488, 600–603, and 609–611. Todd K. Bender, "The Sad Tale of Dowell: Ford Madox Ford's 'The Good Soldier,'" *Criticism*, IV (Fall 1962), 364, makes a passing reference to the kind of narrator that Dowell is not, the unimaginative Gulliver, for example.
17. The two quotations in this chapter from *Gulliver's Travels* are taken from *The Prose Works*, ed. Herbert Davis, 13 vols., XI, Introduction by Harold Williams (Oxford, 1941).
18. Reminiscing about his and Conrad's search for the New Form, Ford writes in *Thus to Revisit* (New York, 1921), p. 44, that they agreed that "the whole novel was to be an exhaustion of aspects, was to proceed to one culmination, to reveal once and for all, in the last sentence, or the penultimate; in the last phrase, or the one before it—the psychological significance of the whole."
19. See James Trammell Cox, "Ford's 'Passion for Provence,'" *ELH*, XXVIII (December 1961), 383–398. Discussing the relevance of the two words in the epigraph, Miss Ohmann, p. 111, writes that "in choosing them, Ford has indicated the controlling design of his novel. His protagonists all refused to face the fact of their own human nature but pursued instead an impossible standard of innocence. It was precisely because they tried too far to walk in the way of honor that they were neither blessed nor stainless."
20. Robert J. Ray, "Style in *The Good Soldier*," *MFS*, IX (Spring 1963), 61–66, shows how Dowell's language exhibits certainty when describing the objective environment but uncertainty when describing human action.
21. For the presence of Aphrodite in *The Good Soldier*, see Thomas A. Hanzo, "Downward to Darkness," *SR*, LXXIV (Autumn 1966), 832–855.
22. *Rossetti* (New York, 1902), p. 189.
23. See *Rossetti*, pp. 164–169 and *The March of Literature*, p. 774. For a short discussion of Ford's criticism of Pre-Raphaelitism, see Cassell, pp. 11–19.
24. The *Vita Nuova*, p. 110.
25. *The Masks of God* (New York, 1959), p. 143.

26. *Ibid.*, p. 368.
27. *Poems, Ballads and Sonnets,* ed. Paull Franklin Baum (Garden City, New York, 1937).
28. C. Lattey, S.J., "Jeremias," in *A Catholic Commentary on Holy Scripture,* ed. Dom Bernard Orchard *et al.* (New York, 1953), p. 584.
29. What Ford added to the facts which supplied the germ for this scene gives us an insight into the design of the novel. For his summary of the hospital experience, see his letter of September 6, 1916, to Conrad, in *Letters,* p. 74. For his account of Arthur Marwood's amusing himself by reading the Encyclopaedia Britannica, see *It Was the Nightingale* (Philadelphia, 1933), p. 208. Marwood, the friend with whom Ford founded the *English Review,* is in some respects the model for Christopher Tietjens. He died in 1917.
30. *The Poetical Works,* ed. William Michael Rossetti (London, 1908).
31. See *It Was the Nightingale,* p. 208.
32. *A Good Soldier,* p. 4. Equally provocative is Ambrose Gordon, Jr., *The Invisible Tent,* pp. 66–85.
33. Miss Ohmann, p. 121, writes, "Strictly speaking, the whole tetralogy to this point has prepared for this chapter, just as the chapter in turn prepares for the rest of the tetralogy."
34. See Don Cameron Allen, "Vaughan's 'Cock-Crowing' and the Tradition," *ELH,* XXI (June 1954), 94–106; Charles Dahlberg, "Chaucer's Cock and Fox," *JEGP,* LIII (July 1954), 277–290; Mortimer J. Donovan, "The 'Moralite' of the Nun's Priest's Sermon," *JEGP,* LII (October 1953), 498–508; and Bernard S. Levy and George R. Adams, "Chauntecleer's Paradise Lost and Regained," *Mediaeval Studies,* XXIX (1967), 178–192.
35. *Elizabethan Lyrics,* ed. Norman Ault, 2nd ed. (New York, 1928).
36. *The Works,* ed. F. E. Hutchinson (Oxford, 1959).
37. According to a letter of November 27, 1931, to Percival Hinton, in *Letters,* p. 204, Ford judged *The Good Soldier* his best book technically "unless you read the Tietjens books as one novel in which case the whole design appears."
38. It is interesting to compare this scene with the description of the temple of Venus in Chaucer's *The Parliament of Fowls,* lines 246–287, in *The Works,* ed. F. N. Robinson, 2nd ed. (Boston, 1957): "Hyre gilte heres with a golden thred / Ibounden . . . / And naked from the brest unto the hed / . . . / The remenaunt . . . wel kevered . . . / Ryght with a subtyl coverchef" lies the goddess "in a prive corner" with "hire porter Richesse."

For Ford's analysis of Chaucer's greatness, see *The March of Literature*, pp. 351 and 406–422.

39. *The Bodley Head Ford Madox Ford*, III (London, 1963), p. 5. Meixner, pp. 217–218, sums up the evidence from Ford's writings for considering *Parade's End* a trilogy or a tetralogy. The strongest evidence that Ford wanted it to be read as a trilogy is his letter of August 17, 1930, to Eric Pinker, in *Letters*, pp. 196–197.

40. *Tannhäuser*, ed. and trans. Natalia MacFarren (New York, n. d.). Italics indicate stage directions.

41. E. V. Walter, "The Political Sense of Ford Madox Ford," *New Republic*, CXXXIV (March 26, 1956), 17.

42. *Letters*, pp. 245–246.

THE OLD GOD IN A NEW WORLD

1. Rosenfield, pp. 173–176.

2. In a totally different context, Miller, pp. 5–7, sees Conrad as pointing the way for the poets of the twentieth century: "Conrad's work does not yet turn the malign into the benign, but it leads to a reversal which prepares for the daylight of later literature."

3. Letter of February 23, 1914, in *Letters from Joseph Conrad: 1895–1924*, p. 245.

4. Letter of September 4, 1892, in *Letters of Joseph Conrad to Marguerite Poradowska: 1890–1920*, pp. 45–46.

5. *The March of Literature*, p. 355.

Selected Bibliography

Alighieri, Dante. The *Commedia.* Translated by John D.
Sinclair. 3 vols.: the *Inferno,* the *Purgatorio,* and the
Paradiso. New York: Oxford University Press, 1961.
———. The *Vita Nuova.* Translated by William Anderson.
Baltimore: Penguin Books, 1964.
Allen, Don Cameron. "Vaughan's 'Cock-Crowing' and the
Tradition," *ELH,* XXI (June 1954), 94–106.
Allen, Jerry. *The Sea Years of Joseph Conrad.* Garden
City, New York: Doubleday, 1965.
———. *The Thunder and the Sunshine: A Biography of
Joseph Conrad.* New York: G. P. Putnam's Sons, 1958.
Andreas, Osborn. *Joseph Conrad: A Study in Non-Con-
formity.* New York: Philosophical Library, 1959.
Arnold, Matthew. *The Poems,* ed. Kenneth Allott. New
York: Barnes and Noble, 1965.
Aubry, Georges Jean. *Joseph Conrad: Life and Letters.* 2
vols. Garden City, New York: Doubleday, Page, 1927.
———. *The Sea Dreamer: A Definitive Biography of Jo-
seph Conrad.* Translated by Helen Sebba. Garden City,
New York: Doubleday, 1957.

Baernstein, Jo-Ann. "Image, Identity, and Insight in *The Good Soldier*," *Critique*, IX, 1, 19–42.

Baines, Jocelyn. *Joseph Conrad: A Critical Biography*. New York: McGraw-Hill, 1960.

Bancroft, William W. *Joseph Conrad: His Philosophy of Life*. New York: Haskell House, 1964.

Beach, Joseph Warren. *The Twentieth Century Novel*. New York: Appleton-Century-Crofts, 1932.

Bender, Todd K. "The Sad Tale of Dowell: Ford Madox Ford's 'The Good Soldier,'" *Criticism*, IV (Fall 1962), 353–368.

Bergonzi, Bernard. *Heroes' Twilight: A Study of the Literature of the Great War*. New York: Coward-McCann, 1966.

The Holy Bible. The Douay Version of the Old Testament; the Confraternity Edition of the New Testament. New York: P. J. Kenedy and Sons, 1950.

Bort, Barry D. *"The Good Soldier:* Comedy or Tragedy?" *TCL*, XII (January 1967), 194–202.

Boyle, Ted E. *Symbol and Meaning in the Fiction of Joseph Conrad*. The Hague: Mouton, 1965.

Bradbrook, M. C. *Joseph Conrad: Poland's English Genius*. New York: Russell and Russell, 1965.

Braybrooke, Neville. "The Walrus and the Windmill," *SR*, LXXIV (Autumn 1966), 810–831.

Campbell, Joseph. *The Hero with a Thousand Faces*. Bollingen Series. No. XVII. New York: Pantheon Books, 1949.

———. *The Masks of God: Primitive Mythology*. New York: Viking, 1959.

Cassell, Richard A. *Ford Madox Ford: A Study of His Novels*. Baltimore: Johns Hopkins Press, 1962.

Chaucer, Geoffrey. *The Works,* ed. F. N. Robinson. 2nd ed. Boston: Houghton Mifflin, 1957.

Conrad, Jessie. *Joseph Conrad and His Circle*. New York: E. P. Dutton, 1935.

——. *Joseph Conrad as I Knew Him*. Garden City, New York: Doubleday, Page, 1926.

Conrad, Joseph. *Complete Works*. Canterbury Edition. 26 vols. Garden City, New York: Doubleday, Page, 1924.

——. *Conrad to a Friend: 150 Selected Letters from Joseph Conrad to Richard Curle*, ed. Richard Curle. Garden City, New York: Doubleday, Doran, 1928.

——. *Conrad's Polish Background: Letters to and from Polish Friends*, ed. Zdzislaw Najder. Translated by Halina Carroll. London: Oxford University Press, 1964.

——. *Letters from Joseph Conrad: 1895–1924*, ed. Edward Garnett. Indianapolis: Bobbs-Merrill, 1928.

——. *Letters of Joseph Conrad to Marguerite Poradowska: 1890–1920*. Translated from the French and ed. John A. Gee and Paul J. Sturm. New Haven: Yale University Press, 1940.

——. *Joseph Conrad: Letters to William Blackwood and David S. Meldrum*, ed. William Blackburn. Durham: Duke University Press, 1958.

Conrad, Joseph and Ford Madox Ford (Hueffer). *The Nature of a Crime*. London: Duckworth and Company, 1924.

Corrigan, Beatrice, ed. *Italian Poets and English Critics, 1755–1859: A Collection of Critical Essays*. Chicago: University of Chicago Press, 1969.

Cox, James Trammell. "The Finest French Novel in the English Language," *MFS*, IX (Spring 1963), 79–93.

——. "Ford's 'Passion for Provence,'" *ELH*, XXVIII (December 1961), 383–398.

Crankshaw, Edward. *Joseph Conrad: Some Aspects of the Art of the Novel*. New York: Russell and Russell, 1963.

Curle, Richard. *Joseph Conrad and His Characters*. Fair Lawn: Essential Books, 1958.

——. *The Last Twelve Years of Joseph Conrad*. Garden City, New York: Doubleday, Doran, 1928.

Dahlberg, Charles. "Chaucer's Cock and Fox," *JEGP*, LIII (July 1954), 277–290.

Davis, Harold E. "Conrad's Revisions of *The Secret Agent:* A Study in Literary Impressionism," *MLQ*, XIX (September 1958), 244–254.

Donovan, Mortimer J. "The 'Moralite' of the Nun's Priest's Sermon," *JEGP*, LII (October 1953), 498–508.

Eliot, T. S. *Collected Poems: 1909–1962.* New York: Harcourt, Brace and World, 1963.

———. *Selected Essays.* 3rd ed., enl. London: Faber and Faber, 1951.

Elizabethan Lyrics, ed. Norman Ault. 2nd ed. New York: Longmans, Green, 1928.

Evans, Robert O. "Conrad's Underworld," *MFS*, II (May 1956), 56–62.

Firebaugh, Joseph J. "Tietjens and the Tradition," *Pacific Spectator*, VI (Winter 1952), 23–32.

Flamm, Dudley. "The Ambiguous Nazarene in *Lord Jim,*" *ELT*, XI (1968), 35–37.

Fleishman, Avrom. *Conrad's Politics.* Baltimore: Johns Hopkins Press, 1967.

Follett, Wilson. *Joseph Conrad: A Short Study.* . . . Garden City, New York: Doubleday, Page, 1915.

Ford (Hueffer), Ford Madox. *Ancient Lights and Certain New Reflections.* London: Chapman and Hall, 1911.

———. *Joseph Conrad: A Personal Remembrance.* Boston: Little, Brown, 1924.

———. *The English Novel: From the Earliest Days to the Death of Joseph Conrad.* Philadelphia: J. B. Lippincott, 1929.

———. *The Good Soldier: A Tale of Passion.* New York: Alfred A. Knopf, 1951.

———. *It Was the Nightingale.* Philadelphia: J. B. Lippincott, 1933.

———. *Letters of Ford Madox Ford,* ed. Richard M. Ludwig. Princeton: Princeton University Press, 1965.

————. *The March of Literature: From Confucius' Day to Our Own*. New York: Dial, 1938.

————. *Parade's End*. New York: Alfred A. Knopf, 1961.

————. *Return to Yesterday: Reminiscences, 1894–1914*. London: Victor Gollancz, 1931.

————. *Rossetti: A Critical Essay on His Art*. New York: E. P. Dutton, 1902.

————. *Thus to Revisit: Some Reminiscences*. New York: E. P. Dutton, 1921.

————. *The Young Lovell: A Romance*. London: Chatto and Windus, 1913.

Friederich, Werner P. *Dante's Fame Abroad: 1350–1850*. Rome: Edizioni di Storia e Letteratura, 1950.

Gillon, Adam. *The Eternal Solitary: A Study of Joseph Conrad*. New York: Bookman, 1960.

Goldring, Douglas. *South Lodge: Reminiscences of Violet Hunt, Ford Madox Ford and the English Review Circle*. London: Constable, 1943.

————. *Trained for Genius: The Life and Writings of Ford Madox Ford*. New York: E. P. Dutton, 1949.

Gordan, John D. *Joseph Conrad: The Making of a Novelist*. Cambridge, Mass.: Harvard University Press, 1940.

Gordon, Ambrose, Jr. *The Invisible Tent: The War Novels of Ford Madox Ford*. Austin: University of Texas Press, 1964.

Gordon, Caroline. "The Elephant," *SR*, LXXIV (Autumn 1966), 856–871.

————. *A Good Soldier: A Key to the Novels of Ford Madox Ford*. Davis: University of California Library, 1963.

Gose, Elliott B., Jr. "'Cruel Devourer of the World's Light': *The Secret Agent*," *NCF*, XV (June 1960), 39–51.

————. "Pure Exercise of Imagination: Archetypal Symbolism in *Lord Jim*," *PMLA*, LXXIX (March 1964), 137–147.

————. "The Strange Irregular Rhythm: An Analysis of *The Good Soldier*," *PMLA*, LXXII (June 1957), 494–509.

Graves, Robert. *The White Goddess*. Amended and enl. ed. New York: Noonday, 1966.

Greene, Graham. Introduction to *The Bodley Head Ford Madox Ford*, III. London: The Bodley Head, 1963.

Guerard, Albert J. *Conrad the Novelist*. Cambridge, Mass.: Harvard University Press, 1958.

Guetti, James. *The Limits of Metaphor*. Ithaca: Cornell University Press, 1967.

Gurko, Leo. *Joseph Conrad: Giant in Exile*. New York: Macmillan, 1962.

Hafley, James. "The Moral Structure of 'The Good Soldier,' " *MFS*, V (Summer 1959), 121–128.

Hagan, John, Jr. "Conrad's *Under Western Eyes*: The Question of Razumov's 'Guilt' and 'Remorse,' " forthcoming in *Studies in the Novel*.

————. "The Design of Conrad's *The Secret Agent*," *ELH*, XXII (June 1955), 148–164.

Hanzo, Thomas A. "Downward to Darkness," *SR*, LXXIV (Autumn 1966), 832–855.

Harkness, Bruce, ed. *Conrad's "Heart of Darkness" and the Critics*. Belmont: Wadsworth, 1960.

————, ed. *Conrad's "Secret Sharer" and the Critics*. Belmont: Wadsworth, 1962.

Harvey, David Dow. *Ford Madox Ford, 1873–1939: A Bibliography of Works and Criticism*. Princeton: Princeton University Press, 1962.

Haugh, Robert F. *Joseph Conrad: Discovery in Design*. Norman: University of Oklahoma Press, 1957.

Hay, Eloise Knapp. *The Political Novels of Joseph Conrad*. Chicago: University of Chicago Press, 1963.

Heimer, Jackson W. "Betrayal, Confession, Attempted Redemption, and Punishment in *Nostromo*," *TSLL*, VIII (Winter 1967), 561–579.

Herbert, George. *The Works,* ed. F. E. Hutchinson. Oxford: Clarendon Press, 1959.

Herndon, Richard. "The Genesis of Conrad's 'Amy Foster,'" *SP,* LVII (July 1960), 549–566.

Hewitt, Douglas. *Conrad: A Reassessment.* Cambridge: Bowes and Bowes, 1952.

Hodges, Robert R. *The Dual Heritage of Joseph Conrad.* The Hague: Mouton, 1967.

Hoffman, Stanton de Voren. "Conrad's Menagerie: Animal Imagery and Theme," *BuR,* XII (December 1964), 59–71.

————. "The Hole in the Bottom of the Pail: Comedy and Theme in *Heart of Darkness,*" *SSF,* II (Winter 1965), 113–123.

Hoffmann, Charles G. *Ford Madox Ford.* New York: Twayne, 1967.

————. "Ford's Manuscript Revisions of *The Good Soldier,*" *ELT,* IX (1966), 145–152.

Howe, Irving. *Politics and the Novel.* New York: Horizon, 1957.

Hynes, Samuel. "The Epistemology of *The Good Soldier,*" *SR,* LXIX (Spring 1961), 225–235.

Joyce, James. *Ulysses.* New ed., corrected and reset. New York: Random House, Modern Library, 1961.

Jung, C. G. *Symbols of Transformation.* Translated by R. F. C. Hull. 2 vols. New York: Harper Torchbooks, 1962.

Kaehele, Sharon and Howard German. "Conrad's *Victory:* A Reassessment," *MFS,* X (Spring 1964), 55–72.

Karl, Frederick R. *A Reader's Guide to Joseph Conrad.* New York: Noonday, 1960.

Kashner, Rita J. "Tietjens' Education: Ford Madox Ford's Tetralogy," *CritQ,* VIII (Summer 1966), 150–163.

Kenner, Hugh. *Gnomon: Essays on Contemporary Literature.* New York: McDowell, Obolensky, 1958.

Kramer, Dale. "Marlow, Myth, and Structure in *Lord Jim*," *Criticism*, VIII (Summer 1966), 263–279.

Lattey, C., S.J. "Jeremias," in *A Catholic Commentary on Holy Scripture*, ed. Dom Bernard Orchard *et al*. New York: Thomas Nelson and Sons, 1953.

Leavis, F. R. *The Great Tradition*. London: Chatto and Windus, 1948.

Leer, Norman. *The Limited Hero in the Novels of Ford Madox Ford*. East Lansing: Michigan State University Press, 1966.

Levy, Bernard S. and George R. Adams. "Chauntecleer's Paradise Lost and Regained," *Mediaeval Studies*, XXIX (1967), 178–192.

Lid, R. W. *Ford Madox Ford: The Essence of His Art*. Berkeley: University of California Press, 1964.

Lohf, Kenneth A. and Eugene P. Sheehy. *Joseph Conrad at Mid-Century: Editions and Studies, 1895–1955*. Minneapolis: University of Minnesota Press, 1957.

Macauley, Robie. Introduction to *Parade's End*. New York: Alfred A. Knopf, 1961.

MacShane, Frank. *The Life and Work of Ford Madox Ford*. New York: Horizon, 1965.

McCann, Charles J. and Victor Comerchero. "Setting as a Key to the Structure and Meaning of *Nostromo*," *RS*, XXXIV (June 1966), 66–84.

McFate, Patricia and Bruce Golden. "*The Good Soldier*: A Tragedy of Self-Deception," *MFS*, IX (Spring 1963), 50–60.

Mégroz, Rodolphe L. *Joseph Conrad's Mind and Method*. New York: Russell and Russell, 1964.

Meixner, John A. *Ford Madox Ford's Novels*. Minneapolis: University of Minnesota Press, 1962.

Meyer, Bernard C. *Joseph Conrad: A Psychoanalytic Biography*. Princeton: Princeton University Press, 1967.

Miller, J. Hillis. *Poets of Reality*. Cambridge, Mass.: Harvard University Press, 1965.

Mizener, Arthur. Afterword to *Parade's End*. 2 vols. New York: New American Library, 1964.

Modern Fiction Studies. I, No. 1 (February 1955) and X, No. 1 (Spring 1964). Issues devoted to Joseph Conrad.

Modern Fiction Studies. IX, No. 1 (Spring 1963). Issue devoted to Ford Madox Ford.

Morf, Gustav. *The Polish Heritage of Joseph Conrad*. London: Sampson Low, Marston, 1930.

Moser, Thomas. *Joseph Conrad: Achievement and Decline*. Cambridge, Mass.: Harvard University Press, 1957.

Mudrick, Marvin, ed. *Conrad: A Collection of Critical Essays*. Englewood Cliffs: Prentice-Hall, 1966.

———. "The Originality of Conrad," *HR*, XI (Winter 1958–1959), 545–553.

Ohmann, Carol. *Ford Madox Ford: From Apprentice to Craftsman*. Middletown: Wesleyan University Press, 1964.

Ray, Robert J. "Style in *The Good Soldier*," *MFS*, IX (Spring 1963), 61–66.

Reid, Stephen A. "The 'Unspeakable Rites' in *Heart of Darkness*," *MFS*, IX (Winter 1963–1964), 347–356.

Reinecke, George F. "Conrad's *Victory*: Psychomachy, Christian Symbols, and Theme," in *Explorations of Literature*, ed. Rima Drell Reck. Baton Rouge: Louisiana State University Press, 1966.

Retinger, J. H. *Conrad and His Contemporaries*. New York: Roy, 1943.

Rosenfield, Claire. *Paradise of Snakes*. Chicago: University of Chicago Press, 1967.

Rossetti, Christina. *The Poetical Works*, ed. William Michael Rossetti. London: Macmillan, 1908.

Rossetti, Dante Gabriel. *Poems, Ballads and Sonnets*, ed. Paull Franklin Baum. Garden City, New York: Doubleday, Doran, 1937.

Said, Edward W. *Joseph Conrad and the Fiction of Autobiography.* Cambridge, Mass.: Harvard University Press, 1966.

Sayers, Dorothy L., ed. The *Commedia.* 3 vols. New York: Basic Books, 1962.

Schneider, Daniel J. "Symbolism in Conrad's *Lord Jim:* The Total Pattern," *MFS,* XII (Winter 1966–1967), 427–438.

Schorer, Mark. "An Interpretation," in *The Good Soldier.* New York: Alfred A. Knopf, 1951.

Seiden, Melvin. "The Living Dead—VI: Ford Madox Ford and His Tetralogy," *London Magazine,* VI (August 1959), 45–55.

———. "Persecution and Paranoia in 'Parade's End,'" *Criticism,* VIII (Summer 1966), 246–262.

Sherry, Norman. *Conrad's Eastern World.* Cambridge: University Press, 1966.

Stallman, R. W., ed. *The Art of Joseph Conrad: A Critical Symposium.* East Lansing: Michigan State University Press, 1960.

———. "Time and *The Secret Agent," TSLL,* I (Spring 1959), 101–122.

Stein, William Bysshe. *"Almayer's Folly:* The Terrors of Time," *Conradiana,* I (Summer 1968), 27–34.

———. "Conrad's East: Time, History, Action and *Maya," TSLL,* VII (Autumn 1965), 265–283.

———. "The Eastern Matrix of Conrad's Art," *Conradiana,* I (Fall 1968), 1–14.

———. *"Heart of Darkness:* Bodhisattva Scenario," *Orient / West,* IX (September–October 1964), 37–46.

Swift, Jonathan. *The Prose Works,* ed. Herbert Davis. 13 vols. Oxford: Basil Blackwell, 1939–1959.

Tanner, Tony. *Conrad: "Lord Jim."* Studies in English Literature. No. 12. London: Edward Arnold, 1963.

Thale, Jerome. "Marlow's Quest," *UTQ,* XXIV (July 1955), 351–358.

Tindall, William York. *A Reader's Guide to James Joyce*. New York: Noonday, 1959.

Toynbee, Paget. *Dante in English Literature: From Chaucer to Cary*. 2 vols. London: Methuen, 1909.

Unterecker, John, ed. *Approaches to the Twentieth-Century Novel*. New York: Thomas Y. Crowell, 1965.

Van Gennep, Arnold. *The Rites of Passage*. Translated by Monika B. Vizedom and Gabrielle L. Caffee. Chicago: University of Chicago Press, 1960.

Van Ghent, Dorothy. *The English Novel*. New York: Rinehart, 1953.

Visiak, E. H. *The Mirror of Conrad*. London: Werner Laurie, 1955.

Wagner, Richard. *Tannhäuser*, ed. and trans. Natalia MacFarren. New York: G. Schirmer, n. d.

Walter, E. V. "The Political Sense of Ford Madox Ford," *New Republic*, CXXXIV (March 26, 1956), 17–19.

Warner, Oliver. *Joseph Conrad*. London: Longmans, Green, 1951.

———. *Joseph Conrad*. Writers and Their Work. No. 2. 3rd ed., rev. London: Longmans, Green, 1960.

Warren, Robert Penn. Introduction to *Nostromo*. New York: Random House, Modern Library, 1951.

Wiesenfarth, Joseph, F.S.C. "Criticism and the Semiosis of *The Good Soldier*," *MFS*, IX (Spring 1963), 39–49.

Wiley, Paul L. *Conrad's Measure of Man*. Madison: University of Wisconsin Press, 1954.

———. *Novelist of Three Worlds: Ford Madox Ford*. Syracuse: Syracuse University Press, 1962.

Wright, Walter F. *Romance and Tragedy in Joseph Conrad*. Lincoln: University of Nebraska Press, 1949.

Yelton, Donald C. *Mimesis and Metaphor*. The Hague: Mouton, 1967.

Young, Kenneth. *Ford Madox Ford*. Writers and Their Work. No. 74. London: Longmans, Green, 1956.

Zabel, Morton D. *Craft and Character: Texts, Method, and Vocation in Modern Fiction.* New York: Viking, 1957.

———. Introduction to *The Portable Conrad,* ed. Morton D. Zabel. New York: Viking, 1954.

———. Introduction to *Under Western Eyes.* Garden City, New York: Doubleday, Anchor Books, 1963.

Index

DATE DUE